THRIVING AS A WOMAN IN LEADERSHIP IN HIGHER EDUCATION

STORIES AND STRATEGIES FROM YOUR PEERS

———————

EDITORS

ELIZABETH ROSS HUBBELL, M.A.
DANIEL FUSCH, PH.D.

———————

ACADEMIC IMPRESSIONS | 2021
DENVER, CO

ANOTHER BOOK YOU MAY ENJOY

Fix Your Climate: A Practical Guide to Reducing Microaggressions, Microbullying, and Bullying in the Academic Workplace

Microaggressions, microbullying, and bullying are the silent destroyers of a university's climate. In this handbook, two leading experts on hierarchical microaggressions – Dr. Myron Anderson and Dr. Kathryn Young – present in-depth scenarios, strategies, and worksheets for addressing these issues on your campus.

https://www.academicimpressions.com/product/campus-climate-microaggressions-bullying/

CONTENTS

PART 3
CONFLICT MANAGEMENT

PART 4
INFLUENCING WITHOUT AUTHORITY

PART 5
LEADING AND THRIVING
AS WOMEN OF COLOR

PART 6
RELATIONSHIP BUILDING
AND OPENING THE DOOR FOR OTHERS

PART 7
MAKING THE CASE FOR YOURSELF
AND YOUR INITIATIVES

PART 8
ADVOCATING FOR EQUITY IN
HIRING AND THE ALLOCATION OF WORK

PART 9
NEGOTIATION

PART 10
DEFINING YOUR SUCCESS

INTRODUCTION

by Elizabeth Ross Hubbell, M.A.
Senior Program Manager, Academic Impressions

In November of 2016, Academic Impressions hosted its first *Women's Leadership Success in Higher Ed* conference in St. Louis, Missouri. What struck us from the very beginning was the authenticity, the vigor, and the passion in the voices of the presenters and the attendees. They spoke of renewed focus on promoting women to leadership positions, both formal and informal, on their campuses. They talked about the challenges of balancing modern career ambitions with the timeless responsibilities of nurturing their families. They spoke of the need to listen, connect, and learn from others who were on similar journeys and of the relief in learning that their experiences do not occur in isolation.

Following that initial gathering, we have hosted dozens of programs with the sole mission of advancing women's voices in higher education. We have cheered as we learned of new presidents being confirmed during our events and have collectively offered our support and empathy as colleagues shared their frustrations.

It became apparent over the years that the voices of the conference presenters and attendees alone weren't enough. So many women had stories to tell and advice to give that didn't yet have a platform. This book is our first foray into providing that platform—of which we hope there will be many others. Throughout this collection of 34 essays, you will hear voices

1

from every level of leadership and across every sector of higher education. You will read stories of strength, advocacy, and support as well as be privy to the pain, frustration, and resilience that is part of being a woman in higher education. Most importantly, you will hear their advice for moving forward—whether for those pivotal moments in meetings or making career-impacting decisions or launching campus-wide initiatives.

These chapters are intended to be teachable nuggets you can use. You can either read this book straight through or use it as a just-in-time guide around particular issues and challenges you are facing. Throughout, the authors and the editors have provided reflection questions to consider as you read. Our hope is that this collection of essays will become a workbook and journal as you navigate your leadership journey.

A Roadmap for This Book

This compendium has been divided into ten broad themes. These themes come from conversations with attendees, questions we receive, and interest shown in the events we've hosted around these timely topics. These themes are:

1. **Risk taking and authentic leadership** – We hear from so many women that they want to "take the leap" and take on a new and daring challenge in their careers, but that fear of repercussion gets in the way. These authors offer honest insights into their successes and roadblocks as they took risks.

2. **Confronting the imposter syndrome** – Even those at the highest levels of leadership experience it. This section will give you tools for overcoming those moments of doubt.

3. **Conflict management** – While conflict can feel intimidating, it can often lead to deep conversations and to better understanding of one another. In this section, you'll hear how various authors managed their conflicts on campus.

4. **Influencing without authority** – Whether you're leading up, down, or across, having social capital and being able to influence others will help you achieve professional goals for yourself and advocate for others.

5. **Leading and thriving as a woman of color** – In this section, you will hear powerful voices from women of color who are navigating their path to leadership with success.

6. **Relationship building and opening the door for others** – In our quest for equity in the workplace, we must not only focus on our journey, but also on the paths of women who follow us. The authors in this section offer ways to be an advocate for women and under-represented populations in higher ed.

7. **Making the case for yourself and your initiatives** – Successfully moving your initiatives forward not only requires bringing your passion for your work, but also showing how your idea can aid the overall goals and mission of your team, department, or university. These

authors write about their experiences in advocating for new solutions.

8. **Advocating for equity in hiring and the allocation of work** – Working towards gender equity not only involves those who work at the institution currently, but also focusing on the pipeline of our future leaders. This section will offer scenarios for creating a more equitable environment on your campus.

9. **Negotiation** – Women are much less likely than men to negotiate their salary or other components of their work. The authors in this section write about their experiences and offer scenarios for you to consider.

10. **Defining your success** – Each of our paths is different and how we define "success" should be as unique as each individual. Having a better understanding of your personal goals and what you will deem successful at the end of your career will help you to consider various options as you move forward.

Remember, this book does not necessarily need to be read straight through, but rather can be used as a resource as you grapple with challenges you face. Each chapter contains reflection questions or tasks for you to use. At the end, we have included deeper reflective questions to help you synthesize all that you've read. Here are where you will find chapters addressing each theme:

INTRODUCTION

Theme	Chapters
Risk taking and authentic leadership	1-3
Confronting the Imposter Syndrome	4-9
Conflict management	10-12
Influencing without authority	13-14
Leading and thriving as a woman of color	15-20
Relationship building and opening the door for others	21-22
Making the case for yourself and your initiatives	23-26
Advocating for equity in hiring and the allocation of work	27-29
Negotiation	30-32
Defining your success	33-34

This book wouldn't have been possible without the support of our CEO, Amit Mrig, and without the guidance of our Chief Strategy Officer, Beth Rotach. Daniel Fusch and I pored over every submission and compiled the final manuscript together, but it was his sharp intuition and tireless commitment that made the book you're holding possible. I am grateful to these individuals for helping to bring an idea to fruition.

Finally, to the women who were willing to lay out their vulnerabilities and lessons for all the world to see in hopes they might offer another colleague a light of guidance—we sincerely thank you.

PART 1

RISK TAKING AND AUTHENTIC LEADERSHIP

CHAPTER 1
THE GENUINE AUTHENTICITY IT TAKES TO LEAD

by Mary Dana Hinton, Ph.D.
President, Hollins University

There is little question that higher education needs to do more to develop and support women's leadership. In the United States, women comprise 57% of higher education students (U.S. Department of Education, 2019) and earn more than 50% of degrees at most higher education levels (Johnson, 2017). Compare those numbers to faculty, of which women only comprise 31% (Kelly, 2019). Women are more common in administrative roles, holding more than 50% of such positions. However, a woman's journey up the organizational chart dramatically narrows, with only 40% of senior positions (cabinet-level) held by women. Only 30% of college presidents are women. Of course, when we overlay additional identities, in this instance race, the numbers are even more disheartening. Overall, women of color comprise less than 10% of the higher education workforce (Jasper, 2018) and hold only 5% of college presidencies. The data makes a clear and compelling case for women's leadership development.

Several questions immediately arise in the face of these numbers: What are the barriers women face in our sector? What strengths and opportunities should we be utilizing and leveraging in higher education as women and as leaders? What skills do we need to develop and enhance?

These questions are helpful as we ponder leadership on a global scale. However, a key leadership skill that women need to embrace is doing the internal work of identifying and being their authentic selves. This chapter aims to encourage you to think through your authentic leadership voice, as defined by you and your intersecting identities, and to imagine how you can leverage your authentic voice to excel. It has been the unearthing, knowing, revealing, and leveraging of my authentic strengths and understanding my identities that has enabled me to persevere and excel as a leader.

Genuine Authenticity is More than Just Showing Up "As You Are"

Authenticity is a popular word in the leadership lexicon today. One has only to glance at the thousands of articles readily available to see the importance of being an authentic leader. A recent *Harvard Business Review* article stated, "Withholding your true self puts a cap on trust and on your ability to lead" and highlights that the inability to be authentic hampers effective leadership. Bringing one's wholehearted, authentic self to the workplace engenders support, empowerment, and a shared commitment to leadership (Frei and Morriss, 2020).

While many may think that just showing up "as you are" is what it means to be authentic, genuine authenticity demands much more. There seems to be a consensus that authentic leaders spend time exploring their own identities, strengths, and weaknesses and know themselves well; are willing to share and build trust with all they work with; are disciplined in their pursuits; are reliable, trustworthy colleagues; seek and accept feedback; and are committed to a personal mission to achieve success for their organizations and themselves. At its core, authentic leadership comes from knowing our many identities and deploying those identities in pursuit of our personal mission (George, 2016). My authentic identity is comprised of being a woman, an African American, a member of Generation X, someone who comes from a lower socioeconomic status, and from having spent much of my life in predominantly white institutions (PWIs).

For example, my leadership was shaped early on by the fact that I grew up among a generation of women who were told authenticity and vulnerability are anathema to being a good leader. We were told to separate our personal lives from our professional lives, and that we had to act and dress like men to be successful and accepted as leaders. If you chose to pay attention to something as frivolous as appearance, did not learn to play golf, or took time off to go on a field trip with your child, it was proof that you were not a leader.

Therefore, I grew up with a pervasive notion that good leaders are strong and decisive men, and that authenticity and vulnerability are inherently incompatible with good leadership. While I, like many, have had to unlearn these notions, the majority of participants in a 2018 study continued to think of effective leaders as men. Those same characteristics emerge as predominant in our culture (Murphy, 2018).

As a result, as women we find ourselves, and our identities, wrestling with cultural notions of what it means to be a leader. However, this cultural, or generational, influence on how we understand and carry out our leadership is not the only—and for many, not even the pervasive—identity that defines us. Our identities as they relate to race, gender, and economic status often play a dominant fashioning role.

The Cost of "Shifting"

We each have identities—for me, it is my race—that force us to have to double down on proving ourselves as a leader and questioning how we can reveal our authentic voice. As a woman of color, daily, I must confront many preconceptions about my level of intelligence, how I attained my current position, my ability to think complexly about issues beyond race, and my willingness to nurture all students I serve, not just students of color. When I bring my authentic voice to bear as a black woman, I am often challenged.

Charisse Jones and Kumea Shorter-Gooden explore black women's struggles with authenticity in the professional world at great length and find that in an effort to support and comfort others, black women must often suppress and silence their own authentic needs. The authors write:

"Our research shows that in response to their relentless oppression, black women in our country have had to perfect what we call 'shifting,' a sort of subterfuge that African Americans have long practiced to ensure their survival in our society. . . Black women are relentlessly pushed to serve and satisfy others and made to hide their true selves . . . From one moment to the next, they change their outward behavior, attitude, or tone. . . And shifting has become such an integral part of Black women's behavior that some adopt an alternate pose or voice as easily as they blink their eyes or draw breath—without thinking, and without realizing that the emptiness they feel and the roles they must play may be directly related."

Yet in order to lead effectively, to know myself, to engender the trust of others, to be disciplined in the pursuit of my personal and institutional mission, I cannot be left empty. Leaders must have a wellspring of courage and ideas from which to draw and cannot sacrifice that for the sake of others. To successfully navigate and persevere as a leader, you must also be willing to embrace and express those identities, despite the challenges they may elicit. For me to lead authentically and effectively, I have to embrace my identity, and my story that supports that identity.

My identity, my authentic voice, was nurtured in rural North Carolina. My origin story, comprised of poverty and too many racist experiences to count, is not one that one shares when attending a New England liberal arts college or when leading in PWIs. My "delightful" and "quaint" southern accent only served to mark me as other. So, my voice and my story, and things that could help you discern my story, were silenced and quietly packed away because they marked me as vulnerable. As weak. As not a leader.

Eventually, the tiresome work of shifting, as so aptly defined by Jones and Shorter-Gooden, began to exact an outsized personal toll and limit my ability to lead. Fortunately, I came to realize that those things which made me vulnerable also made me strong. This realization and subsequent recalibration had a powerful and transformative impact on my leadership. I found that sharing my authentic voice and making myself vulnerable with others strengthened my leadership ability and encouraged others in their desire and ability to lead. For example, I share with students that I couldn't do the things in college that many can take advantage of—play a sport, study abroad, buy a college sweatshirt—because I didn't have the money. I share that I know what it's like to feel like an outsider on a college campus and an interloper when I return home. When I share these vulnerable feelings, I am able to connect with those who are currently having a similar experience and encourage them to use their authenticity and vulnerability to inspire and sustain them as leaders.

As a result, students began to share their stories and identities with me. I know of homeless students who decided to pursue education to prove their value to their families. I have embraced students who have had every material need met but have questioned their human value and self-worth. I have prayed with students who need the love and support of a campus community to get through personal crises. The same is true for faculty and administrative colleagues who have chosen to share their hearts with me because I was willing to authentically share mine with them.

These moments of connection are what enable me to lead effectively. Successful leadership, while demanding content expertise, is rarely determined by an ability to master a spreadsheet, budget, or other tactical skills. Successful leadership hinges upon your ability to be in deep relationship with those you are leading. To create those relationships, inspire and engage others, be disciplined in your pursuits on behalf of your organization, and fulfill your mission, you must embrace your authentic voice.

Questions for Reflection

As you think about who you are, the complexity of your identities, and the authentic voice you want to bring to leadership, please ask yourself the following questions:

1. What is your authentic leadership voice?

2. What are your intersecting identities?

3. How do you work through all of those identities as you lead? How do you understand what compels your leadership?

4. How do you share and live your authentic identities and voice in ways that enhance your leadership,

within a world that may not fully understand or value those multiple and overlapping identities?

5. What resources can you look to as you strive to answer Questions 3 and 4? (Hopefully, this book can help add to your resources and network!)

Answering these questions is an essential first step in revealing and leveraging your essential leadership voice.

Of course, many structures and policies need to change to better support women leaders. Some of those realities we can control by asserting and enforcing our rights in the workplace and equipping ourselves with the skills needed to succeed. Some of those structures require a collective effort to right, such as pay equity or paid family leave, and it is critical to acknowledge and seek to address those structures.

That said, it is also critically important to focus on our internal leadership capacity. At the end of the day, no structural changes—no amount of support, no number of networking events, no advanced degrees—will work unless you believe in and are able to reveal your authentic self. Too often, our most dangerous messages come from within, as we suppress who and what we are in an effort to please others. Instead, we must believe in our value and authentic voice, in our worthiness, if we are going to embrace who we are—as women and as leaders. Because who we are is, simply put, enough.

Resources

U.S. Department of Education, National Center for Education Statistics. (2019). *Digest of Education Statistics*, 2018 (NCES 2020-009), Chapter 3.

Frei, Frances X., and Anne Morriss. "Everything Starts with Trust." *Harvard Business Review*, May 2020. hbr.org/2020/05/begin-with-trust.

George, Bill. "The Truth About Authentic Leaders." *HBS Working Knowledge*, Harvard Business School, 6 July 2016, hbswk.hbs.edu/item/the-truth-about-authentic-leaders.

Johnson, Heather L. 2017. *Pipelines, Pathways, and Institutional Leadership: An Update on the Status of Women in Higher Education.* Washington, DC: American Council on Education.

Jones, Charisse, and Kumea Shorter-Gooden. *Shifting: The Double Lives of Black Women in America.* Perennial, 2004.

Kelly, Bridget Turner. "Though More Women Are on College Campuses, Climbing the Professor Ladder Remains a Challenge." The Brookings Institution, 29 Mar. 2019. www.brookings.edu/blog/brown-center-chalkboard/2019/03/29/though-more-women-are-on-college-campuses-climbing-the-professor-ladder-remains-a-challenge/.

McChesney, Jasper 2018. *Representation and Pay of Women of Color in the Higher Education Workforce* (Research report).

CUPA-HR. Available from:
https://www.cupahr.org/surveys/research-briefs/

Murphy, Heather. "Picture a Leader. Is She a Woman?" *The New York Times*, 16 Mar. 2018.
www.nytimes.com/2018/03/16/health/women-leadership-workplace.html.

About the Author

Mary Dana Hinton is the thirteenth president of Hollins University in Roanoke, VA. She is an active and respected proponent of the liberal arts and inclusion, and her leadership reflects a deep and abiding commitment to educational equity and the education of women. Active in the national higher education arena, she is a member of the Board of Directors for the American Association of Colleges and Universities, the National Association of Independent Colleges and Universities, Interfaith Youth Core, Saint Mary's School, and the University Leadership Council. She founded the Liberal Arts Illuminated Conference.

Dr. Hinton's scholarship focuses on higher education leadership and inclusion in higher education. She is the author of *The Commercial Church: Black Churches and the New Religious Marketplace in America* and is a frequent op-ed contributor across higher education publications.

Dr. Hinton earned a Ph.D. in religion and religious education with high honors from Fordham University, a Master of Arts degree in clinical child psychology from the University of Kansas, Lawrence, and a Bachelor of Arts degree in psychology from Williams College. She is the recipient of the Bicentennial Medal from Williams College and an honorary Doctorate of Humane Letters from Misericordia University.

CHAPTER 2
AUTHENTIC LEADERSHIP: BRINGING YOURSELF TO THE LEADERSHIP TABLE

by Karen M. Whitney, Ph.D.
President Emerita, Clarion University

Introduction

Often when presenting workshops or giving talks on leadership, I am asked if you can be yourself *and* be a successful leader. The questioner often gives me the impression that they feel like they must somehow choose between their true self or succeeding as a leader in their organization. I respond back to the questioner, and now to you, the reader, that it is a false choice to believe you have to choose between who you are and how you can be a successful leader. The truth is that you define and then you choose how you will show up to work. The only real question to ask yourself is: To what extent are you satisfied with how you show up to work and with the results you are getting? The other spoiler to this false choice is that you somehow have to be someone else to be a leader. Being an authentic leader is more about how well you know yourself, how committed you are to developing a full array of leadership skills, and the extent to which you are willing to adjust your leadership skills to achieve the results you have been hired to achieve. You will be a leader when you get the results you were hired to achieve. Let's walk through the skills, lessons learned, and actions you can take to be an authentic leader.

An Essential Skill: Ability to Reflect

For me, one of the biggest differences between successful leaders and folks who never quite succeed as leaders is their ability to reflect upon their leadership with an unfiltered and unflinching honesty. Reflection is simply how you see yourself as others see you—as legitimate feedback that regularly informs how you approach your work. As such, the authenticity of leadership is based on reflection and the willingness to learn and develop.

Reflection is hard and scary and requires 1) the courage to want to see yourself accurately the way others see you; 2) the clarity to know exactly how you want to be seen as a leader; and 3) the confidence to welcome regular feedback on your approach to leadership from those around you. This is a tall order in that you have to be willing to not get defensive or dismissive when feedback is given. Instead you have to be willing to adjust strategically or change to be the leader you want to be going forward. This effort requires the courage to allow a mix of compliments and criticisms to inform how you choose to show up to your work in the future. Real reflection done regularly is the key to keeping your approach to leadership relevant and effective.

Lessons Learned (The Hard Way)

At a mid-point in my administrative career, I was suddenly thrown into responding to a series of student-led protests, as the SSAO (senior student affairs officer). During this time, I was caught completely by surprise as to how disconnected I had become with the pulse of a significant student constituency. I had, up to this point, believed that one of my strengths was being in tune with the student body and keeping ahead of the hot button issues of the day. As you might imagine, I was thrown into an existential crisis of confidence, wondering how I could have been so out of touch and so unprepared. This crisis of confidence led me to realize that I did not have any feedback routines in place that would ensure a rigorous reflection and evolution for my approach to leadership.

Once the student protests were managed through, I spent several months having very candid conversations with the folks who reported to me, with my peers, and with my supervisor, the university CEO. The initial purpose was to debrief and arrive at lessons learned from the series of critical incidents. I also took this moment to explore and pose good questions to garner feedback regarding my own leadership. I asked over and over again, as the SSAO, what could or should I have done differently in order to prevent, mitigate, or respond to the students. Fortunately, I had sufficient relational currency and trust built with folks that they told me the truth. The truth hurt and helped. Because I was more committed to being an effective leader than to justifying my current approach to leadership, I was willing and able to take the feedback and allow it to inform me. My goal was to become much more intentional as a leader going forward. As a result of the feedback, I integrated a very specific leadership and team-building model into my leadership approach and I developed a list of leadership behaviors that I went about developing further. I also came to terms with a list of behaviors that I needed to change and, in a few cases, stop doing, because they were hampering my effectiveness. The details of the specific leadership model and behaviors I adopted that transformed my leadership approach is not important. The convergence of my willingness to be vulnerable, the humility to admit that after 20 years in higher education and holding an executive position, I still had much to learn and that there continued to be opportunities for me to improve my leadership, is what is noteworthy. Today, 20 years later, I still regularly acquire critical feedback about my leadership and I continue to be willing to grow, evolve, and improve in order to be both the leader that is true to who I am and the leader the organization needs me to be. For me, the convergence of self and organization forms my authentic leadership style.

How to Bring Your Real Self to the Leadership Table

There are many ways to reflect as a way of bringing yourself to your leadership table. First, you have to want to be an authentic leader more than you want to be comfortable. I say this because the road may be uncomfortable or difficult. Reflecting on who you really are, what your natural "go to" approach to leading involves, understanding what your current university/college needs from you as a leader, and aligning all of these parts gets you your successful, authentic approach to leadership. You are not a leader in the abstract; you have been hired to get results. You are leading at a certain moment in time that encompasses the organization's history, culture, mission, vision, values, and goals, which forms an organizational context. Your authenticity is how you come to be true to who you are and how you choose to lead within a particular context.

There are actions you can take to be your authentic leadership self:

Know yourself.

Ask yourself the following questions: What good in the world do I want to do through my leadership? What is my leadership mission, vision, and values? What are my leadership priorities? What are my best leadership skills? What leadership skills need improving? How do I want others to see me? How do I want to "show up" to my position?

Take action: Reflect and respond honestly to these questions. Write down your answers either in the Roadmap provided in the next few pages or make your own map. The purpose is to know yourself so you can consider where and how to make any shifts or changes.

Know how others see you.

Ask those who know you at work the following questions: As a leader, what do I do that you hope I would keep doing?

As a leader, what do you hope I would stop doing? What advice do you have for me that would help me be an even better leader?

Take action: One of the challenges to understanding how others see you is how to obtain honest and helpful feedback. Often people are reluctant to talk candidly about each other's approach to leadership. The reluctance may be a fear that they will hurt your feelings or somehow damage the relationship they have with you. I am a big fan of 360° feedback reviews. If a "360° review" is a new concept, I suggest you explore this item further on your own. The very short description is that you obtain feedback about your leadership from everyone in your circle (360 degrees) of work—you, your boss, peers, and direct reports. The feedback can be obtained through an online survey or from an independent consultant interviewing folks. You invite those in your circle to respond and, through the survey and/or consultant, the feedback is given to you anonymously, which allows the respondent the space to be honest. Regardless, the outcome is a summary of descriptions of how you are seen as a leader by yourself and by others. From this information you can understand how the way you see yourself compares to how others see you. With this information you can consider how you want to be seen in the future. You may then consider the specific leadership behaviors you choose to develop, change, or stop. For example, Academic Impressions (www.academicimpressions. com) offers workshops and webinars on their leadership model called *The 5 Paths to Leadership*. The model is also supported by an online 360° survey that your 360° circle completes. Having your 360° circle complete the survey gives you feedback presented within the model from which to consider skills/behaviors to improve upon going forward.

Know the context within which you have been hired to lead.

Ask yourself the following questions: What are my organization's mission, vision, values, and priorities? What are my boss's priorities? Are my leadership mission, vision, values, and priorities in alignment with my organization and with my boss?

Take action: Read your organization's planning documents that would describe mission, vision, values, and priorities. As you can, talk with your boss and ask them about their vision, mission, values, and priorities regarding their leadership. Your purpose is to piece together these elements that comprise the context you are leading within. Use the chart below to outline what you learn.

Arriving at Your Authentic Approach to Leadership

Once you are grounded through a process of reflection as to who you are, how you show up, and the context in which you are leading, you are ready to put it all together and create your roadmap to becoming a more authentic leader. See the next several pages for a worksheet to assist in developing such a roadmap.

AUTHENTIC LEADERSHIP

THE ROADMAP TO AUTHENTIC LEADERSHIP

Key items	Me (what I know about Myself)	My current approach to leadership
Mission		
Vision		
Values		
Priorities		
Desired Results		
Other Important/Urgent Items		

My organization's approach to leadership	Is there alignment? (If *yes*, great. If *no*, what is the work to be done?)	Key items
		Mission
		Vision
		Values
		Priorities
		Desired Results
Other Important/Urgent Items		

Notes	
What do I do best? *(My self-assessment plus feedback from others)*	**What could I do better?** *(My self-assessment plus feedback from others)*

Resources

Academic Impressions: Locate a multitude of resources including: 360° online assessments, The 5 Pathways to Leadership webcast, a variety of leadership assessment and development tools, blogs, articles, webinars, conferences, coaching, and more offered with membership. See www.academicimpressions.com.

Brown, Brené. *Dare to Lead: Brave Work. Tough Conversations. Whole Hearts.* Random House Publishing Group, 2018.

Lencioni, Patrick. *Five Dysfunctions of a Team.* Jossey-Bass, 2002.

About the Author

Karen M. Whitney, Ph.D.
Interim Chancellor, University of Illinois Springfield (2020-2022)
Interim Chancellor Pennsylvania System of Higher Education (2017-2018)
President (2010-2017) & President Emerita, Clarion University

Throughout her 40-year career in higher education, Dr. Karen Whitney has held a variety of executive and leadership positions with increasing levels of responsibility, beginning as a Director to Associate Vice President, Vice Chancellor, President, and Chancellor. Karen is also a nationally recognized organizational and leadership development writer, speaker, consultant, and advisor. Karen is currently working with system heads, institutional presidents/chancellors, and a variety of higher education leaders to tackle higher education's toughest problems. She holds a doctorate from the University of Texas at Austin in Higher Education Administration and is a certified leadership coach through the Center for Executive Coaching.

She advocates for courageous and confident leadership that is needed now more than ever in higher education, particularly since the challenges and threats to leadership success seem to be increasing. In working with every leader to succeed, Karen's approach is to combine a proven track record of higher education leadership with a variety of engagement approaches, including advising, coaching, facilitating, and training. Drawing on her vast experience at every level of leadership, she customizes an individually-structured process to ensure each leader achieves their highest professional and institutional priorities.

CHAPTER 3
LEARNING TO TAKE RISKS

by Liz Rockstroh, Ed.D.
Senior Associate Director of Communications and Programs, Student Union, UT San Antonio

Are you a risk-taker?

If we could climb the mountain of the future and look back on the entirety of our professional journey, there are seemingly endless decisions dotting the landscape of our careers with a series of question marks:

> *Do I apply for the promotion in my department?*
> *Am I willing to negotiate for a higher salary?*
> *Can I relocate for a better opportunity?*
> *Do I take time off to have children?*

The list goes on, as life presents new challenges and opportunities with each passing year.

Faced with these endless decisions, we are also faced with taking risks, and the stakes are high. Often, taking a calculated professional risk can vastly change the trajectory of your career. A better title, a higher salary, a supportive mentor, and a job we are passionate about all result in a greater foundation for a successful professional life. However, a complicating factor remains that men are more likely to take risks than women. Although this gap may be narrowing over time, there are still serious implications for women today who are less likely to take risks compared to their male peers, including significant differences in professional advancement, financial security, and healthy work-life balance.

Learning to explore opportunities and evaluate risk is a skill, and one that can be developed to help women succeed in higher education. The process of taking calculated risks requires us to address fear, be vulnerable, set meaningful goals, and strategically analyze how to reach them. The benefit of strengthening this skill is creating new opportunities in a deliberate way. In higher education, this advancement is particularly important for women, as we work to narrow pay inequity and gender bias in academia.

Tackling Fear and Rejection

When presented with a new opportunity, the biggest barriers we often face are fear and rejection. Fear is the nagging voice in our head envisioning worst-case scenarios.

> *What if I don't get the promotion? How will I face the embarrassment of staying in my current role?*

> *What if I take a year off to study and then can't find another equivalent position for years?*

Ad nauseum.

Another hurdle is rejection. Every new opportunity requires us to become vulnerable. If we are taking a risk, we will inevitably face our share of rejection. A conversation comes to mind that I had with a good friend of mine who is a mathematician. He went to an elite school, finished his studies early, and landed a post-doc at an ivy league institution. He seemed to skate effortlessly through the process with grace and efficiency. Yet when I sat down with him for coffee, he confided about the grueling hours he spent applying for over 100 faculty positions and post-doc opportunities before receiving only one acceptance. Even after securing a meaningful offer, he was still deflated under the cumulative weight of so much rejection. Each woman reading this book knows that finding the right job, at the right time, in the right place, for the right salary in academia is a daunting task. We face rejection from hiring boards, editors, conference planning teams, supervisors, and even peers. Fear and rejection are two reasons not to take risks, and they both serve as reminders of why it's important to approach risk-taking as a skill to be cultivated.

Overcoming Fear

When I think about risk-taking in my professional career, several salient examples rise from the lake of my memory. These examples highlight different perspectives on risk-taking, and I will share how these decisions impacted my overall career.

Wanderlust

In my late 20s, as I approached the end of my doctorate, I started seriously considering taking a year off to travel and study abroad. The decision was complicated. I had already worked professionally for many years and was plagued by how a decision to travel would impact my career. I had a coveted job with the City and County of San Francisco, and peers at my institution joked that people never left positions once vested. With secure health and retirement benefits, I felt I had a lot to lose. Plus, I had put in years of hard work to build my career.

Could I professionally afford to walk away from my position?

Could I personally afford to live for a year without salary and health insurance while paying off student loans?

In the end, I decided there wouldn't be another time in my life I could travel for a year. I finished my doctorate, and shortly thereafter put in my two weeks' notice at work. Many colleagues questioned my decision. I felt a stigma of irresponsibility in others' perception of my choice, and I had to wonder if a young man would have been perceived the same way.

I spent a meaningful year living and traveling abroad, but there were consequences associated with the risk I took. I came back to America practically penniless and re-entered the workforce at a significantly lower position than when I left. I will admit I felt the sting of embarrassment and questioned my worth. Yet the benefits were also significant. While living abroad I visited many institutions, studied language courses, and greatly expanded my professional network and personal perspective about higher education.

One of my biggest fears was explaining a year-long gap on my resume. This seemed impossible to explain to a prospective employer, yet over the last 10 years I've found it is a great conversation starter. To my knowledge, it has never held me back from an opportunity, but perhaps has helped me stand out among committees considering dozens of applicants. While the overall financial cost was high, I've never regretted taking that risk, making that decision to travel and study abroad for a year.

The Grass is Greener

After settling back into my career following my year of traveling, I found myself in a more stable environment. I moved home to San Antonio, Texas, and got married. I landed a great job in a leadership role at an institution where I really felt like I could dig in and do good work. I was grateful for the opportunity and felt there were many prospects for growth and advancement. I was about eight months into the position when I got a call from Human Resources from a different college. They had my resume from months prior when I was applying en masse. At first, I considered telling them I wasn't interested, but I listened to their offer. A bump in title, double my salary, and my commute shortened by 30 minutes.

The risk I took was, in fact, risky. In my excitement over a better title and salary, I took a position that didn't fully align with my career goals and research interests. Further, by leaving the state education system, I lost out on valuable years of service in terms of retirement and health benefits. Ultimately, my new position was cut after two years. While I don't regret the risk I took, I learned an important lesson about the value of strategic and long-term thinking in career planning.

They Call Me Mommy

I married into motherhood, instantly becoming a stepmom to three children, and then had two of my own. When I decided to have kids, I wasn't fully aware of the risk I was taking professionally. Having kids has influenced my career in uncountable ways. From day-to-day decisions such as aligning drop-off times with day care, to professional development opportunities such as coordinating childcare during a conference, being a mom touches innumerable elements of my work.

While I didn't truly comprehend the risk I was taking when I decided to have kids, being a mom has taught me some important lessons about risk-taking. First is the understanding that there is risk in everything we do, no matter what decision we make. Since becoming a mom, I think more critically about the ricochet that choices may have throughout my career. Additionally, choosing to be a mom taught me a powerful lesson in aligning risk with values. Being a mom is the greatest joy in my life, and therefore taking the risk is easy for me. I am unapologetic about being a mom first when it comes to my professional life. When we take risks, there is power in owning decisions that connect closely with personal values.

Risk-taking comes in many forms. Sometimes it feels intentional and brave, like stepping off the carefully planned career path to follow a dream and travel for a year. Other decisions require true strategic planning and benefit greatly from practiced analytical reasoning, like choosing to accept a new professional position. Still other risks for women are not so much a choice, but rather tied to gender. Each of these examples provide a valuable case-study lesson in how decision making and taking calculated risks can influence career path and success in higher education.

Are you ready to take risks?

I hope the information presented in this chapter provides a prompt for you to think deeply about your goals and identify where and when you can take risks to meet your ambitions. There is risk in every decision. Sharpening your skill in risk-taking can help you identify when it is the right time to take a risk that might help you succeed on your leadership journey.

I encourage you to take the next week and dig deep into building your risk-taking skillset.

Dedicate 15-30 minutes a day to work through the prompts provided below:

1. **Monday: Address your fears**

    - What fears are getting in the way of your decision to take a risk?

- Journal about your fears, worst-case scenarios, and any concerns about rejection.

- Brainstorm possible solutions or workarounds for these fears.

2. **Tuesday: Practice vulnerability**

- In order to be open to new opportunities and growth, you have to be vulnerable.

- Thinking about the fear exercise, how can you take a step towards vulnerability in pursuit of a professional risk?

- Who can you reach out to for support?

- Who is one person in your life who demonstrates vulnerability as part of their leadership philosophy? Pick up the phone and call that person to ask them about the role of vulnerability in their success.

3. **Wednesday: Set meaningful goals**

- Sit down and make a list of your 20 top goals for your life. Note which goals are personal or professional. Narrow the list down to your top 10 and circle those goals.

- Spend some time thinking about how you can reach those goals. Weigh what risks you can take to reach those goals.

- What goal will you tackle first?

4. Thursday: Strategize and analyze

- First, learn about your personality type. Are you a logical thinker? Strategic thinking and analysis may or may not be a strength for you.

- Learning about yourself is an essential step to strengthening your decision-making skill surrounding risk.

5. Friday: Learn from the past

- Examine your past decisions. What risks have you taken and how have they contributed to your success or failure? What did you learn from those failures?

- Look to other people you consider successful. Consider what decisions led them to their success.

- Ask your mentor what risks they've taken that ultimately supported their successful leadership.

After you spend a week working through these exercises and thinking deeply about risk, put accountability measures in place so you continue to grow in this area. Consider setting aside 30 minutes to 1 hour each week to review your goals and pursue opportunities. Partner with a mentor or colleague to have lunch once a month and discuss how risk can help you advance your career. Continue this discussion and consider building your risk-taking skill as part of your toolset to help you thrive as a leader in higher education.

ADDITIONAL RESOURCE: WORKSHEET

At the end of this book, under the "Worksheet: 15 Questions for Reflection," Academic Impressions has provided a matrix that you can use to evaluate the risks you are considering in your professional or personal life.

Resources

Books

Pink, Daniel H. *When: The Scientific Secrets of Perfect Timing.* Riverhead Books, 2019.

> *Why you should read it:* This book is full of insightful hacks about timing in life and will help you understand how to maximize your productivity and how to evaluate risks you're about to take.

Brown, Brené. *Dare to Lead: Brave Work. Tough Conversations. Whole Hearts.* Random House Publishing Group, 2018.

> *Why you should read it:* Brené Brown describes vulnerability as "uncertainty, risk, and emotional exposure" and artfully connects vulnerability as both the core of shame and the

birthplace of joy and creativity. She reminds us that failure is a natural part of leadership, success, and innovation.

Workshop

True Colors
https://truecolorsintl.com/personality-assessment-3/

> *Why you should attend:* Learning about your personality strengths can help you understand how you make decisions, what you value, and what opportunities might be successful for you.

About the Author

Liz Rockstroh is a professional in higher education with over 15 years of experience in Student Affairs and higher education marketing. She holds a doctorate in educational leadership from the University of California at Davis. Currently, she works at the University of Texas at San Antonio as a Senior Associate Director for the Student Union. Liz is a Texas native, and currently resides in San Antonio with her husband, five kids, and a dog.

PART 2

CONFRONTING THE IMPOSTER SYNDROME

CHAPTER 4
IMPOSTER SYNDROME: ABANDONING THE FALSEHOODS FOR MORE PRODUCTIVE TRUTHS

by Katie Jackson, Ed.D.
Director of Student Conduct & Conflict Resolution,
University of Minnesota in Duluth

In December of 2012, I was sitting in the window seat of an airplane, bound for Minneapolis from St. Louis, on my way to spend time with family over the holiday. My tray table was down and I had my head resting on it. I had just landed a new leadership position. The job was inside higher education, but in an area that was completely new to me. My salary had nearly doubled. My peers in the division were my parents' age. I ranked above employees who had begun working in the department in the early '90s.

I had officially arrived. And I could hardly believe it.

I began my new position right after the New Year. At the same time, I was about to embark on my final semester of doctoral coursework. Over the next several months, my feelings of disbelief evolved into feelings of fear and self-doubt. A constant loop of unhelpful thoughts impacted my behavior with my new team. *Could this be right? I'm not sure I deserve this. This might be a mistake. Oops, I didn't know that; everyone must think*

I'm not cut out for this. It's probably only a matter of time before I get fired.

My experience isn't unique. One of the largest stumbling blocks for women in higher education is the fear of being exposed as a poser or fraud in a position they are uncertain they even deserve. Imposter syndrome was first identified in higher education's own backyard—the college counseling center. Pauline Clance (1978) observed that women students often questioned their own abilities and even suspected that their admission was the result of an error. Referring to imposterism as a syndrome undercuts how common it actually is, with nearly 70% of Americans having experienced at least one episode in their lifetime (Sakulky, 2011). It is an experience of cognitive distortion, where mistakes, doubts, and failures are deeply ingrained in the mind, whereas accolades, successes, and achievements barely register (Gravois, 2007). Further, the belief that we are not worthy, or not capable enough, results in a hesitancy to pursue opportunities.

One of my favorite authors, Gretchen Rubin, says, "Research is 'me-search,' so write the book you want to read." As I began my own work on this chapter, I knew I'd experienced imposterism in the past, and that I've felt some improvements in recent years, but I wasn't entirely clear on what strategies had counteracted it, or why it still crops up from time to time. Luckily, this piece provided me the space and motivation to locate and read the work of Valerie Young, a subject-matter expert on imposterism who identifies five cognitive errors that can and will implicate your leadership behavior if left unchecked (Young, 2011). The first step to overcoming imposter syndrome is to find a firm handle on what it looks like in our everyday thoughts and how that in turn impacts our behaviors. In naming these thoughts and exposing their falsehoods, you'll make space for new truths and more effective behavior.

Young's Cognitive Errors

1. Perfectionism

Perfectionists believe that a minute error is equivalent to a complete and utter failure. If you are a perfectionist, you hold impossibly high standards for yourself. Further, you may refuse to adjust expectations about what you must accomplish, regardless of circumstances. No matter what, you expect the best of yourself *and* you expect to be the best or top-ranked performer. Moreover, your brain has a habit of one-upping any accomplishment. For example, you got a promotion, but you remind yourself of someone else who has gone further. You get published, but you're suddenly unsatisfied by the scope or ranking of the publishing authority. You've done something well in academia, but there is someone else who has more funding, more publications, and more media coverage.

2. Success is fast and easy

While imposters are prone to perfection, they also expect their successes to come fast and easy. You might believe that success is only success if it comes from innate talent, as opposed to a lot of hard work, paired with trial and error. For example, if you share a document with a colleague, you feel deflated when you receive their suggestions for additions or modifications. You expect your first staff meeting to run as smoothly and as effortlessly as others who have led such meetings for 25 years. This way of thinking goes beyond tasks and carries into identity. You believe your capacity to be any of the following is fixed at birth—a writer, a leader, a teacher, or a public speaker. Despite the fact that higher ed is, in and of itself, advanced in nature, when you encounter work that feels challenging or difficult, you find yourself thinking *it must be me.*

3. Refusing to dive in ill-informed or inexperienced

The next cognitive error can function as a Catch 22—while imposters expect success to come fast and easy, at the same time, they are hesitant to jump into a role until they have surpassed a high threshold of knowledge and experience. You may think that unless you know absolutely everything about a topic, you aren't prepared to speak about it. Or, if you have fewer years of experience, you should defer to others in meetings, or in pursuit of opportunities. The level of absolute knowledge you believe you need is infinitely impossible to obtain.

4. Going at it alone, from scratch

Yet another cognitive error for imposters is the idea that you're not a success if you don't accomplish something 100%

on your own by starting completely from scratch. Your insatiable desire to demonstrate groundbreaking work without any help from anyone requires that you must know it all, and you must know it first, or else your knowing does not count. Next, you do not expect that anyone will see your work as a clear success if you share your work with others. A diverse project requiring a variety of knowledge, skill, and numerous person-hours, must be performed all alone.

5. Having it all

Finally, imposters are prone to desire success in diverse venues. For you, it is not enough to be the Einstein of the group, you feel compelled to demonstrate your Martha Stewart capacity as well. Not only do you want to be the best, you wish to be the best at essentially everything. You must win all the awards, receive the most compliments at the potluck, report the fastest 5K time, don the best work wardrobe, share the funniest water cooler stories, and drive the nicest car.

My Imposter Story

I see myself as a recovering imposter. I relapse here and there, but in recent years, I decided that changing my mind in some specific ways could only benefit my long-term success. That said, the road to recovery was bumpy. I realized that imposter-fueled behaviors aren't super relatable or likeable. Instead, I've found there is joy to be found in making authentic, honest connections with people.

So, without further ado, here is my honest experience with the five cognitive errors of imposterism.

Perfectionism

While working in alumni relations, my team hosted special events to honor donors and alumni. These once in a lifetime events were characterized by red carpets, fine cuisine, ice sculptures, scripts, tuxedos, commemorative art installations, and the like. Late one afternoon, I had finally signed off on the programs for one such event after months of collecting information, drafting, designing, editing, and finalizing. When they arrived back from the printer, I pulled one out and began paging through. On page 6, I saw something that looked like a wet spot. I felt anxious and pulled out a second copy. It wasn't a wet spot; it was on every single program. My heart was pounding, and I fired off an email to my supervisor, explaining the wet spot, taking responsibility for it, and offering to pay over $400 dollars out of my own pocket to have the programs reprinted. My supervisor asked me to calm down and invited me in to speak with her. She also brought in another colleague for a second opinion. She specifically asked, "Should we have a cow over this?" My colleague confidently stated, "No. No cow, no moo." It was fine. The programs were designed to have the look of parchment and the variance of the background was intentional. I insisted others might comment on the spot, and I contacted the designers to fix it and have a small quantity of copies reprinted for our guests of honor and their families.

For leaders in particular, perfectionism negatively impacts others. This particular incident didn't win me any credit with our design team, who I depended on daily. Aiming to impress others, I actually caused my supervisor to develop doubts about something she likely would not have even noticed or interpreted as a concern. And I spent time and effort re-doing something everyone else deemed completely unnecessary. Over time, I have come to the conclusion that perfectionists aren't all that easy to work with, or more importantly, work for. In drawing this conclusion for myself, I have let perfectionism go.

Success is fast and easy

While I have spoken with supervisors nearly every day of my career, there are a few conversations that I've retained in my long-term memory. One such conversation, occurred early on in an entry-level position. Specifically, I shared that I was job searching, and that I had applied to several director-level positions. My supervisor reflected that I struck her as someone who wanted to fast-track my career. While I think she shared this with the intention of having me reevaluate my plan, instead, I fully agreed with her. I went on to explain that I had a goal of being a doctor and a director by age 30. Fast forward a few years. I failed to meet either goal by my intended ages. When I met both goals at age 31 and 33, respectively, the success was subdued. When you apply an arbitrary time limit on a goal that you do not entirely control, you are setting yourself up to fail, and you then feel less accomplished when you actually meet your goal shortly thereafter. More recently, my current supervisor reminded me that I have a "long runway ahead." She's wise and I've come to agree—you do not need everything all at once. There is joy in the process.

Refusing to dive in ill-informed or inexperienced

My experience with this particular error demonstrates the capacity for recovering imposters like me to experience minor relapse. When the call for submissions for this book about *Thriving as Women in Leadership in Higher Education* landed in my inbox, my interest was piqued. Quickly thereafter, a thought floated through my brain: *Perhaps I don't really have the expertise for this though?* An hour later, my mind cycled back to this opportunity. Only then did I realize that I do in fact hold a doctorate in educational leadership and I am a woman with nearly two decades of leadership experience. These facts suggest I was better suited to the task than my psyche originally led me to believe. Still, I began canvasing for information on this topic. First, I watched all the TED talks. Then, I read a dozen blog posts. Next, I listened to several podcasts. Finally, I dove into my university's library research database and spent half a day pouring over peer-reviewed studies. Lastly, I bought a book on the topic. Still, I felt somewhat unsatisfied with my level of knowledge. *Certainly, I am capable of deeper research, like I did when I wrote my dissertation.* The idea that a dissertation-type dive is necessary for non-dissertation-like tasks is problematic. Knowledge is infinite. You cannot know it all, nor do you need to. If you are writing a dissertation, take a deep dive. If you are not, adjust accordingly. Also, take heart in the fact that other people are capable of knowing stuff too. And, if you're working together, you can show appreciation for the expertise they bring to the table.

Going at it alone, from scratch

A colleague once told me that the Diet Coke tap in our office was not working. I was new, but I noted he entrusted me to solve this problem and so I immediately busied myself with finding a solution by myself. I called the company to find out when they could come out and take a look at it. Next, I sent an email to the whole office with any update about the action taken along with a plan I had made to work with the company moving forward. The irony here is that this was actually someone else's task and it had been for a very long time. She emailed me the following day and admitted this had bothered her all night and she inquired why she couldn't work with the vendor anymore. Had I been willing to ask for help early on, I would have quickly learned that someone else had this covered. In taking care of it myself, I actually hurt my employee more than I helped her. If you try to do everything alone, you will likely make the same mistake of infringing on others' territory.

Having it all

In my 20's I had a desire to be surprisingly good at a lot of different things. For me, I was particularly keen on the idea of having an impressive career *and* an immaculate domestic showing. I wanted to wow people at home and at work. I often brought pieces of home to work (baked goods, a lot of décor, etc.) and likewise pieces of work came home (emails, project research, etc.). Things reached a boiling point during my doctoral program. Not only was I working full time in a position that required travel, I was commuting two hours each way to attend classes in person. I eventually made the decision to fire myself from domestic perfection. And I hired a wonderful woman who truly valued the opportunity to help me out with maintaining the household. Cleaning could be and *actually was* her business. It didn't have to be mine, and there was nothing more freeing than the feeling of letting go of that work, and that exhausting double-life.

Shutting the Syndrome Down

In my experience, imposterism lives in your head and comes out in your behavior. The best way to deal with it is to change the way you think about success, and Young's five cognitive errors provide an excellent road map to do this work. Additionally, here's a handful of other helpful tips I've found useful:

Navigating a networking event

Entering a room filled with strangers for small talk can be intimidating to anyone—it's not just you. The key to success in these venues is to consciously stop thinking about your feelings, and instead, direct all your energy and attention to others. Find someone who hasn't quite found their own 'in.'

Now, stop fanning the flames on your own fraud feelings and make it your goal to help them feel comfortable and welcome at the event. Be curious, listen, and keep the conversation light and friendly. After a few minutes, you'll both start enjoying yourselves, and don't be surprised when others join your group. Help facilitate introductions, even if you've just met.

Reveal that dirty little secret

Part of feeling like an imposter is the fear you could be 'found out.' Perhaps you've even decided there are some specific facts about you that, if revealed, will automatically disqualify you from the roles you hold. Former Chief Technology Officer of Hewlett-Packard, Phil McKinney, asks, "What happens when you share the secret that has been feeding your impostor syndrome for more than 25 years?" Turns out, for him, it meant absolutely nothing. His secret—the fact he never graduated from college, was published on the front page of the newspaper. In sharing his secret, it officially lost its power.

Develop a growth mindset

Psychologist Carol Dweck posits the value of abandoning a fixed mindset in favor of a growth mindset. A growth mindset is essentially the belief that skills are built, rather than born. From this perspective, every opportunity, challenge, mistake, and success presents an opportunity to learn and grow. Operating from a growth mindset, some of life's worst moments and biggest errors leave us with a choice—to focus on what we've lost, or to look for what we've gained. And some of life's biggest challenges make us exactly who we are meant to be.

Resources

Clance, Pauline R., and Suzanne A. Imes. "The Impostor Phenomenon in High Achieving Women: Dynamics and Therapeutic Intervention." *Psychotherapy: Theory, Research and Practice.* 15 (3): 241–247, 1978.

Sakulku, Jaruwan, and James Alexander. "The Impostor Phenomenon." *The Journal of Behavioral Science*, 6(1), 75-97, 2011.

Gravois, John. "You're Not Fooling Anyone." *The Chronicle of Higher Education*, 54(11), A1, 2007.

Young, Valerie. *The Secret Thoughts of Successful Women Why Capable People Suffer from the Impostor Syndrome and How to Thrive in Spite of It.* Crown Publishing, New York, NY, 2011.

Additional Reading

Read the original research on the Imposter Phenomenon:

> http://mpowir.org/wp-content/uploads/2010/02/
> Download-IP-in-High-Achieving-Women.pdf

Valerie Young is a subject-matter expert. Her book is *The Secret Thoughts of Successful Women*, her Twitter is @ValerieYoung, and her website is impostersyndrome.com. You can also:

Take her Imposter Syndrome Quiz:
https://impostorsyndrome.com/quiz/

Check out her Ted Talk:
https://www.youtube.com/watch?v=h7v-GG3SEWQ

Listen to her podcast episode:
https://www.stitcher.com/podcast/life-and-leadership-podcast/the-life-and-leadership-podcast/e/63363485

Here are additional curated TED talks on Imposter Syndrome:

https://www.ted.com/search?q=imposter+syndrome

Check out the Growth Mindset Training Hub:

https://trainugly.com/growth-mindset-hub/

When you experience a doozy of an imposter moment, take some time to deconstruct it. Here is a useful tool that will guide you through the deconstruction in seven steps:

https://www.getselfhelp.co.uk/docs/ThoughtRecord Sheet7.pdf

About the Author

Dr. Katie Jackson currently serves as the Director of Student Conduct and Conflict Resolution at the University of Minnesota-Duluth. She earned B.A. degrees in Psychology and Religion from Concordia College. She completed an M.Ed. in College Student Personnel from The University of Southern Mississippi. She earned her Ed.D in Education Leadership and Policy Analysis from the University of Missouri. Her dissertation research was titled "Fit Between Student Conduct Administrators' Personal Values and Professional Codes of Ethics."

She was the 2019 recipient of the Outstanding Staff Award presented by the Chancellor at the University of Minnesota-Duluth. In 2014, she was a finalist for the Dan Cockrell Ed.D. Dissertation of the Year Award. She currently serves as Chair for the Association for Student Conduct Administration's Research Committee. She is listed on the Minnesota Supreme Court roster of qualified neutrals. In her position as Conduct Director, she led her office in a name change and effectively expanded their service offerings to include a full suite of alternative resolutions and outreach on conflict mediation. She has experience leading teams in residence life, alcohol and drug prevention, alumni relations and annual giving, student conduct, and student affairs.

CHAPTER 5
OVERCOMING INTENTIONAL INVISIBILITY IN THE WORKPLACE

by Rosann Bar, Ph.D.
Dean, School of Business and Social Sciences
Ocean County College

Be FDR

"Be FDR! Franklin Delano Roosevelt, that is. Be the face of your 'New Deal.'" These words from my mentor, Carol Brown, former president of several community colleges, identified a critical skill that I lacked—the ability to put myself out in front, articulate my accomplishments, gain exposure, and receive appropriate credit for my achievements. Ultimately, being unnoticed can impact performance reviews and hinder career mobility. It was a false assumption on my part that my efforts would be seen without my making them visible. Little did I know at the time that I was practicing behaviors that have recently been termed, "intentional invisibility," by Stanford researchers Swethaa Ballakrishnen, Priya Fielding-Singh, and Devon Magliozzi. They define this concept as "a set of risk averse, conflict-avoidant strategies that women professionals... employ to feel authentic, manage competing expectations in the office, and balance work and family responsibilities... intentionally remaining behind the scenes in attempts to avoid backlash and maintain a professional status quo." As highlighted by these researchers, I navigated the "workplace labyrinth" in ways aligned with my personal identity (Ballakrishnen, et al.).

Collaboration is at the core of my management style, and working with others as a team is my preferred way of leading. For me, as Dean, this translated into my rolling up my sleeves and actively assisting my faculty when needed in completing projects and running campus events that were elements of my vision for our school. However, my favorite place to "perform" at work was always behind the curtain, backstage, far away from the spotlights and the audience. I took pride in being a quietly effective but relatively invisible leader, working hard directing and guiding others behind the scenes, yet making things happen. I spent countless hours in multiple meetings where I provided advice, creative ideas, and pathways toward completion of projects with those I supervised. Anytime problems arose or resources were needed, I brainstormed with my faculty and worked to guarantee that they had sufficient resources to complete what I referred to as "their projects." I was happy to empower those I managed to be the "stars" of the show. For me, their success was my success, and just knowing that important work that benefitted our students and the college community was being accomplished was sufficient.

In addition, I am not a good self-promoter, nor do I admire that behavior in others. I am wary of those who feel the need to manipulatively brag about their accomplishments, "grab the mic" and talk loudly over others to gain attention, claim credit for work done by others, or recycle other's ideas with a commanding tone that makes it seem that the ideas belong to them.

My mentor was astute enough to realize my dilemma: how to gain appropriate recognition for accomplishments that could enhance my career mobility, while at the same time letting me stay in my comfort zone and not resort to what I was socialized to believe were negative behaviors. As a historian, she shared the leadership style of Franklin Delano Roosevelt and the "New Deal" with me. The term "New Deal" emerged from FDR's 1932 acceptance speech for the Democratic Party's nomination for President. Since then, FDR and the "New Deal" have become synonymous. Yet, the names of Roosevelt's Brains Trust (among them Adolf Berle, Rexford Tugwell, and Benjamin V. Cohen), who assisted in shaping the policies related to relief, recovery, and reform inherent in the New Deal are probably lost on all but those who have made an effort to study this historical period.

In challenging me to be FDR and the face of my "New Deal," my mentor was motivating me to peek out from behind the backstage curtain and establish myself as the point person for the work that was being done collaboratively with and by others in support of my vision—my "New Deal"—for my school. Even if others helped me create or execute an idea, event, or plan, I needed to be associated with it. I still struggled with this concept until we discussed one more important idea. Being the face of your vision does *not* equate to self-promotion, which involves the failure to recognize the work of those around you. The FDR model provided me with a means to raise my profile at work in a manner that I was comfortable with and to move gradually a few steps beyond "intentional invisibility." While I still shine the spotlight on others who command the stage, I have learned to share the stage with them for a brief moment, just enough to have my face associated with the initiative.

What I Learned

Recognizing my invisibility was the first step in working to overcome it. This occurred when I was invited, along with a colleague, to attend a prominent leadership training program. This program was intense and sometimes difficult because it forced me to really take a hard look at my leadership skillset. It also paired me with a mentor and a coach to assist me in my self-reflective journey. One of the program requirements was to complete a 360° review that compared my perception of my leadership skills with that of my supervisor and colleagues. There was a discrepancy in scores between my manager and me on two components of Kouzes and Posner's leadership model: "challenging the process" and "inspiring a shared vision." My manager scored me lower than I scored myself and lower than my peers ranked me. One of my goals of the leadership training was to explore the gap. In doing so, it became obvious in discussions with my supervisor that he was unaware of my role in many different initiatives. He attributed discrepancies in the scores to my inability to articulate all of my accomplishments. This was also reflected in my annual performance review. It was at that point, in consultation with my mentor, that the realization of my invisibility came to the forefront.

Time to be FDR! What, in practice, did that mean? I was challenged to take a step toward visibility by introducing those involved next time a school event or initiative was going to take place. When I explained my mentor's challenge to my supervisor, he was very supportive. The first situation where that occurred was in a presentation to the Board of Trustees on stackable credentials and use of technology in our Accounting Program. While I clearly acknowledged the work done by my faculty in developing the program and gave them center stage to present the core ideas, I introduced them and identified the importance of this effort and its place within our school. The presentation as a whole was well-received. The FDR model worked for me! It raised my visibility but still permitted me to showcase my faculty's efforts. I was very comfortable with this level of visibility because it matched my personality, collaborative nature, and allowed me to be authentic. Since then, I have made it a point to be on the program for other events such as our honor society induction ceremonies, Addictions Summit, and entrepreneurial "Sink or Swim" contest. These brief appearances link me to the "alphabet" of initiatives of my "New Deal" and heighten my profile as a leader.

One last caveat: As a sociologist, I support social and organization change that leads to greater gender equity. At the same time, I recognize that changing the structure and culture entrenched in one's workplace can be a difficult task and is not always possible in the short term. In addition, sometimes the very socialization process of women holds them back and makes them prefer the invisibility that aligns with the "woman as helper" role. So, I stand behind the FDR model, which encourages women to change and grow, while fully understanding that there is a broader goal to embrace: recognizing all leadership styles, both those favored by men and women alike.

Putting This into Action

A) Be conscious of your organizational culture

1. The values, ethics, and overall culture of your organization will impact your satisfaction with your work situation. Does your organization recognize the potentially different work styles of both men and women? How do you know?

2. Culture can undergo major change or change in subtle ways. Is the culture of your organization amenable to change? What steps might you take to promote needed change?

3. Promotion and advancement requirements vary within organizations and among different super-visors. Is visibility an important factor in career mobility where you are employed?

B) Engage in self-reflection

1. You reveal your management style at work when interacting with colleagues. Do you practice "intentional invisibility"? If so, why? Is it related to avoiding conflict? Or to being in sync with your personality? Or is it related to balancing personal and professional obligations?

2. There is a continuum of degrees of visibility. How visible do you want to be? What are the pros and cons of becoming more visible? Are there some initiatives for which higher visibility is more important than it is for others?

C) Find an empowering mentor

1. Choosing an appropriate mentor is critical. Is your mentor sincere in helping you as your mentor? Trustworthy and honest? An enthusiastic role model? An experienced professional willing to share his/her successes <u>and</u> failures?

2. As good as we are, we can always be better. Are you open to accepting constructive criticism?

D) Plan a strategy

1. Identifying goals is the first step in achieving them. What are your short- and long-term goals for your presentation of self in your capacity as a manager?

2. Goals must be practical and feasible in order for you to attain them. What series of steps will you take to achieve them?

Resources

Ballakrishnen, Swethaa, Priya Fielding-Singh, and Devon Magliozzi. "Intentional Invisibility: Professional Women and the Navigation of Workplace Constraints." *Sociological Perspectives* 1-19, 2018.

"Step into the Spotlight," Discussion Guide: Women at Work, 2019. *Harvard Business Review*. Retrieved 22 May 2020. https://hbr.org/resources/pdfs/podcast-discussion-guides/WAW_DG_S3_E2.pdf

Kouzes, James and Barry Posner. *The Leadership Challenge: How to Make Extraordinary Things Happen in Organizations.* Jossey-Bass, 2017.

About the Author

Rosann Bar received her Ph.D. in sociology from Columbia University. She worked as a production editor for Globe Fearon, a division of Simon and Schuster, before becoming a full-time, tenured faculty member and Chair of the Department of Sociology and Criminal Justice at Caldwell University, Caldwell, NJ. There, she taught numerous sociology and anthropology courses for nearly 20 years. She educated students in culture and social life by designing multiple travel abroad seminars to various destinations in Europe, Asia, South America, and the Caribbean. Dr. Bar is currently Dean, School of Business and Social Sciences, at Ocean County College in Toms River, NJ, where she has worked on behalf of students since 2015.

CHAPTER 6
HOW TO BANISH "I WISH I WOULD HAVE SAID" FOREVER

by Ella Ingram, Ph.D.
Associate Dean for Professional Development; Professor, Biology &
Biomedical Engineering, Rose-Hulman Institute of Technology

Leaders strive for effective communication, that is, communication that meets the objective of each interaction. Unfortunately, women leaders can experience challenges in communication stemming from gender-based communication patterns. For example, you may recognize the experience of "speaking while female," describing situations like sharing an idea that is later attributed to a male colleague, or being repeatedly interrupted, especially by junior male colleagues. You may also use language that is considered tentative (linguistic research confirms this tendency in women): expressing uncertainty, adding disclaimers, using qualifiers and hedges, and phrasing statements as questions. Such language choices combined with externally-imposed "speaking while female" and other gendered microaggressions undermine your authority and influence others' perceptions of your competence.

One antidote to these challenges, including the tendency to use tentative language, is to build a vocabulary of phrases that empower the speaker and demonstrate assertive commun-ication. I call this vocabulary my "stock phrases." A stock phrase is one that you as the leader can use without hesitation in difficult situations, and it therefore banishes tentative language. The stock phrase gives you confidence, because you have pre-determined your response and therefore it is consistent with your leadership philosophy and approach. The stock phrase helps you claim your position at the table and assert your leadership strengths and authority.

Preparing the Stock Phrases

An important feature of stock phrases is having them "at the ready." To be ready to deploy a stock phrase means you have practiced it out loud and with your "pass the salt" voice (the unheated, neutral tone you would use to request the salt at the dinner table). A member of your leadership council is a good choice of partner for this role-playing practice; these individuals are likely to know enough of the scenario and people involved to create authentic responses. I can't overstate the importance of this practice to get the inflection and tone of your statements to be neutral and firm.

When the situation presents, share your stock phrase and then stop talking. Additional explanation, backtracking, or follow-up reduces the power of your message and implies you are not convinced by your own message. You can take control of the interaction and ownership of your perspective by stating the phrase in a firm, clear, succinct manner and then being quiet. Repeating the same phrase again when your conversational partner goes another round on the topic is effective in ending the conversation, with your message as the dominant message.

To be clear, the situations I am writing about are not the interactions where everything goes right, all parties leave with smiles on their faces, and objectives are met. The scenarios I am addressing here are the ones where you get back to your office and know that it did not go the way you wanted it to go. They often involve disappointments, conflicts, disagreements, saying no, correcting behavior, or other conflict scenarios. Because these situations can involve conversational partners across the organizational hierarchy, I have included below examples of interactions and phrases for colleagues, examples for conversation with your team members, and examples for conversation with your supervisor.

The Stock Phrases

Interactions with Colleagues

SITUATION: A COLLEAGUE DISPARAGES ANOTHER COLLEAGUE OR SUPERVISOR, ETC.

Stock Phrase: "I don't want to talk about someone without them here."

Stock Phrase: "I'm sure Marsha wouldn't want us talking about her when she isn't here to set the record straight."

SITUATION: YOU LEARN A COLLEAGUE HAS DISPARAGED YOU TO OTHERS.

Stock Phrase: "Please do not discuss my behaviors, performance, or personality with anyone but me."

Stock Phrase: "If you are unhappy with my contributions to our project, I expect you to address them with me so we can meet the objectives of the work, not discuss them with people uninvolved in the project."

SITUATION: COLLEAGUE TALKS OVER YOU OR CUTS YOU OFF IN A MEETING.

Stock Phrase: "Excuse me, Bill, I'd like to finish sharing my thought. As I was saying..."

Stock Phrase: "Bill, you interrupted me. Please don't do that again. My main point was..."

SITUATION: A COLLEAGUE SAYS SOMETHING TO WHICH YOU STRONGLY DISAGREE.

Stock Phrase: "I'm having a strong reaction to that suggestion."

Stock Phrase: "I appreciate hearing your perspective, Robert. I disagree with that suggestion. My major point of disagreement is...."

Interactions with Team Members

SITUATION: A TEAM MEMBER ASKS YOU FOR YOUR DECISION TOO SOON OR IN AN INAPPROPRIATE SETTING.

Stock Phrase: "I'm not ready to make a decision on that issue. When I decide, I will alert you."

Stock Phrase: "I previously indicated I would have a decision made on that topic by next Monday."

SITUATION: A TEAM MEMBER SAYS THINGS LIKE "YOU OWE ME" OR "THAT'S NOT FAIR."

Stock Phrase: "I owe you no more and no less than I owe everyone in our unit."

Stock Phrase: "These expectations are reasonable and achievable, even in the absence of an official policy."

SITUATION: A TEAM MEMBER PROPOSES OVERSTEPPING HER DECISION-MAKING AUTHORITY.

Stock Phrase: "I'd like to be involved in that decision."

Stock Phrase: "That decision is one that requires my input and oversight."

SITUATION: A TEAM MEMBER EXPRESSES DISAPPOINTMENT WITH SOMETHING YOU'VE DONE.

Stock Phrase: "I'm sorry to learn that you are disappointed; however, your disappointment doesn't change my decision."

Stock Phrase: "Thank you for expressing that sentiment."

SITUATION: A TEAM MEMBER QUESTIONS THE BASIS FOR A DECISION GIVEN NEW INFORMATION.

Stock Phrase: "I made this decision with the best information available at the time, keeping in mind our mission to provide individual attention and support to our students."

Stock Phrase: "At the time of my decision, I knew that we faced a budget deficit of 12%. Now that I know the deficit is 17%, I will take appropriate action."

SITUATION: A TEAM MEMBER ASKS FOR SOMETHING COMPLETELY OUT OF BOUNDS.

Stock Phrase: "I'm sorry that I won't be able to fulfill that request."

Stock Phrase: "That request is inconsistent with our stated priorities. Therefore, I cannot grant your request at this time."

SITUATION: A TEAM MEMBER WANTS SOMETHING YOU DON'T HAVE THE AUTHORITY TO GRANT.

Stock Phrase: "Unfortunately, that decision is out of my hands."

Stock Phrase: "That decision is made above my level, and at this time, I don't intend to raise it with my supervisor."

SITUATION: A TEAM MEMBER SUBMITS UNACCEPTABLE WORK.

Stock Phrase: "This work does not meet my expectations with respect to tone, error removal, and formatting. Please re-submit it with those expectations fulfilled."

Stock Phrase: "This work is not usable in its current form. I want to work with you to ensure this doesn't happen moving forward."

Interactions with Your Supervisor

SITUATION: YOUR SUPERVISOR REVERSES A DECISION YOU MADE.

Stock Phrase: "I understand why you reversed this decision. Please inform me in advance if this occurs again."

Stock Phrase: "The decision I made was based on our agreed-upon goals. Has something changed I don't know about?"

SITUATION: YOUR SUPERVISOR COMMITS YOU TO A MAJOR PROJECT WITHOUT CONSULTING YOU FIRST.

Stock Phrase: "I need your assessment of which current activities I should put on the backburner to fulfill this request."

Stock Phrase: "This new work will delay delivery on the curriculum reform project."

SITUATION: YOUR SUPERVISOR ASSIGNS WORK DIRECTLY TO YOUR TEAM MEMBER WITHOUT CONSULTING YOU FIRST.

Stock Phrase: "This puts me in an awkward position with my team member. Please discuss work assignments with me first."

Stock Phrase: "I don't think we are in agreement here. I would like to have a meeting to figure out our priorities before I speak with my team member."

SITUATION: YOUR SUPERVISOR DISPARAGES ONE OF YOUR PROJECTS OR PROGRAMS.

Stock Phrase: "If you were unhappy with this project, I wish you had expressed it earlier. What specific features do not meet your expectations?"

Stock Phrase: "That program is important to me and my team. Your constructive feedback will help us improve it."

When I first started practicing phrases like the ones listed here, I thought I would sound like I was giving a canned speech or would be perceived as unempathetic and rigid. In other words, I feared the stock phrases approach would decrease the power of my communication. The opposite has been true; by having pre-decided what I will say in many challenging situations, the power of my communications has increased based on the metric of meeting the objectives for my conversations. And the positive influence on my day-to-day experience was profound. I was released from constantly rewinding the tape on these conversations.

Putting Stock Phrases into Action

As you can see from the examples, the concept of a stock phrase is broadly applicable. As you practice this skill, your reliance on the specific words will reduce. Also, I suspect you will discover other scenarios you frequently encounter that could benefit from the stock phrase treatment. Use these scenarios as a starting point, find that role-playing partner, and give it a try. A next step would be to extend the stock phrase strategy to other behaviors—such as a team member repeatedly coming to work a few minutes late, a colleague rolling his eyes in a meeting, a team member or colleague wearing inappropriate clothing, your supervisor's crushing handshake, or the colleague who starts the meeting before time and before everyone is present.

Another next step could be crafting the words of the stock phrase to suit your language conventions. You might say "I'm uncomfortable with that suggestion" rather than my preferred "I'm having a reaction to that suggestion." You might also craft the stock phrase to feature some aspect of your leadership like your decision-making approach, your coaching philosophy, or your strategic thinking. For example, when asked by a team member to support an out-of-scope project, you might say "I want to support your initiative. Please bring me a revision that better fits with our unit's goals," rather than "I'm sorry that I won't be able to fulfill that request."

The skill of having an authoritative statement ready for the most common situations allows you as a leader to project your confidence, leadership, and competence. These phrases by their nature conflict with the tentative language women leaders often use, and these phrases represent an empowering way to address gendered microaggressions. These phrases can highlight your authority, competence, strengths, position, and influence, and therefore help you as a leader fully enact your role. Try a stock phrase or two; you won't be sorry.

Resources

Gender, Communication, and the Leadership Gap (2017, eds. Cunningham, Crandall, and Dare) is a comprehensive analysis and solutions book—every chapter is excellent, but especially McKenzie and Halstead's chapter on combatting micro-aggressions.

The concept "speaking while female" was popularized in Sheryl Sandberg and Adam Grant's op-ed series "Women at Work" in *The New York Times.*

Jennifer Coates' *Women, Men, and Language* (3rd ed. reissued, 2016) is a highly cited and accessible exploration of gendered language.

Meggin McIntosh's *Emphasis on Excellence* (meggin.com) is focused on faculty success and productivity. Her special gift is to make all advice actionable. I learned about the concept of the "pass the salt" voice from her workshops on establishing personal policies and eliminating drama. You may find her *Top Ten Productivity Tips for Women* series especially valuable. (See www.toptenproductivitytips.com/women.)

David Perlmutter and Alison Vaillancourt each have columns in *The Chronicle of Higher Education* that regularly address issues of strategic, effective communication for leaders. Perlmutter's *Admin 101* series has entries focused on communication during stressful situations (https://www.chronicle.com/package/admin-101/). Vaillancourt's series *The Management Corner* often includes quotes from tested leaders that would make great stock phrases (www.chronicle.com/package/the-management-corner/). Both columns are uniformly excellent and worth every minute to read.

Patterson, Grenny, McMillan, and Switzler's book *Crucial Conversations: Tools for Talking When Stakes Are High* (2nd ed., 2011) lays out a complete conversational model for difficult situations. The model relies on having a plan in advance of a discussion and on being firm yet empathetic. I'd consider this book the advanced course in stock phrases that are focused on problem-solving, rather than simply addressing an in-the-moment experience.

About the Author

Ella Ingram earned her B.A. in biology and mathematics from Augustana College (IL) and her Ph.D. from Indiana University in ecology and evolution. She joined the faculty of Rose-Hulman Institute of Technology in 2004, then assumed duties as Director of the Center for the Practice and Scholarship of Education in 2013. She was appointed Associate Dean for Professional Development in 2017. Dr. Ingram received the highest honor of her career in 2016 when she was named an Honorary Alumna of Rose-Hulman. She was also named the Board of Trustees Outstanding Scholar in 2017. Recently, she joined the NSF ADVANCE ASCEND project to promote advancement of women in STEM. Dr. Ingram has blended her work in the classroom with work in scholarship of teaching and faculty development. She instituted or improved multiple programs: the new faculty mentoring program, the writing accountability programs, the promotion support group, the endowed chair program, and more. When not teaching or working with faculty, Dr. Ingram enjoys spending time on her family farm with her husband and their seven dogs and relaxing with a sewing project.

CHAPTER 7
DEVELOPING YOUR POSITIVE INNER VOICE

by Laurie Friedman, M.A.
Strategic Business Consulting

In my work as a leadership and executive coach I have met and worked with many women leaders in education and across industries who, from the outside looking in, seem to be accomplished and successful in their careers, rising stars and heads of academic departments, and yet when their door is closed, they fear they are "not enough." The fear can be both debilitating and motivating, depending upon the moment. The truth is, many people, whether male or female, experience the fear that they will be found out "as imposters, and worry that they are not good enough." This phenomenon, although not just a women's problem, has commonly been suggested as one of the factors that can hold women back in their careers.

Women who learn to develop their "positive inner voice" to counteract the *imposter voice* are more likely to minimize the imposter voice's impact. Brain science confirms that "the pain of criticism is much stronger than the pleasure of praise." (See "How to Counteract the Power of Negative Thinking," *The Wall Street Journal*, December 28-29, 2019.) It takes five "atta girls" or positive affirmations, to one criticism, to break the negativity chain.

THE IMPOSTER VOICE IN A HIGHER EDUCATION SETTING

Women in university/academic settings still lag behind men when it comes to holding senior leadership positions. Many theories attempt to account for the reasons why more women do not crossover or climb up to senior academic positions. There is not enough data to suggest that the imposter syndrome plays a *primary* role; however, data does suggest "the imposter voice" could contribute to why women do not rise to their full potential. The bottom line for women is that to be successful they must go out on the ledge, do things that they have never done before, and be prepared to quiet their inner negative voice.

One client shared this example; she was in a meeting with her team and she looked out around the room and thought, *"Why are they listening to me?"* Another client confessed that her internal negative ruminations kept her up at night. If these types of internal messages or negative self-talk keep you from being your best, you are not alone. Studies suggest that more than 70% of women suffer from the imposter syndrome. This should tell you that *you are in good company*.

Below are some strategies to override the *imposter voice* and build your positive inner voice.

Overriding the Imposter Voice: Your Five Step Action Plan

1. Become aware of your inner voice.

In those moments when negative voices are in your head, it is important to acknowledge these voices and counter them with a positive voice. Imagine if Michael Jordan, the famous basketball player, told himself, "I cannot make that shot." We can learn from sports the importance of positive psychology. Positive psychology provides us with the template to manage our negative inner voices. Brain research shows that certain parts of the brain are lit up when we are given positive feedback, and these recognitions serve as motivators to be our best selves. When we provide positive affirmations for ourselves, we are building our own positivity brain roadmaps. By becoming aware of your negative voices, you can train yourself to override the negative messaging with positive ones. Often, we are so accustomed to our negative voice that we are not truly conscious when those negative voices show up. Awareness is the first step.

2. Track it.

Once you become aware when your negative voice shows up, *get curious*. Is it every day? With certain people? In certain situations? Many of my clients express surprise when they develop a greater awareness not just of their negative voice but of the behaviors that show up based on their negative thoughts. One client described "shutting down" in staff meetings because her negative voice told her "no one is listening to me." When she felt "not listened to," she was sure it was because she was "not good enough." By developing your awareness, you can build your counter strategy, not just to your negative voice but to the negative behaviors that may also show up because of your inner voice.

This next exercise may sound arduous, but I promise you it will make a difference. For a few weeks, write down the negative voices you hear in your head. Track your words and, if possible, your behavior or reactions in those situations. The longer you do this, the better. I often recommend thirty days; this provides enough data to identify patterns so that you can build your strategic counter strategies. Your secret thoughts, once brought out into the light, can lead to new insights, including identification of blind spots and career derailers. Negative thoughts are sneaky mental habits that, if left unchecked, will lead you to places where you do not want to go.

Scott Adams, the Dilbert comic strip creator, coined the phrase "loser think." *Loser think* is a made-up phrase to illustrate and provide insights into how we think and the mental models that keep us in a negative mindset. When you have negative thoughts or negative beliefs, we handicap ourselves. If we use the concept of *loser think* as an opportunity to hold a mirror to ourselves, we can identify those patterns of behavior that may be trapping you or keeping you in place. Ask yourself, what mental habits keep you trapped in your negative mindset?

3. Talk to yourself.

Research supports the antidote: "You can change behavior by talking to yourself" (Van Raalte). Develop your positive words to override the negative thoughts. Trade "I can't" for "I can." Prepare in advance to be ready and armed with positive affirmations.

One of my clients created visual reminders on her phone and computer to regularly remind her to practice positive habits. Developing a positive mindset takes practice; like learning any new skill, it requires the three P's: *preparation*, *practice*, and *patience*:

- Prepare your action plan in advance so you are ready to counteract your negative thoughts.

- Practice and track your successes and opportunities to be better.

- Be patient and be compassionate with yourself.

One of my clients told me he lives by the mantra, "Get it done and get it right the first time!" Recognize your inner critic at work and be kind to yourself. Many imposter theorists believe "the imposter syndrome and perfectionism go hand-in-hand." (See *5 Different Types of Imposter Syndrome and 5 Ways to Battle Each One* by Melody J. Wilding, melodywilding.com.) Are you tough on yourself? Do you look for perfection? Is it difficult to let your work go forward before you deem it perfect? Do you tell yourself that it is just easier if you do it yourself because you know it will be done right? If you answered *yes* to any of these questions, you might want to explore whether perfectionism is playing a role in your negative thinking.

4. Remember you have a choice as to whether to allow that negative voice in.

Picture your front door and imagine closing your door to the negative voice that is taking up space in your head. Stop and change the narrative. *Develop your positive mantra and repeat.*

5. It takes five "atta girls" to counter one negative criticism.

This rule of thumb has been adapted from the marriage literature of Dr. John Gottman, who suggests that for successful married couples the ratio of positive to negative words is five to one. For every negative interaction, it takes five positives to counteract the one negative. Why do we tend to hold on to the negative experiences more than the positive experiences? If we think about negative feedback as threats, scientists theorize that our ancestors, those hunters and gatherers, passed on this bias to us. This phenomenon, known as the "fight or flight response," has been adapted from our caveman days where danger was around every corner. Although our sensitivity to negative data can still be useful today, it helps to remember to use positive psychology to counteract our natural tendency to focus more on negative than positive inputs. When your internal voice tells you that "you are a failure for not getting that report in on time," you will need to find five positive experiences to counteract your one negative thought. Your inner voice requires the same care and feeding as your body. Feed your mind with positive words, and you will change the way you think and behave.

One more for good measure:
6. What gets measured gets done.

The old adage "what gets measured gets done" is true here. If you don't track your game plan, if you don't record your positive to negative ratios, you will not know your success formula. Set your goal, create your game plan, and check in with yourself. Adjust your thinking and behavior as needed. You can change your negative habits with practice, compassion, and positivity. There are many reasons women in academe are not rising into leadership positions in the same numbers as men—but if one of the causes is the imposter syndrome, the good news is that with intentional, customized, personal strategies, women can counteract patterns of negative thoughts and change one of the factors that may be holding them back. Women can be as strong on the inside as they are on the outside.

Final Thoughts

As I reflect on my many clients who have described the imposter voice as a prevalent friend and foe in times of stress, I think of one client in particular, whom I mentioned earlier. She described the torture of sitting in a conference room, leading a team, all eyes looking at her while thinking to herself,

"Why are they listening to me?" She told me that she had tried therapy, medicine, and meditation to get rid of the nagging negative voices inside her head. Although the voices had not derailed her career, the stress of trying to stop her imposter voice was exhausting.

We worked together to develop an action plan. She began by tracking when, with whom, and how often her negative voices showed up. After careful review we discussed change strategies that she could implement at the moment the imposter voice "spoke up." Some of the tools included counteracting the negative thought with an immediate positive one. This took practice until she found the words or thoughts that calmed her in those moments. She also identified a visual tool that supported her change.

Brené Brown, the wise and compassionate leadership guru, titled her New York Times bestselling book, *The Gifts of Imperfection*. In her book, videos, and podcasts, Brené Brown provides a hopeful roadmap to guide you in "letting go of who you think you're supposed to be" and to "embrace who you are." The practice of muting the imposter voice follows the same guidelines. By seeing the negative voice as part of your *gift of imperfection*, practicing self-awareness, and embracing strategies to build your positivity muscles, the path to greater freedom from negativity can be achieved.

As for what happened to my client—a year or two later I met her at a coaching conference. She proudly showed me her visuals still in practice and told me that after retiring from her executive position, she became a certified coach. She thanked me for supporting her and told me our work together had inspired her to become a coach so that she could help other women who are also struggling with their negative voices.

Her story inspires me every day. In my career, I too have struggled with turning off the negative voices inside my head. I have learned to practice a positivity mantra, and I begin every day—ok, almost every day—with the practice of gratefulness. These practices are hard, and hard won. When we learn how and when our negative thoughts guide or derail us, it is like toothpaste coming out of the tube. You cannot put the toothpaste back.

There are three things I have learned as a coach, as a mentor, and as a Mom. We are not defined by how others see us, we are not defined by our negative voices; we are defined by the choices we make when faced with a personal challenge and when we allow our vulnerability and truth to light the way. I think Carolyn Hax said it best in her "Dear Carolyn" column in *The Washington Post* (July 22, 2020): "Engage with the good, disengage from the bad."

About the Author

Laurie Friedman is founder and CEO of Strategic Business Consulting, an independent consulting firm that provides both strategic and tactical tools to enhance leadership development and improve organization, team, and individual performance. She holds a Master's in Human Resources and Organization Development from The George Washington University and she is a certified Myers Briggs Type Indicator, DISC, and Action Learning facilitator. Laurie has worked in both the public and private sector, and she has held leadership positions at Deloitte Consulting and Washington Gas. Laurie has published numerous business articles on strategic thinking, employee engagement, and building teams. Her most recent publication is a chapter in the book titled *Compassion@Work: Creating Workplaces that Engage the Human Spirit.* In 2015 Laurie was awarded the Sherpa Coach of the Year award in recognition of mastery and advancement of Sherpa Coaching.

IMPOSTER SYNDROME WORKSHEET

In the past week I have experienced _____# of negative thoughts.

I have noticed those thoughts when:

_____

The words I hear are:

_____

One change I can make immediately is:

_____

One way I can remind myself to stay positive is:

_____

(*e.g. put a message on my computer*)

My positive word/words are:

_____

My accountability partner is:

_____

(For your accountability partner, identify someone whom you trust and are comfortable sharing your imposter change goal with. Remember once you share your vulnerability with someone, you are shining a light out from the darkness.)

I will check in with myself *(circle)*:

Weekly | Daily | Monthly

I will check in with my accountability partner:

Weekly | Daily | Monthly

One way I will know if I am successful is:

_____

Did I "shut the door" to my negative thoughts? Yes | No

I can be better next time if

_____

I gave myself these five "atta girls" after one negative thought:

_____

_____

_____

_____

_____

Today I learned:

_____

My plan to keep getting better is:

_____

I have been kind and compassionate with myself! Yes | No

Bravo! Congratulations! You are on the road to a life well lived and a job well done.

CHAPTER 8
OVERCOMING THE IMPOSTER SYNDROME THROUGH AUTHENTIC COGNITIVE RESTRUCTURING

by Susan Thomas, Ph.D.
President, Truman State University

Intellectual phoniness, persistent beliefs of inadequacy despite evident success, concerns about being discovered as a fraud—these are hallmark feelings of the imposter syndrome. While these feeling sow significant seeds of doubt, there is no doubt about interest in the subject. Google "imposter syndrome" and 3,920,000 results are produced; google "women and imposter syndrome" and 826,000 results are produced; google "women in higher education and imposter syndrome" and 523,000 results are produced. Results include definitions, symptoms, prevalence, impacts, and advice about how to overcome it. The gist of all of the posts is that the imposter syndrome is pervasive for accomplished and/or highly educated people, and perhaps especially for accomplished and/or highly educated women. Celebrities such as Serena Williams, Lady Gaga, Maya Angelou, Sonia Sotomayor, and Michelle Obama have owned experiencing the imposter syndrome, doubting their accomplishments and fearing they would be exposed as frauds.

Interestingly, while there is a prolific discussion of the imposter syndrome in the popular press, according to a 2020 systematic review of the empirical literature (Bravata, et al.), there is no published research that examines treatments to mitigate the symptoms. Although there is no empirical support for any particular approach to addressing the imposter syndrome, conceptually, cognitive restructuring (also known as cognitive reframing) has great promise, and I have found it to be very effective.

Through mastering the skill of cognitive restructuring, you can modify or replace the automatic negative, inaccurate, or irrational thoughts associated with the imposter syndrome. It is these cognitive distortions that are connected with the negative outcomes of the imposter syndrome, including, amongst others, self-doubt, self-criticism, self-sabotage, and anxiety. Each of these negative outcomes is a common barrier women face in academe, as each can impair your sense of self and your confidence and make you more likely to play small and not achieve the level of success you otherwise could.

Cognitive restructuring involves identifying and challenging cognitive distortions and replacing them with more accurate, positive, and beneficial ways of thinking. Changing your way of thinking takes time, practice, and cognitive energy. It starts with increasing your awareness and recognition of your negative imposter thoughts. This is much easier said than done, as many of these thoughts have most likely become automatic. It is also difficult to address your negative thoughts head on, especially given that they occur simultaneously with negative emotions. You must be intentional, vigilant, and strong enough to willingly take on emotionally charged thoughts. Once you recognize these thoughts, you cannot just accept them as inevitable; you must do the work to modify them.

There are a variety of techniques that can be used to accomplish cognitive restructuring. The one I have found to be the most effective is the Socratic Questioning method. Essentially, this method involves determining evidence for and against a thought and utilizing this evidence to analyze the thought. Once the thought is analyzed, the analysis can be used to restructure the thought to be more accurate, positive, and beneficial.

Utilizing your knowledge of your authentic self is enormously helpful in both the analysis and the cognitive restructuring of the imposter thoughts. For example, for many of us who experience or have experienced the imposter syndrome, the perspective "the more you know, the more you know you don't know" sums up the concerns about being exposed as a fraud. While on the surface this perspective appears to be negative, as it places a focus on what you do not know, I realized that when applying my own self-knowledge, it is not negative for me.

As the president of a university, while many look to me to have all of the answers, I realized it is not important to my self-identity to have all of the answers or to have others believe I have all of the answers. In everything I do, I want to make the best decision. As I have learned on many occasions, even if I must make the ultimate decision, my best decisions come from gathering relevant information and insights from others. True teamwork is very important to me and I do not need the credit or want the spotlight. By reflecting on who I am and what is and is not important to me, I was able to cognitively restructure the originally negative thought of "the more you know, the more you know you don't know" into a positive, by embracing the fact that others knowing more than me ensures I can make better decisions by willingly and proactively considering and incorporating their knowledge, skills, and talents into my decisions.

Fortuitously, a real-time positive impact of this cognitive restructuring actually enhanced this chapter. In line with proactively gathering others' perspectives, I asked my provost if she would review the chapter, and she graciously agreed. In her review, she shared a powerful insight that the imposter syndrome may prevent leaders from building the strongest teams. To avoid being exposed as a fraud, those who suffer from the imposter syndrome may be reluctant to hire or include team members who are smarter, more talented, or challenging of ideas, etc. Thus, restructuring "the more you know, the more you know you don't know" into a positive doesn't just improve your decisions; it can also significantly heighten the effectiveness of a team.

Perhaps surprisingly, my insight about the value of cognitive restructuring to negate the imposter syndrome did not come from a major event. Rather, it was a seemingly insignificant decision that ultimately ended up significantly impacting my ability to be confident and authentic as a leader. I was a faculty member at the time and was serving in my first lower-level administrative role as the chair-designate of a council that reported directly to the chancellor and of which the chancellor was an *ex officio* member. The chair-designate served in an apprentice role for a year before assuming the chair role for three years. At the time, and almost without exception, the chair role was held by a senior male faculty member. I was a relatively new associate professor. I was quite surprised that I was nominated and selected to serve in the role, and I was quite cognizant that I was different in many ways from the previous chairs.

The council met every week for 1.5 hours and addressed major budget and planning issues. It was a very labor-intensive council, with very dedicated members. Given this, I was expecting some formal recognition of the work of members who were leaving the council, but the last meeting of my chair-designate year was no different than any other meeting. There was no recognition of the chair's four years of service on the council or the service of others rotating off the council. As someone who believes in the importance of recognizing the great work and accomplishments of others, this lack of recognition was unsettling for me.

Fast forward to the end of my first year as chair of the council. I very much wanted to recognize the work of the individuals who were rotating off the council but was hesitant to do so. I was hesitant because there was no history of such recognitions and I was afraid that it would be seen as an unprofessional, silly, feminine thing to do. However, since recognition is very important to me, I mustered up the courage to ask the chancellor if he would be comfortable with me doing a formal recognition of service, complete with refreshments and plaques, at the last meeting. Much to my surprise and delight, rather than finding the idea to be silly, he supported the idea and stated that it should have been happening for a long time.

The chancellor's reaction opened the door for my first cognitive restructuring as someone new to an administrative role. I was able to see how my initial thought was inaccurate and irrational, and that a thought derived from my authentic self, although different than the thoughts of previous council chairs who I saw as being higher, better, and worthier than me, could be a positive rather than a negative. I am enormously grateful for that door being opened, as it gave me the opportunity to understand the power of cognitive restructuring to address the imposter syndrome and cognitive distortions—and allowed me to see that I could be myself *and* be an effective administrator.

Since that first experience, I have employed the cognitive restructuring skill whenever I have doubts (either self-imposed or imposed by others). I have found it to be invaluable in addressing a wide range of experiences, from being asked how I was going to fill the shoes of a beloved previous president (I can't fill his shoes, but he can't rock four-inch heels!) to how to effectively move the university forward through the COVID-19 pandemic (teamwork and routinely taking stock of what has been accomplished under very trying circumstances). Cognitive restructuring doesn't prevent doubts; I still routinely question myself. What it does provide is an effective way to deal with the doubts and the self-questioning to ensure you take the necessary steps and not play small.

Will cognitive restructuring work for you? It certainly can, but you will need to have the motivation and energy to free up some mind space to do the work. Cognitive restructuring is not a quick fix. As it is a skill, cognitive restructuring requires strength and focus, and needs to be honed with practice. Once developed, cognitive restructuring can be an incredibly useful tool to address the imposter syndrome and other cognitive distortions.

To get started, Ackerman (2019) has a good, basic list of questions you can use to identify cognitive distortions:

1. Is this thought realistic?

2. Am I basing my thoughts on facts or on feelings?

3. What is the evidence for this thought?

4. Could I be misinterpreting the evidence?

5. Am I viewing the situation as black and white when it's really more complicated?

6. Am I having this thought out of habit, or do facts support it?

To this list I would add: How does this thought fit with my authentic self/self-knowledge?

Once you have identified a cognitive distortion through the use of these questions, you can use the analysis to defuse it and restructure it to be more positive, accurate and beneficial. After the thought is restructured, you can take strength from it to move forward.

Harkening back to my belief that providing recognition for those who were rotating off a work-intensive council would be seen as an unprofessional, silly, feminine thing to do, the answers to the six questions provided by Ackerman clearly reveal that this belief was a cognitive distortion. While I did not ask myself these questions at the time, in retrospect, I could have identified my belief as a cognitive distortion more quickly if I had done so. While I might have believed that the thought was realistic, in actuality it was not. Moreover, the belief was not based on facts, but rather, was based on a feeling for which I had no direct evidence. Even worse, I automatically assumed the chancellor would respond in a stereotypical way. This assumption made my belief inappropriately black and white.

In spite of the fact that my belief was a cognitive distortion that I did not realize at the time, what allowed me to muster the courage to make the request of the chancellor was the realization that this belief did not fit with my authentic self—an authentic self that embraces the importance of recognizing the great work and accomplishments of others. This realization, coupled with the chancellor's response, provided the foundation from which I could question my initial belief and cognitively restructure it from a negating thought to a self-affirming thought that continues to influence my approach to administration to this day.

As Irene C. Kassorla eloquently affirms, "The pen that writes your life story must be held in your own hand." Cognitive restructuring gives you a powerful tool to hold your own pen. If you are holding your own pen, you cannot be an imposter.

Resources

Abrams, Abigail. "Yes, Impostor Syndrome Is Real: Here's How to Deal With It." *Time*, 20 June 2018, time.com/5312483/how-to-deal-with-impostor-syndrome/.

Ackerman, Courtney E. "CBT's Cognitive Restructuring (CR) For Tackling Cognitive Distortions." *PositivePsychology.com*, 13 Oct. 2020, positivepsychology.com/cbt-cognitive-restructuring-cognitive-distortions/.

Bravata, Dena M., et al. "Prevalence, Predictors, and Treatment of Impostor Syndrome: a Systematic Review." *Journal of General Internal Medicine*, vol. 35, no. 4, 2019, pp. 1252–1275., doi:10.1007/s11606-019-05364-1.

Clance, Pauline R., and Suzanne A. Imes. "The Impostor Phenomenon in High Achieving Women: Dynamics and Therapeutic Interventions." *http://www.paulineroseclance.com/Pdf/ip_high_achieving_women.Pdf*, Psychotherapy: Theory Research and Practice, 15, p. 241-247, 1978.

Sewer, Marion. "Overcoming Impostor Syndrome." *American Society for Biochemistry and Molecular Biology*, 1 Dec. 2015, www.asbmb.org/asbmb-today/careers/120115/overcoming-impostor-syndrome.

About the Author

Dr. Susan L. Thomas is the seventeenth President of Truman State University and holds the academic rank of Professor of Psychology. She serves on the Missouri Coordinating Board for Higher Education (CBHE) Commissioner's Advisory Group and is an appointed commissioner of the Midwestern Higher Education Compact. She also serves on the Executive Committee of the Council of Public Liberal Arts Colleges (COPLAC), is chair of the Council on Public Higher Education in Missouri (COPHE) and the vice chair of the Great Lakes Valley Conference (GLVC), and is a member of the Board of Directors of the Girl Scouts of Eastern Missouri. Dr. Thomas is a member of the National Honor Society of Phi Beta Kappa, the National Honor Society of Phi Kappa Phi, the Psychology National Honor Society of Psi Chi and the Business National Honor Society of Beta Gamma Sigma. She earned her Ph.D. and Master of Arts degree in Social Psychology as well as her MBA in Administrative Management from the University of Missouri-Columbia and a Bachelor of Arts degree in Psychology from Allegheny College in Meadville, Pennsylvania. Her recent teaching and scholarly interests include underrepresented students in STEM, mentor effectiveness, and psychological grit.

CHAPTER 9
NO ONE HAS EVER CALLED ME SMALL

by Roberta O'Hara, M.A.
Associate Vice President for Donor Relations
Rutgers University Foundation

No one has ever called me small. I'm 5'10" on a barefoot day; 6' in heels. And yet, despite my height, like many women, I have often felt small in the organizations I have worked for—sometimes so small, I am darn near invisible.

I know I am not alone in that experience. You may have experienced that sinking feeling, too, that you are not being seen or heard. I can recount many times when I have found myself at a meeting, speaking up, sharing input, offering an opinion, only to be met with nods of heads but no further recognition... and then moments later to have the male two seats down from me share identical thoughts and be met with lots of feedback, commentary, and even praise. Whatever its intent, this conscious or unconscious behavior on the part of male (and sometimes female) colleagues can be downright humiliating and can throw this girl off her game. It's a confidence detractor, at a minimum; for some, it can be downright debilitating.

Have heart. Because it truly doesn't have to be that way. There are many tips and techniques that can assist you in removing the invisibility cloak and building back up your confidence.

10 Tips

1. Remember who you are.

You are a subject expert. You would not have been invited to the table, meeting, nor, in fact, to the organization if you weren't. You have something to offer to the conversation. Don't forget that. Remind yourself every day. One small exercise you can do every day (or even multiple times a day) is to just say to yourself as you are sitting down for that meeting or logging in for the virtual call, "I know what I am doing." I have personally done this before walking into a defining or pivotal meeting; I keep the phrase "I know what I am doing" running in the back of my head during the welcoming remarks and introductions. It is so simple, but so affirming. Because you *do* know what you are doing. As women, we sometimes forget this and in doing so become our own worst enemy: the self-doubting self. Try instead to be the self-supporting self. You know what you are doing, and you are there to do it.

Need another reminder of who you are? Read over your LinkedIn profile or your resume as if you're reading someone else's. Impressed? You should be. Full confession time here: When I participate in conferences or speaking engagements, I am always asked to submit a bio. Before I hit send to convey it, I typically update it with the latest from my career, whether it's my title, publications, awards, or a new project. Next, I read it as if I am reading a list of accomplishments submitted for a job application, and I ask myself, "Does this person know their stuff, or what?" Your answer about yourself should be the same as mine: Yes!

2. Prepare.

Now just because you are a subject expert doesn't mean you should ignore the Boy Scout motto: *Be prepared.* Always, always prepare for a discussion. Write down your thoughts before a meeting. Gather the facts and figures that support your ideas. In fact, prior to a group conversation, you might try creating a digested version of what you want to contribute to the session and then sending it to the meeting participants with the promise that you will elaborate further in person. By doing this habitually, you will have put yourself on notice that you will be participating in the meeting and you will have made yourself accountable to the other attendees. This may feel like putting pressure on yourself, but if you get into a routine of doing this you will soon find that it essentially has the opposite effect; it relieves pressure. Women in particular are often afraid of being dubbed imposters by our colleagues or being "found out" for not truly knowing our stuff, and we sometimes sit in that pressure rather than finding ways to alleviate it. When we take the time to prepare, to arm ourselves, we are exhibiting that in fact we are the opposite; we are smart, capable, and valuable contributors.

3. Don't be shy.

Don't be silent. It can often be difficult to speak up when you feel that you are surrounded by very little support, but the more you articulate your thoughts the more comfortable you will be with hearing your own voice at the table. You will come off as confident. A fringe benefit of this is that others, too, will become accustomed to hearing from you and will begin to look to you for your input. And do so early in any organizational gathering. The longer you wait in a 60-minute session, the more likely you are to not converse and to start experiencing the self-doubt that we want to exorcise, not propagate. I have done this, ended a meeting still holding onto a thought I should have shared but for whatever reason didn't. I have also experienced those moments when someone else voices my thought, and I kick myself under the table. Don't do this to yourself. Share. Share often.

Practice by doing this in other settings, too. Make it a habit to stop by someone's office to discuss a topic, grab someone's ear in the hallway to give them a quick update, drop an email or make a call to ask questions. All this practice in hearing your thoughts articulated helps build your comfort level in work discussions and labels you as proactive.

4. Create the interaction you want.

You are a subject expert, you have prepared, and you've spoken up. Still getting silence or the perfunctory head nod? Try this simple technique: End your comments with a question to the group, forcing others at the table to not only acknowledge that you have spoken but to engage in conversation around your remarks. Don't ask a yes or no question; ask colleagues to examine what you've presented or to respond directly to your input.

Here's an example: I once presented on the topic of discontinuing a major event; after I'd presented my analysis and listed the pros of moving away from an antiquated event model, I ended by asking the group: What might we do instead of this event? That is a big question that draws people in and allows for an exchange of ideas. This one question ignited a great conversation about alternatives and then consensus on a new model. All are more likely to remember your input if it sparked an engaging conversation and resulted in people giving their feedback. (The bonus here is that you aren't just sharing your thoughts and ideas, you are collaborating. You're seeking interaction and input.)

5. Own the next steps.

Take the lead on summing up what was discussed and what the next steps are, if it would not be stepping on the host's toes. If the host or someone else has taken that lead, make sure to participate by committing to the next steps verbally and by reiterating your own role in those steps. What does this accomplish? It identifies you as integral to the process, and it cements your role and authority (to whatever degree that might be).

6. Eye contact and recognition.

Grab eye contact with your audience or with the speaker. In particular, you should try to connect visually with the person conducting the meeting. Nod your head in acknowledgment of what is being said. Use verbal cues, too, to demonstrate that you are listening. I'm not advocating an "Amen" after everything your boss says, but brief reactions signal that you are present in the conversation.

7. Take a deep breath.

My mother gave me a lot of life advice that is so useful in the workplace, and "remember to breathe" was probably the best. Take a deep breath before you begin speaking, whether you are presenting or just responding to a query. Those few seconds help you collect your thoughts and spread relaxation throughout your body. Physiologically, your heartbeat slows and your blood pressure drops; deep breathing is a great way to fight stress. I find it particularly helpful to do this when someone lobs a question at me that could be construed as confrontational.

8. Strike a pose.

Harvard professor Amy Cuddy calls it Power Pose; my sister calls it Wonder Woman Pose. Whatever you call it, put your hands on your hips when you're talking. Hold that pose. Visualize and embody strength and authority. It's another simple physical device, but it, too, works. It conveys a strength that isn't imposing but is confident.

Once, in a particularly difficult conversation with an alum, I found myself physically shrinking during his barrage of negativity about the institution and recent decisions that he didn't agree with. We've all faced unanticipated onslaughts of conflict or criticism in the workplace, those torrents that feel like you're drowning and there is no way to get your head above water. It took everything I had to take a deep breath (thank you again, Mom), throw my shoulders back, and assume the position, but once I had, I could politely interrupt the alum's outpouring and counter what he was saying. Sure, he was momentarily flustered, probably because no one else had ever stopped him in the past, but once the realization of the moment struck him, he listened to me and his tone calmed. And in the end, while we were probably never going to see eye-to-eye, he felt heard and I felt respected. My confidence, boosted by my pose, won out that day.

Poses to avoid: arms across your chest (you'll appear closed to new ideas); leaning too far back (you'll appear too relaxed or unengaged); and slouching (you'll appear uninterested).

9. Find an organizational mentor.

Finding a mentor is one of the smartest things you can do for yourself professionally. Look for someone who has several years of experience on you, both in the field and on the job. You will want an individual you feel comfortable confiding in and someone whose opinion you trust. Identify a person who can teach you "the ropes." The ropes can include office politics, the history of the organization, the vision and mission of the place, the trends in the field. Most importantly, you want a voice from which you can accept constructive criticism, because a good mentor is someone who won't shy away from giving you advice, guidance, and motivation. Look for a role model, perhaps one in authority. And, while this may sound counterintuitive, don't dismiss the idea of a male mentor, who can share perceptions from the male perspective.

In my lifetime I have had several mentors. Most recently my boss, who may not even have realized it, was a mentor to me.

She long had a reputation for being a strong manager who valued her employees, promoted excellence, candidly offered advice, motivated and thanked staff, and enjoyed a bit of healthy competition with other teams. Some lessons are quietly taught, and witnessing how she interacted with her staff, how she conveyed criticism, and how she made sure her voice was heard were all master tutorials on servant leadership.

10. Find an organizational ally.

You are probably asking yourself, "What's the difference between a mentor and an ally?" While a mentor will stand behind you and hold you up, an ally is someone standing next to you in a supportive role. An ally will be present to assist you whether you are preparing a presentation in front of a board or ideating a new concept you want to share more broadly. And, most importantly, an ally will have your back even when you aren't in the room. Don't forget to find female allies. Too often we women don't support each other in the workplace, and we need to correct that.

I hope that these ten tips help. Try one, or ten.

6 Habits to Stop

If you're anything like me, you probably have some habits that you'll want to stop, too. Here are a few suggestions.

1. Stop beating yourself up over errors.

In my career, I have made my share of mistakes; if we're being completely honest with ourselves, we all have. Making mistakes is not a crime, but how you react to those blunders might be a personal offence. Do your best to "let go" of the desire to scold yourself and instead try to focus on what you learn as a result of the foible. Johnny Cash, the man in black, once said, "You build on a failure. You use it as a stepping stone. Close the door on the past. You'd don't try to forget the mistakes, but you don't dwell on it. You don't let it have any of your energy, or any of your time, or any of your space."

2. Stop speaking in a small voice.

Stop deferring to your perception of authority. Don't be afraid to speak up! Your ideas add value. Don't think that only leadership should have a say. Good leaders recognize that they hired you for the contributions you will make, so make them.

3. Stop self-censoring.

This goes hand in hand with not being shy. Try this: In advance of a meeting set a number of times you will speak up. And stick to it. If this is particularly difficult for you, start with one—one time that you'll contribute. Trust me, you'll feel good that you did it. And the next time won't be as painful.

4. Stop saying, "I'm sorry."

I had a horrible, horrible habit. Whenever I would knock on the door of a colleague I would inevitably and automatically start by saying, "I'm sorry, can I interrupt you for a second?" Why was I apologizing? Sure, it seems like a polite thing to do, but it immediately puts one in a passive place compared to the person you are approaching. But if I had just phrased the interruption in a different way, such as, "If you have a moment, could we please talk about X," I would be starting on a level playing field. Pay attention to how often you say "I'm sorry" when it's not truly necessary. Apologize if you've eaten my mint chocolate chip ice cream or if you've run over my bike with your car. But don't start a thought or a conversation with an apology.

5. Stop ignoring your gut feelings.

And this one applies to more than just that feeling of invisibility or smallness. Intuition is often the result of years of practice and knowledge. In other words, it goes hand-in-hand with you being a subject expert. If your instincts are telling you to do something, heed that guidance. Don't overthink it; trust your first inclination. Which leads me to…

6. Stop overthinking.

If I had a nickel for every time I overthought something and ended up missing an opportunity or second-guessing myself… Ugh. I have lost sleep from "snow globing"—letting the thoughts float around in my brain untethered, basically clouding my vision and direction. This has also stopped me from voicing my opinion. If you are in this situation, find something to distract yourself when you start to do this. Even something as simple as focusing on your favorite daydream (Hugh Jackman) for 15 seconds—do it. The diversion will help you clear, reset, and speak up.

And, finally, remember the words of Maya Angelou: "Stand up straight and realize who you are, that you tower over your circumstances." You are not small.

Resources

For more on the subject of confidence, try these resources:

Busch, May. "How to Speak in Meetings with Confidence and Authority." *Ladders*. 28 Oct. 2019, www.theladders.com/career-advice/how-to-speak-in-meetings-with-confidence-and-authority.

Council, Forbes Coaches. "Council Post: 15 Ways You Can Find the Confidence to Speak Up." *Forbes*. 25 Oct. 2017. www.forbes.com/sites/forbescoachescouncil/2017/10/25/15-ways-you-can-find-the-confidence-to-speak-up/.

Mullen, Caitlin. "This Is When Confidence at Work Peaks for Women." *Bizjournals.com*. 8 Aug. 2019. www.bizjournals.com/bizwomen/news/latest-news/2019/08/this-is-when-confidence-at-work-peaks-for-women.html?page=all.

Wheatman, Debra. "Increasing Self-Confidence in the Workplace." *LiveCareer.* 22 Sept. 2020. www.livecareer.com/resources/jobs/networking/increasing-self-confidence-in-the-workplace.

About the Author

Roberta O'Hara is the Associate Vice President for Donor Relations at the Rutgers University Foundation. Previously Roberta was the senior leader in the Office of Stewardship at Princeton University. Roberta was a founding member of the New England Stewardship Conference, the precursor to the Association of Donor Relations Professionals (ADRP). Roberta served as inaugural Treasurer; content chair and chair for the 2014 and 2015 International Conferences, respectively; and Chair for GATHER@ADRP for senior donor relations leaders. Roberta volunteered as Donor Relations Best Practices Chair for AASP and Relationship Manager for ADRP/AASP. Roberta's Princeton team won the 2014 CASE Circle of Excellence Bronze Award and the 2015 Gold and Silver Awards for donor recognition pieces, and Roberta received the 2015 CASE Quarter Century Service Award and 2019 ADRP Founder's Award. A frequent speaker for Academic Impressions, CASE, ADRP, AASP, and other groups, Roberta has also published extensively on the subjects of donor relations, stewardship, events, surveys, leadership, and other fundraising-related topics. Roberta holds a B.A. in psychology and English from Rutgers University, where she graduated Phi Beta Kappa, and an M.A. in English Literature from Northeastern University.

PART 3

CONFLICT MANAGEMENT

CHAPTER 10
HOW MUCH TRANSPARENCY IS TOO MUCH?

by Dr. Carol Moore
Former President, Columbia College

Talk with most trustees, faculty, alums, and students, and they will agree on a common aspiration for their institution's leadership: transparency. Sure, simple enough, right? For public institutions, which represent 42% of U.S. colleges, it's a given; they are by state requirements transparent, aren't they? On the other hand, private colleges, while under some state and federal regulations to reveal internal data, vary considerably in their desire to share critical institutional details.

After four decades in higher education as a faculty member and union vice president, chief academic officer and president, I find myself pondering the spoken thirst for transparency and concluding that there's rarely a one-size-fits-all solution. Trustees and faculty, in particular, may be adamant in their demand for facts and unvarnished truths, but ill-equipped to deal with the realities that come with true transparency. While the boundaries between unbridled candor and nuance aimed at maintaining a collective calm vary depending on the history and current context of the college, I have found—time and again—that there is an impenetrable limit to how much reality trustees and faculty are prepared to accept, especially if you are a woman in the senior or mid-level administrative ranks. After all, women are warm, nurturing, and reassuring—mothers

121

who, at all costs, shield their charges from ugly truths that threaten their future. It is the male who is the purveyor of reality, who can lay down the law to unquestioning stakeholders: "we need money" or "we have to cut programs."

How can women leaders gauge the tolerance level of the college community for tough decision-making and balance reality with "happy news," while remaining true to transparency and authentic communication? This skill—to be a transparent cheerleader—is critical to leadership success, and a particular challenge for those of us who are women.

3 Scenarios

Let me share with you a few experiences at different colleges to illustrate the transparency challenge for women leaders.

SCENARIO 1

Three weeks into my presidency at a small, regional, public college, I was informed that the college was showing a deficit of $800,000 on a budget of $16 million. I immediately contacted the chancellor, who had just hired me. While he was shocked that admissions numbers had been allowed to slide so precipitously during the presidential transition, he left me with little doubt that the problem was mine to solve. The board's mantra, "a dollar short, a president short," was not comforting. Nor was the news that system reserves could be used only for physical plant emergencies. I was on my own.

In launching my new leadership, I was determined to build on transparency, I announced our budget deficit to the college community that September. A few goodhearted faculty assured me the chancellor's office would bail us out and refused to believe me when I told them that was not going to happen. Several less well-meaning faculty spread the notion that I had fabricated the deficit to camouflage changes I wanted to make.

After a little over a month in office and a dearth of useful suggestions from faculty, I was still struggling to identify ways to tackle the shortfall. Given this experience, I began to question the value of "telling it like it is," but remained steadfast to the concept of transparency, albeit with a tempered edge.

SCENARIO 2

Next, I moved into the private sector, charged with the turnaround of a very small, arts-oriented college. After a preliminary assessment of the dismal financial status, I called the community together to outline the situation and the skeletal plan to position the college for sustainability. I had some trepidation given my previous experience, but I felt the community had a right to know what we were facing, and I knew I would need their cooperation if we were to stabilize the finances. The response of the community was quite different this time. Faculty and staff had suspected the truth but were appreciative of being told the facts and being asked to take an active role in addressing the fiscal crisis. This time I was not going it alone.

After a year of hard work, we were on the road to a balanced budget and on the verge of bringing in the largest class in the college's history. Unfortunately, however, the college had been on accreditation probation for almost two years and, as the community was painfully aware, we were facing the threat of accreditation suspension. As graduation and the accrediting decision were scheduled for the same weekend, I posed a difficult question to the community: Did they want the accreditor's decision as soon as it was available, which would have been the day before graduation? The consensus of the entire community was *no*. Let us celebrate with the students and families; nothing should dampen the graduation celebration. So, the Monday after graduation, we gathered and I shared the news that our accreditation had been suspended, meaning that we would have to make plans to close the college. Here was a community mature enough to handle transparency and to postpone transparency for the sake of the students.

SCENARIO 3

I next moved to a small, private college in the southeast, recently placed on the Federal Financial Watchlist. In hiring me as interim provost/president, the Board and faculty clamored for transparency; they had been kept in the dark by the previous administration and told only "good news," with the more troubling realities facing the college kept carefully shrouded. My tendency toward transparency was well received at first, and the candid financial appraisal welcomed, especially after years of obfuscation. But the thirst for financial transparency lost its halo in a few short years. Although the college had successfully been removed from the Watchlist—a huge accomplishment— much more work was required to financially stabilize the college. Just as we were prepared to turn the corner financially, the Board and faculty reverted to old habits, demanding only positive news and holding tight to the fantasy that we had scaled our financial hurdles and there was plenty of money. As president, I was buried in the details of the turnaround and in my commitment to transparency, I missed the signals—signals that fore-shadowed a growing intolerance for transparency.

Summary and Lessons Learned

Women frequently lean toward communicating openly. Yet experience reveals that stakeholders have varying levels of tolerance when challenged with news regarding the sustainability of the institution. As an increasing number of colleges are financially stressed, many leaders are faced with the challenge of juggling reality and a "false" sense of stability.

So what have we learned? And how can we best apply these lessons?

As a woman leader:

Make sure transparency is on your radar.

Whatever your role (program director, registrar, controller, assistant dean), ask yourself these questions about the information your office produces:

- Who could benefit from having this data?

- Why do they or why don't they have access now?

- Are there historical reasons for restricting access to certain constituencies?

- Do those reasons make sense to you?

- Could you be in a position to contribute to data-distribution decisions?

- What are your supervisor's thoughts on data access, and would he or she support your efforts to increase transparency?

- What are the potential consequences of making this information available?

- Are there legitimate concerns about how the data might be misunderstood or misused?

- Does transparency dampen the environment or enlighten the community?

Pushing projects forward every day does not allow for evaluating the culture and reading the signals. To keep constituents on your transparency radar, plan a work-at-home-day either Friday or Monday for reflection only on the temperature of various constituencies. For working moms, this is hard; working at home always stares down the dishes, laundry, etc. However, go to the local library, if the laundry keeps calling.

Take careful stock of the college's culture and judge the resilience of stakeholders.

Different groups may use or react to the information that your office provides differently. Consider whether a weekly admissions report or a monthly financial report can be used most effectively by the cabinet alone, or whether there are benefits to distributing it to all faculty and staff, to the trustees, or the alumnae/i leadership. When is it too much information? Can you play an important role in encouraging broader distribution of information, or is your institutional culture such that lobbying for greater openness could be risky professionally? If your college has a history of tightly controlled information, you may need to proceed slowly and cautiously.

To keep the campus somewhat upbeat when you've been doling out grim news regarding the finances, switch up the topic. For example, talk about positive aspects of the future—maybe a new initiative that might bring in new revenues once cost containment efforts have taken hold. Remember, bad news is more easily accepted from men, but a little good news goes a long way.

Continually pause and read your stakeholders, monitoring the ability of each group to cope with challenges.

It is important to maintain a constant awareness of how the information you provide is being received. A first step should be to identify individuals within each group whom you can trust and use feedback from those individuals to gauge the general reaction to your reports. Consider, too, how timing may change the way information is received. There may be times when an announcement of good news is particularly needed. Let's think, for example, about faculty morale following a difficult semester in which several programs were discontinued. In this case, I asked trustees to vote on faculty tenure and promotion decisions several months early—in December, rather than the following April—to provide the needed "shot of good news." Faculty could then end the semester on a high note, buoyed by tenure and promotion announcements.

Balance reality with good news and optimism, recognizing that constituent groups have shorter-term vision and less tolerance for long-term objectives than leaders do.

This works both ways. While it's important to infuse positive news into situations that have been dominated by the execution of difficult and unpopular decisions, as in the example above, it's just as crucial to avoid shrouding reality in communications that focus only on good news. Consider the institution that historically flooded its alumnae/i with positive news, a practice that continued even as the leadership grappled with serious financial challenges. When bits of information began to seep out, alumnae/i began to suspect some financial instability. The delicate task that lay before me in my first address to the Alumnae Council was to give them a balanced report that would reinforce their trust and their optimism. With a penchant for transparency, I presented an honest picture of the current finances, along with plans to balance the budget for the coming year, and to develop new programs that would reinvigorate our admissions numbers and our stability. The report was well received, with alumnae/i expressing appreciation for the new level of candor.

Remember to celebrate whatever you can in the midst of RIFs and budget cuts. You might hold up a new initiative, a faculty publication or promotion, or a student achievement. This will help associate you with good news and not always with doom and gloom.

Validate your analysis with trusted individuals amongst stakeholder groups.

In each of the examples above, I was able to vet my response with trusted colleagues and use their feedback to ensure that we had considered how well the information would be received.

While it is obvious I lean toward transparency in managing the flow of information to various stakeholders, I want to emphasize that there is no one-size-fits-all solution. Institutional cultures vary, as do their history of sharing information and the resilience of their stakeholders. You'll find many constituents have the experience but not the desire to stay the course over time without positive glimpses of the ultimate vision. You must know and consider these factors when deciding on the degree of transparency that will best benefit the community.

Keep your finger on the pulse of the community by identifying a few trustees, faculty, staff, students and alums you can trust. Use the group to validate your assessment of the constituencies. When one group is heading for the rabbit hole, reach out strategically to bring people back to center.

In order to achieve a solid path for the overall college you must maintain the support of the community you work in. Turning around a stressed institution or effecting change to prepare the institution for future trends takes patience, time, and a thoughtfully scheduled strategic agenda. Awareness will serve you well.

About the Author

Dr. Carol A. Moore has amassed more than 40 years of experience at both two and four-year institutions of higher education in the private and public sectors. She holds a B.A. and M.A. in Biology from Montclair State University. Dr. Moore holds a Ph.D. in Marine Biology from Northeastern University. Carol began her career as a high school science teacher and then moved into college-level teaching. Shortly thereafter, she began progressively responsible administrative roles.

She has been involved with the National Association of Academic Administration, the New England Estuarine Research Society, and the American Society of Zoologists. She has presented more than 30 scientific and educational papers and is widely published among scientific and educational publications.

In 1992 she was named Provost at Mercy College in NY and in 1998 was appointed President of Lyndon State College, VT. In 2014 she became President of Burlington College in VT. In 2016 Dr. Moore was chosen Provost at Columbia College in SC, later becoming President. She has devoted her career to education, specifically to strategic and curricular planning, program development, retention, and especially to supporting the advancement of women in higher education.

She has been involved with ACE as a former Senior Fellow and previous chair for the Commission on Women. In

February, ACE honored Dr. Moore with its Donna Shavlik Award, which recognizes those who demonstrate a sustained commitment to advancing women in higher education. Her dedication to empowering women is also evidenced by her tenure on the Girl Scouts Council, in which she served on the VT Council from 2001 to 2008.

CHAPTER 11
RESPONDING TO AGGRESSIVE BEHAVIOR IN THE WORKPLACE

by Jana Lynn Hunzicker, Ed.D.
Department of Education, Counseling, and Leadership
Bradley University

Have you ever noticed how you get along great with people until you cross them? Your roommate from college stays in touch regularly until you question the motives of her new boyfriend. Your next-door neighbor is friendly until the spearmint you planted last season begins popping up all over his lawn. You often have lunch with your co-worker, until she discovers your political views. Unfortunately, the consequences of doubting or disappointing others can generate unintentional conflict.

I discovered this reality as an eighth grader taking a test in home economics. I was new to the school and didn't really know anyone in the class. Once the test was distributed, the teacher left the classroom. Immediately, several girls started looking around. "What's the answer to Number Four?" someone whispered. Someone else replied. Within seconds, half the class was exchanging answers. I was horrified.

Without thinking, I blurted, "Stop it, everyone. Just take the test!" The room became silent. Everyone looked at me. Celina, the tallest girl in the class, stood up. "What did you say?" she demanded, as my heart raced. I decided to reason with her: "I said, you need to stop. When the teacher returns, we'll all be in trouble. It's an easy test; just take it!"

I waited. The rest of the class watched. Celina hesitated. After what felt like an eternity, she simply replied, "Okay," and sat back down. Everyone returned to their test without talking, and seconds later the teacher returned, surveyed the room, and took a seat at her desk. I breathed a sigh of relief.

Later, I learned that Celina was one of the school's bullies, but I never heard from her again. She kept her distance for the rest of the semester, and so did I. Outside of class, I saw her in the halls occasionally, but we never came face to face. That day in class, for a short time, I was a target—but not a victim. Whether you're an eighth grader or an adult professional, you don't have to be a victim either.

Inauthenticity Is a Lot Like Cheating

I ended up becoming a teacher, then a principal, and finally a university faculty member and administrator. In my world, cheating isn't right! Inauthenticity, or not being your true self, is a lot like cheating. You cheat yourself when you censor your words and premeditate your actions. Others cheat you when they try to keep you from being yourself.

At the age of 40, I accepted a tenure-track faculty position in higher education, diving in with enthusiasm. For a while, I focused heavily on teaching and research, setting high standards for myself and quickly achieving a good measure of success. I believed I had much to offer in terms of the real world, so I often spoke up during faculty meetings. One day, a well-meaning colleague pulled me aside and suggested that I stay quiet until I earned tenure and promotion.

Although surprised and perhaps a bit angry at first, I understood her intervention as a friendly warning. I had to decide whether to follow the department's cultural norms or find an alternative. Over time, through committees, accreditation tasks, and other service work, I learned to express myself in smaller venues. I also began seeking leadership roles and responsibilities that required me to provide updates during meetings, allowing me to contribute authentically while also abiding by the department's culture. For a while, everyone was happy; I hadn't crossed anyone yet.

The Consequences of Crossing People

The consequences of doubting or disappointing others can be worse when someone has authority over you. Sometimes, you don't even have to do anything wrong. Maybe you got the job when they wanted someone else. Perhaps you successfully completed a big project that no one else bothered attempting. Or maybe you questioned a protocol when norms mandated polite compliance.

As I continued to grow as a faculty member, I began noticing subtle signs of dissatisfaction from my direct supervisor, whom I will call Dr. May. Dr. May never seemed overly friendly toward me, and occasionally I would receive a rude email reply. He downplayed my successes, even as he praised others; and he grudgingly gave me high marks on my annual performance evaluation, but never a perfect score.

Feeling stifled, I began seeking leadership opportunities outside my department and was successful in securing a position that included a 50% course reduction with a direct report to a second supervisor. This provided some relief; Dr. May still evaluated me, but I spent only half of my time in the department and was free to work creatively, grow professionally, and network campuswide the rest of the time. Again, I had found a way to contribute authentically. But then, I crossed him.

At the time, it was very scary. I had not yet earned tenure or promotion. In my leadership role, I made a budgetary decision—approved by my second supervisor—that involved a staff member in my department. Dr. May went through the roof. I was traveling at the time, so a punishing email exchange ensued. Rather than simply acquiesce, I attempted to explain myself. He became angry at the back-and-forth, and his rudeness escalated. Finally, I said it in writing: "I believe you are trying to bully me."

My words set into motion a direct and fierce assault. Upon my return to campus, Dr. May summoned me to his office, having invited a third party unbeknownst to me. He was prepared like an attorney; notes and printed documents spread out in front of him, he examined and cross-examined me relentlessly as he attempted to win favor with the third party.

I was intimidated but knew I had done nothing wrong. I summoned my courage and stood my ground. Fortunately, the third party assumed the role of impartial facilitator and made sure I had as much time as I needed to explain. I started at the beginning and described exactly what I had done and why. Dr. May's attempts to discredit me fell flat. Ultimately, I won the battle that day, but the war raged on. I had crossed him. I had become a target.

Signs that You Might be a Target

In the workplace, attempts to forcefully persuade or retaliate are often covert (Anderson and Young, 2020). When someone is good at it, you may not even recognize what is happening. Dr. May was good at it. Following our infamous meeting, I noticed interpersonal changes in his behavior. If he could avoid greeting me, he would. If he could evade acknowledging my comments or accomplishments, he did. I also began recognizing my department colleagues as insiders and outsiders. Insiders were given department-level titles, high-profile responsibilities, and corner offices. Outsiders were denied opportunities, given difficult teaching schedules, and disparaged behind closed doors. While insiders were praised for completing routine work, even outsiders' special accomplishments were downplayed or not even mentioned.

I was one of the outsiders. Dr. May did all he could to discourage my appointment to a new university-level leadership position, assigned new course preparations to my teaching load several semesters in a row, and tried to give the courses within my area of expertise to others. He withheld information when he could, often waiting until I asked and then delaying his response for days. When curriculum or accreditation work was needed, he never asked me directly, and once the work was completed, I was rarely acknowledged. During meetings, even when questions related directly to my work were asked, he would answer these himself rather than defer to me.

All of this flew under the radar. I am certain that many insiders in my department never even noticed. Moreover, Dr. May was careful to appear supportive on official records. My annual performance evaluations remained strong because there were few weaknesses to magnify. If I needed a letter of support, he would provide it. When someone acknowledged my achievements, he would wholeheartedly agree. Sometimes, though, his mixed messages pushed me off balance. I would begin to relax, thinking that maybe he was beginning to soften. But then, he would strike again. Eventually, I learned that unpredictable behavior is a common tactic of workplace bullies (Anderson and Young, 2020; Stewart, 2018).

Identifying as a target but not as a victim, I didn't take all of this lying down. However, I'm not an overly aggressive person, and sometimes Dr. May's tactics were so subtle that I needed a reality check. About one third of the department faculty were outsiders, which enabled me to compare my perceptions with others'. Sometimes, my perceptions were validated; other times, I was being hypersensitive. Either way, having a support network of trusted colleagues experiencing similar treatment provided the sustenance I needed to continue standing my ground.

When it came time to evaluate Dr. May, I was always brutally honest, which didn't help our relationship, but I believed it was the right thing to do. I also shared some of his injustices with my second supervisors over the years, who sometimes— but not always—intervened. I was always appreciative when others intervened on my behalf, but over time I came to realize that I was more empowered when I stood up for myself. On one occasion, after a back-and-forth email communication that was going nowhere, I articulated my position with specific examples that Dr. May could not refute. As reinforcement, I wrote that I intended to forward the message to my second supervisor so that she was aware of my position, but before I had a chance to do so, he preemptively forwarded it himself. Occasionally, I won a battle, but I never won the war.

Five Practical Strategies to Avoid Becoming a Victim

An abundance of literature exists on the topic of workplace bullying (see the list of Resources at the end of the chapter), but I am careful not to overindulge. While it is important for adult professionals to acknowledge the reality of workplace bullying, how to recognize it, and how to effectively respond, if you dwell on it too much you risk becoming a victim due to the phenomenon of self-fulfilling prophecy (Brearley, 2019). Instead of dwelling on being a target, I offer five practical strategies to help you avoid becoming a victim:

1. Be good at what you do.

The better you are at your job, the less room there will be for legitimate criticism. Prioritize your work responsibilities and go above and beyond when you can. Even if no one else notices, you will have the satisfaction of a job well done, with your curriculum vita, student course evaluations, performance evaluations, and publication records as substantiation.

What can make this difficult: Factors that might work against you include a heavy workload, working in isolation, and low self-confidence. Be sure to prioritize tasks, say no when you can, and build your support network. It is also important to remember that you don't have to be perfect every time. Always do your best and adopt an attitude of continuous improvement.

2. Get along with everyone.

A good friend of mine once said, "There's never an excuse for rudeness." Even when you are treated disrespectfully, always respond graciously. Don't engage in gossip, avoid making snarky comments, and go out of your way to support your colleagues—both insiders and outsiders. Even when the time comes to stand up for yourself, do so respectfully.

What can make this difficult: Getting along with everyone can be challenging when others are not trying to get along with you. Sometimes, the best response to an insult is simply to smile and say nothing. Personal defensiveness might be another barrier. Know your hot buttons and prepare in advance not to let them trigger responses that you might later regret. Remember that it is okay to make mistakes, and that you don't always have to get due credit for a job well done.

3. Positively influence cultural norms.

Remember that effective leaders lead by example. When you are good at what you do and get along with everyone, you will increase your capacity to positively influence others, because they will respect and admire you. Even if people know you are a target, they will watch and listen to you. Over time, this will render opportunities for you to make observations, pose questions, and offer suggestions that might encourage others to think and behave differently.

What can make this difficult: Even as adults, it can be surprisingly uncomfortable to stand up against the crowd. In a toxic workplace culture, appropriate behavior is often disparaged in favor of maintaining the unhealthy status quo (Ryan, 2016). Instead of sweeping reform, think in terms of one-on-one relationships, subtle behavioral changes, and small displays of courage. And be patient. Cultural norms don't change overnight, but one step at a time.

4. Be a courageous and creative problem solver.

Now we're getting to the hard part. Harden-Moore (2019) reminds us:

> In order to address academic bullying, victims of academic bullying must be willing to both share their experiences and call out their bullies. While that can be very difficult, particularly when considering the potential professional and personal consequences, it must be done in order to bring attention to this issue (para. 8).

Similar to my confrontation with Dr. May, sometimes you'll have to speak up, stand up, or take action. But contrary to the relationship I described between Dr. May and myself, the idea in these interactions is not to "win the battle," unless that is your only choice. Instead, aim to collaborate authentically with others—including your Dr. May—to examine all sides of pressing issues and to develop innovative solutions that benefit everyone.

What can make this difficult: Unfortunately, not everyone likes to collaborate. In fact, in a toxic workplace culture, people are more likely to keep to themselves as a means of self-protection (Ryan, 2016). When individuals are entrenched in dysfunction, it can be very difficult to think outside the box, let alone join others in doing so. Keep in mind that you don't have to be courageous and creative in every situation. Choose your opportunities and take heart in small victories.

5. Keep pushing forward.

Above all, don't allow yourself to become discouraged, angry, or burnt out. That would make you a victim. Utilize your support network. If your goal is to earn tenure and promotion, focus on that. If you aspire to a particular leadership position, prepare yourself. If you continually fail to rebuild a damaged relationship, keep trying. Maria Shine Stewart (2018) reminds us that "it takes awareness and guts to change a culture, to confront someone out of bounds and to strive to create a healthier climate" (para. 12). No one said it was easy. Always remember that you are in control of your thoughts, beliefs, attitude, feelings, and behavior. You alone get to decide the direction of your future. Make it big!

Closing Thoughts

Just as I learned in my eighth-grade home economics class, if you are true to yourself, sooner or later you will cross someone. And when you do, there is a good chance that you'll become a target. Maybe the situation will resolve itself quickly, as it did with Celina and me. Maybe it will stimulate self-reflection, as it did with my well-meaning colleague. Or maybe it will launch an ongoing saga similar to my experience with Dr. May. Whether you're an eighth grader or an adult professional, you've got this. Even when you're a target, you don't have to be a victim!

REFLECTIVE QUESTIONS

1. What are my strengths, both professionally and interpersonally? What can I do to build upon my strengths?

2. What are my areas for improvement, both professionally and interpersonally? What people and resources might I call upon to develop in these areas?

3. In terms of my work relationships, am I doing everything I can to get along with everyone? Am I doing anything that might be contributing to toxicity in my workplace culture?

4. How have I positively influenced cultural norms in my work environment, both large and small? How might I be able to positively influence individuals or groups in the coming weeks and months?

5. What requires courage in my workplace? What requires creativity? What acts of courage and creativity—small and large—have I exhibited recently? What opportunities for courage and creativity might I be willing to prepare for or pursue in the future?

6. How robust is my support network? To whom can I reach out for friendship? To whom can I offer support?

7. What is one thing I can do today to ensure that even if I'm a target, I don't have to be a victim?

Resources

Anderson, Myron R., and Kathryn S. Young. *Fix Your Climate: A Practical Guide to Reducing Microaggressions, Microbullying, and Bullying in the Academic Workplace.* Academic Impressions. Denver, CO. 2020.

Brearley, Ben. "How a Self-Fulfilling Prophecy Will Make or Break Your Team." *ThoughtfulLeader.com*, 4 June 2019, www.thoughtfulleader.com/self-fulfilling-prophecy/.

Harden-Moore, Tai. "Academic Bullying: Higher Education's Dirty Little Secret." *Diverse.* 16 Aug. 2019. diverseeducation.com/Article/152566/.

Legg, T.J., and C. Raypole. "How to Identify and Manage Workplace Bullying." *Healthline.* 29 Apr. 2019, www.healthline.com/health/workplace-bullying.

Lester, Jaime. (Ed.). *Workplace Bullying in Higher Education.* Routledge, 2013.

Malahy, Sandra. "Workplace Bullying Impacts District Climate." *Illinois School Board Journal*, Illinois School Board Journal, 2016, p.18-20. www.iasb.com/about-us/publications/journal/2016/november-december/workplace-bullying-impacts-district-climate/.

Rockwood, Pamela. "Survey Finds Perception of Adult Bullying among School Leaders." *Illinois School Board Journal*,

2016, p.21-23. www.iasb.com/about-us/publications/journal/2016/november-december/survey-finds-perception-of-adult-bullying-among-sc/.

Ryan, Liz. "Ten Unmistakable Signs Of A Toxic Culture." *Forbes*, Forbes Magazine, 20 Oct. 2016. www.forbes.com/sites/lizryan/2016/10/19/ten-unmistakable-signs-of-a-toxic-culture/.

Stewart, Maria Shine. "How to Deal with Bullies in Higher Education (Opinion)." *Inside Higher Ed*, 1 Aug. 2018. www.insidehighered.com/advice/2018/08/01/how-deal-bullies-higher-education-opinion.

Twale, Darla J. *Understanding and Preventing Faculty-on-Faculty Bullying*. Routledge, 2018.

Twale, Darla J., and Barbara M. De Luca. *Faculty Incivility: The Rise of the Academic Bully Culture and What to Do About It*. John Wiley & Sons, Inc., 2008.

About the Author

Dr. Jana Hunzicker is a professor in the Department of Education, Counseling, and Leadership and associate dean for the College of Education and Health Sciences at Bradley University in Peoria, Illinois. She holds a master's degree in educational administration, a doctorate in curriculum and instruction, Illinois Type 75 administrative certification, and the Illinois superintendent endorsement. In addition to seven years of middle school teaching, she served for nine years as an elementary/middle school administrator before transitioning into higher education.

As a professor, Dr. Hunzicker teaches graduate courses in teacher leadership, higher education administration, and scholarly research, and undergraduate courses in young adolescent development, middle school instruction, and reading/language arts. As associate dean, she oversees the college's curriculum development, coordinates student success initiatives, represents the college on university-level committees, and assists the dean with special projects. Dr. Hunzicker has authored over 50 refereed journal articles and book chapters.

CHAPTER 12
KEYS TO CONFLICT
MANAGEMENT

by Carolyn Perry, Ph.D.,
Professor of English and Director of the Center for Teaching and
Learning, Westminster College

Of all the skills needed by administrators, conflict management is among the most vital. While this chapter will focus on
faculty issues, the principles can be applied across all areas of
higher education. Regardless of the position, the top priority
at any institution is the quality of each student's experience.
Without a team that is focused on the mission and working in
sync with one another, no institution will reach its full
potential, regardless of how talented the faculty and staff may
be. Far too often, unnecessary conflict is allowed to fester
within or between departments or offices, and ultimately it is
the students' experience that suffers. By honing their skills at
conflict management, women in higher education can create a
stronger, healthier working environment.

Managing Conflict Between Faculty

One morning while I was serving as Dean of Faculty at
Westminster College, a young faculty member stormed into
my office, fuming. At many small liberal arts colleges, faculty
know that they have access to administrators most any time,
so I wasn't surprised. I had hired this young woman—we'll

call her "Evelyn"—just a few years earlier, in large part because she was both highly creative and clearly able to hold her own. Given the generational divide in her department, with the faculty leaders having taught at Westminster for decades and used to calling the shots, I looked forward to Evelyn's ability and willingness to shake things up a bit, to challenge the status quo.

After a few minutes at my desk, Evelyn calmed down enough to lay out her complaint: she had spent hours researching and writing a proposal to make changes to the major, and yet the chair of the department dismissed her ideas without discussion. At a recent departmental meeting, he thanked her for her thoughts but stated that he didn't see any need for change and actually feared that change might hurt their program; after all, weren't students continuing to get into graduate programs at a steady pace? As Evelyn had come to expect, no one in her department was willing to challenge the chair's decisions; older faculty trusted his judgment while the younger ones feared potential consequences for speaking up. But Evelyn knew from her research that other institutions were doing a better job of attracting and retaining students interested in their major, and she not only thought the department had room to grow, but also suspected that graduates would be better served by some thoughtful changes.

So what could be done? After carefully listening to Evelyn's complaint, I asked her to do two things: first, to ask the department chair if he would be willing to have a discussion of her proposal with all members of the department—the discussion she had hoped for at the last meeting—and second,

149

to consider a middle ground based on the results of that discussion. Perhaps *some* change would be better than none. If he refused, then she should let him know that she would appeal to the dean.

A few days later the department chair showed up in my office door, fuming, as well. How dare this young faculty member question his judgment? He had standards to uphold, and she had no right to challenge his decision to dismiss her proposal. And what nonsense—taking this mere quibbling to the *dean?* At this point, we were not in a good place, and some repair work needed to be done. I let both the chair and Evelyn know that I wanted to step in and help mediate the situation, and we launched into a series of talks over the next few weeks. (The lessons learned from those talks follow below).

In the end, the department voted to accept 70% or so of Evelyn's recommendations for changing the major, and Evelyn and the chair seemed to be on good terms. The other department members seemed quite pleased, too, and perhaps a bit more willing to voice their opinions. All in all, the mediation was a success. I wish I could report that conflict management always went this smoothly, but people are complicated and relationships are messy, and sometimes a resolution is not going to be found. But with this incident, I learned many lessons that I was able to implement going forward—resulting in a much happier dean, as well.

Evelyn's bursting into my office that morning was no small matter. It led to hours of careful listening, careful thought, and careful action before the matter was resolved. In the end, because Evelyn understood how passionate the chair was about their major, she knew that she needed to be sensitive about "preserving the best" and holding onto key traditions. Likewise, once the chair realized that he could trust Evelyn's motives—that they were rooted in her concern for the long-term health of the department—he was able to listen to her rationale for change, agree that she had provided ample evidence to support her ideas, and come to a reasonable compromise. Over time, Evelyn became an excellent administrator herself—one who was able to listen to and learn from others, but who also brought unique strengths to her work.

Critical Action Steps for Conflict Management

Know when *not* to get involved.

For the most part, I think deans need to steer clear of faculty disputes, as they run the risk of micromanaging, taking sides, or simply being seen as bothersome administrators. I've found that deans—and I think female deans, in particular—want/need to see themselves as problem-solvers, always ready to swoop in and make things right. Therefore, they sometimes need to be reminded that faculty can negotiate most situations just fine. It's also important to avoid sending a message to faculty that they need to run to the dean whenever there's a problem to be solved. Before getting involved in faculty disputes, it's smart to check one's ego, and if possible, stay out of the way.

Be ready and willing to *get* involved.

Any dean who has watched a dysfunctional department year after year, or seen faculty relationships falter and fester, knows that if problems don't get resolved, eventually students suffer. And it truly *is* a dean's job to make sure that the quality of education provided is never sacrificed due to faculty turmoil. Above all, academic deans must be the keepers of faculty and curriculum, ensuring that every aspect of academic affairs remains strong. So there are times when it's not simply practical, but also mission-critical, that a dean step in.

Set expectations early.

A dean's role in conflict management and mediation actually starts months or years before a situation arises. From the beginning of one's tenure, it is important to begin conveying to your faculty your values and priorities as an administrator. Any time you find yourself in front of the faculty, take a few moments to demonstrate your commitment to the institution, its mission, and its values. Remind faculty of why we commit our lives to higher education and of the responsibility we have taken on to educate and inspire learning. Before a faculty meeting, for example, when you're trying to persuade faculty to attend the spring choir concert, don't be afraid of taking that extra step and explain *why*. Take a moment to reset your faculty's focus on the vast potential of a liberal arts education and the role they play within it. We too often assume that faculty know the "why" and don't need to hear it again, but sending a message about the mission or values of your institution reminds faculty of *your* mission and values—and reminds them that you are deeply committed to your college. And that's an important card to have in your hand when you're mediating faculty conflict.

Build trust, and more trust.

At the same time, it will be impossible to mediate faculty conflict if faculty don't trust you and trust you deeply. So it is equally important to convey to faculty your commitment to *them*. Such a commitment can't be demonstrated by words alone; faculty must be convinced that you have their back, whether an unhappy parent has issued a complaint about them, a coach thinks their attendance policy is too strict, or a Board member starts talking about the problems with the tenure system.

Faculty also have to know that you value their creative ideas and their desire for professional development, and it's on you to create opportunities for them to thrive. That doesn't mean that you will always agree with your faculty, but you have to prove over time that you will listen well, be fair and reasonable, and do everything you can to support each one. Again, when sitting down to help mediate a tough situation, you need to be able to establish a strong sense of trust from the onset, and that will be very hard if you haven't poured a solid foundation months or years before.

Put those listening skills to good use.

It's also important that you take the time to listen well *before* engaging in mediation between two faculty members. Hearing out a faculty member—*really* hearing him or her out—means that you can't start solving the problem before you've heard the whole story. Also, try to tease out as much context as possible in order to give the faculty member a broader perspective to work with. Ask questions such as: Why is this issue/situation such an important one to you right now? What outcome would seem satisfactory to you, and why? What have your encounters with your colleague been like in the past? Have you had opportunities to work together that went well? What do you really want your colleague to hear and understand about the situation? And perhaps most importantly, "when I hear from your colleague, what will he/she tell me about what happened?

While you're listening, take note of possible outcomes, as well as of any positive statements that you hear about the other colleague; these comments may prove useful during mediation as you find ways to build bridges. Think, for example, of the effect of being able to say, "In talking with both of you ahead of time, it became clear that you are equally committed to the wellbeing of our students." Or, "Evelyn, I remember you saying how much you appreciated your chair's support as you worked through the tenure and promotion process." After building trust with you and with the mediation process, the second most important thing you can do is build bridges between the two colleagues, bridges that make finding a resolution feel as natural as possible.

Be satisfied with the good.

Finally, never let the perfect get in the way of the good. Faculty are trained to be critical thinkers, after all, and a perfect ending to mediation might feel false. And if you're a dean worth your salt, you will have shaped the hiring process to attract and hire a faculty marked far more by its diversity of thought than by agreement. It's often the case that two people who are at loggerheads simply need someone to stand between them and provide the first move toward agreement. But they don't need (or expect or want) perfect harmony. Agreeing to disagree—with mutual respect and perhaps slightly more open minds—often sets the stage for healthy working relationships in the future.

QUESTIONS TO CONSIDER

1. In your supervisory role, where do you see conflict festering or potential conflict arising? How might you start building relationships with the faculty or staff involved in case you need to serve as a mediator down the road?

2. What opportunities do you see in your role to reinforce the mission and values of your institution? How can you help focus your faculty/staff attention on shared goals?

3. What do you do on a regular basis to ensure that your faculty and/or staff feel valued and supported by you? What might you need to do to build additional trust?

4. Think about your own strengths and weaknesses. What is easiest for you when it comes to casting a vision, building trust, calling out conflict, listening well, building bridges, and/or bringing conflict to a resolution? Where are you likely to struggle? What can you do to fortify your strengths and work through your weaknesses?

Resources

Berryman-Fink, Cynthia, "Can We Agree to Disagree? Faculty-Faculty Conflict." In Holton, S.A. (Ed.), *Mending the Cracks in the Ivory Tower: Strategies for Conflict Management in Higher Education* (pp. 141-163). Bolton, MA: Anker Publishing Company, Inc., 1998.

Gmelch, Walter H., and James B. Carroll, "The Three Rs of Conflict Management for Department Chairs and Faculty." *Innovative Higher Education* 16, 107–123, 1991.

Price, Patricia L. and Scott Newman, "The Conflict Management Tool Kit." *Inside Higher Ed.* February 20, 2015.

Suárez, Elizabeth, "Navigating Conflict." *Inside Higher Ed.* May 4, 2016.

About the Author

Dr. Carolyn Perry is currently Professor of English and Director of the Center for Teaching and Learning at

Westminster College in Fulton, Missouri. She came to Westminster College in 1991 to teach English and develop the Writing-Across-the-Curriculum program, and she has served in a variety of administrative roles at the College, including Department Chair for English, Division Chair for the Humanities, and Senior Vice President and Dean of Faculty. During the fall of 2017, she served as Acting President of the College.

Carolyn earned a B.A. in English from the University of Missouri and her M.A. from the University of Nebraska. In 1990, she received her Ph.D. from the University of Missouri, with a specialization in Victorian and Modern Literature. She has co-edited three books—*The Dolphin Reader* (with Doug Hunt), *Southern Women's Writing, Colonial to Contemporary* (with Mary Weaks), and *The History of Southern Women's Literature* (with Mary Weaks)—and has presented numerous papers at academic conferences. She is the recipient of the Governor's Award for Excellence in Teaching, the Alpha Chi Teacher of the Year, and the Westminster Parents Association Teacher of the Year. Over the years she has particularly enjoyed traveling abroad with students, supporting the Women's and Gender Studies program and the Remley Women's Center, hosting international students, and serving as the faculty sponsor for EcoHouse and the Environmentally-Concerned Students (ECoS).

PART 4

INFLUENCING
WITHOUT AUTHORITY

CHAPTER 13
INFLUENCING WITHOUT AUTHORITY:
THE 4X4X4 MODEL

by Maureen Breeze,
Principal at Cultivage, Co-Founder of Retreat Reinvent Recharge

and Annette Watkins, Ph.D.
University of Notre Dame Australia

Do you find yourself dealing with the difficult dynamics that result from a confluence of power between administration, faculty, staff, students, and government systems? Being able to influence situations without the authority of a title and/or political capital can be particularly challenging. Yet having the skills to do so on behalf of yourself, your students, your colleagues, and your institution is imperative.

In any given situation it's helpful to consider whether you're looking to influence an overarching system, a guiding policy, or operational procedures. Perhaps it involves all three. Regardless, it comes down to influencing the people behind the systems, policies, and procedures.

As consultants working with education leaders across the globe, we often hear people say they'd do things differently, if only they had the authority. We then help them strategically influence their situation from where they stand.

Recently, a director of advising shared her frustrations about attempts to revamp the advising department at her institution. Her vision included adjusting advisement hours to better reflect the time students were on campus. She also wanted advisors to hold meetings in the student union, which was more centrally located, as their offices were currently on the other side of campus. In addition, she envisioned a more holistic approach to the advising process.

The dean of student services and vice president of academic affairs pushed back. Changing advising operations meant changing employee contracts, hiring procedures, and office logistics, just to name a few things.

In our work together, the director of advising focused on specific targets for change. She then went to work using a tactical skillset for influencing those who had authority.

This tactical skillset includes three domains:

1. Abilities
2. Actions
3. Awareness

We began by exploring her **abilities** or, in other words, what she needed to be able to do to effectively influence the situation. We then outlined **actions** she could take. Finally, we heightened her **awareness** of who she could be as an influencer.

In our coaching work, we've found that when people focus on their abilities, actions, and awareness—whether or not they have authority in a given situation—they are better positioned to influence others and enhance their leadership effectiveness.

Following is our 4x4x4 model to build your influencing skills. Keep in mind that this process is an ongoing part of professional life.

4 Ways to Influence the Situation

To start, let's look at your abilities, or what you can do to influence a situation in four ways:

Step 1: Clarify your 'why'

Consider what you hope to accomplish by influencing the situation. Understand what motivates you and why the timing for influence is now. Challenge your assumptions and get to the heart of your reasoning. There are times when your desire to influence may be both self-serving and organization-serving, which is absolutely fine. However, it helps to be clear about motives. Knowing your 'why' not only solidifies your conviction, but also reveals potential blind spots that might work against you.

Step 2: Adopt a mindset of curiosity

We often engage in the act of influence with a 'power' mindset. We may even unconsciously be thinking, "How can I control this situation?" If so, pause and ask yourself, "What might I learn in this situation?" Have an open mind and genuinely listen to your opposition. Francesca Gino, behavior scientist and Harvard Business School professor, studies the role that curiosity plays in business dealings. Her research concludes that curiosity helps people view situations more creatively, reduces conflict, and broadens perspective. In addition, when a situation is approached from a curious mindset, information flows between parties and people on both sides listen with greater capacity.

Step 3: Search for common concerns

We often approach situations from our 'stance'—how we think a process *should* unfold. It then becomes our stance against someone else's position. Step back and examine the concerns you have in common. What are the potential pain points and opportunities that you share? Knowing this will help you customize your approach to influencing the situation in a way that addresses mutual concerns, versus opposing stances.

Step 4: Sit in a different perspective

Seek to understand what's at stake for the people you're trying to influence. Knowing this will help you craft your message and approach to the situation. How might their current perspective be serving them? What might it cost them to release their current point of view? And finally, how might your perspective benefit or threaten them?

How can these 4 steps be applied to a Higher Education setting?

As the director of advising from our example reflected on **what** she could do to influence her situation, she first **clarified her 'why.'** This step was critical in her process of gaining buy-in from both the campus leadership and her advising team. These changes would be an uphill battle for all, but at their core, she believed they would help the advisors be more effective and meet the needs of the students most likely to drop out. By making these changes, they'd be addressing the institution's retention goals, which was the **common concern** for all involved. She also **reflected** on the **perspectives** of both the VP of academic affairs and the dean of student services. In doing so, she thought about the competing priorities they juggled and estimated the costs of overhauling the advising department. As a result, she prioritized the most important procedures to influence initially and decided strategically to pursue the change in advisors' hours over her other ideas.

4 Ways to Influence Others

Now let's explore four actions that can impact how you influence others.

Action 1: Share a vision for your hoped-for outcome

Take time to paint a vivid picture in your mind for what your ideas will achieve and then share that picture with those you hope to influence. According to Richard Boyatzis' research (2015, 2018) on Intentional Change Theory, a clear vision that illustrates possibility results in a more positive emotional response to change. Engaging others in such a vision activates networks and regions of the brain associated with big picture thinking, motivation, and imagination. Ask yourself, "*What do I envision and how will this vision serve the people I'm trying to influence?*"

Action 2: Use data to support your ideas

Data creates a helpful separation between you and the issue at hand by offering a tangible representation of the situation.

Facts, figures, and honest projections influence analytical reasoning. Return to sitting in the perspective of the person you hope to influence, so that you can determine how to best present your data. Does this person respond well to graphs and illustrations, or do they prefer budgets and spreadsheets? Or would a well-thought-out narrative be better received?

Action 3: Tell a story to relay your vision

Don't stop at analytical reasoning. Stories can help you make an abstract idea concrete. They are powerful sources of inspiration, and they engage our emotions by activating the brain's limbic system, where decisions are made. Brené Brown, a research professor from the University of Houston, says, "Stories are data with a soul. Data wrapped in stories have the ability to move people, to inspire people to take action." What story can bring your idea to life? Who will benefit from your idea, and what will it look like on an individual level?

Action 4: Communicate with collaborative language

We are often encouraged to use powerful and commanding language. However, when looking to influence a situation Adam Grant, Wharton professor and author of *Give and Take: A Revolutionary Approach to Success*, suggests using a more collaborative approach. Words such as "we" and "ours," versus "I" and "my," create a sense of mutual purpose. At the same time, asking questions and listening deeply to the answers creates an opening for discussion. According to

Grant, softening your viewpoint from a declarative statement ("I believe we should change advising hours") to a question ("What might we learn from changing advising hours at this time?") can help to open up another person's mind.

What do the 4 actions for influencing look like in our example?

To determine how to influence those with authority, the director of advising began by **articulating her vision on paper**. In this process, she created a blueprint for a differently-functioning advising department. Her 'five-year-out' view included advising offices more centrally located, services available to students from 8:00 a.m. – 8:00 p.m. with tele-advising options included, a holistic approach to support, and a comprehensive peer-advising component that served students from the summer before freshman year through graduation.

She then **collected data** from 'exit interviews' with students who had dropped out. From the data, she drafted **three compelling stories from students with different profiles** who would have benefited from her envisioned services. Each story included a punch line for how a revised advising department could better impact the institution's retention goals.

> Last of all, she **invited** those with authority to consider what a pilot project with different hours of advisement could teach them all about their students and the institution at large.

4 Strategies to Manage Your Role

To conclude, let's examine four strategies to manage your role as an influencer:

Strategy 1: Build trust, rapport, and visibility

Trustworthiness is an influencer's most critical asset. Leadership expert Stephen Covey identifies two pillars of trustworthiness: competence and character. To be a strong influencer it's important to have the competence—the skills, knowledge, and credibility—to deliver on commitments. It's equally important to have the character—the transparency, integrity, authenticity, and honesty—to be depended upon. Because building trust is a process, it's helpful to take advantage of every opportunity to develop this rapport in low-stake situations. Make the effort to increase your visibility with senior personnel by contributing to their goals, and develop rapport with those you manage by being clear in your direction and diligent with your follow-through.

Strategy 2: Choose your issues wisely

Teachers and parents have long used the phrase "choose your battles wisely" when referring to interacting with young children. It's the same with influencing. Are you likely to fight for every cause that comes your way? If so, you might be seen as someone who is more vested in the fight than the outcome. Be intentional regarding the battles you choose, and you'll have more social capital for influence. Ask yourself, "Is influencing this particular cause the best use of my time, energy, and resources?"

Strategy 3: Think like an innovator

Those who are able to spot opportunities and generate unique solutions are often seen as highly influential. However, you might be inclined to say, "I'm not creative" or "Innovation is not my thing." Innovation is a skillset that can be cultivated by committing time to engage your imagination.

To do this, practice looking to the future and anticipating different outcomes. Ask yourself and others, "How else might we view this?" Connect unrelated dots by considering what the social, political, technological, environmental, and economic implications of a given situation might be. Experiment with asking "What if _____?" multiple times as you think through a dilemma. Train yourself to think like an innovator and your ability to influence situations will improve.

Strategy 4: Cultivate strategic responses

Great influencers avoid knee-jerk responses; they typically take time to reflect on their thoughts and be strategic. In his book *The Pause Principal*, Kevin Cashman discusses a ritual of pausing to help deactivate the fight or flight response system that can emotionally hijack you in high-stake situations. According to Dr. Jill Bolte Taylor, a Harvard-trained brain scientist, it takes 90 seconds after an emotional trigger for the hormonal component of anger to dissipate from the blood and for the automatic physiological response to end. By pausing, you buy critical time and perspective to be more intentional and influential. What can you say to yourself to pause so that you can generate a more strategic response?

What do these 4 strategies to impact your role as an influencer look like in action?

Returning to our director of advising, she made a concerted effort to focus on **building trust and rapport** by being diligent in delivering high quality work on her other projects. She made sure that when given the green light to proceed on her proposed ideas, she'd have people's full confidence in her abilities to manage a change process.

When she first proposed her vision and was told no, she **paused to be strategic**. Instead of either immediately pushing back with her idea or giving up on it, she requested that together they continue thinking about a transformative vision for advising to better serve the students.

Over the next month, she thought **like an innovator**. She asked herself, "If we were to improve retention by 20%, what would advising need to look like?" "What if we established unique partnerships with housing and admissions?" "What if we collaborated with financial services to support students making critical decisions?" "What if we enlisted returning students who had previously dropped out to help inform advising policies?" This process helped her refine her proposal.

Last of all, she selectively **chose her battles**. During this same time the university was considering a new advising and tracking software. When the leadership decided to go with a product that was not her first choice, she went along with the decision. Her advisors could live with this software, and fighting for her first choice of product might hurt her ability to influence her larger vision.

After several months, this director of advising was able to positively influence those in charge, and she garnered approval for changing advisement hours. She is continuing to work on executing her larger vision, and as a result of her process, she has gained credibility for her leadership without having the benefit of official authority.

Resources

Boyatzis, Richard E., & Jack, Anthony I. "The Neuroscience of Coaching." *Consulting Psychology Journal: Practice and Research,* 70(1), 11-27, 2018. https://doi.org/10.1037/cpb0000095

Cashman, Kevin. *The Pause Principal: Step Back to Lead Forward.* San Francisco, CA: Barrett-Koehler Publishers Inc., 2012.

Covey, Stephen M. R., & Merrill, Rebecca R. *The Speed of Trust: That One Thing that Changes Everything.* New York, NY: Simon & Schuster. 2006.

Gino, Francesca. "The Business Case for Curiosity." *Harvard Business Review,* 2018. hbr.org/2018/09/curiosity.

Grant, Adam. *Give and Take: A Revolutionary Approach to Success.* New York, NY: Penguin Books. 2014.

Knight, Rebecca. "How to Increase Your Influence at Work." *Harvard Business Review,* 2018. hbr.org/2018/02/how-to-increase-your-influence-at-work.

About the Authors

Maureen Breeze has over 25 years of experience working in the fields of coaching and senior level management. She is a certified executive coach through the International Coaching Federation and has authored two books on leadership and creative thinking. Maureen has facilitated trainings and leadership development workshops in Europe, Asia, and throughout North America. She is the Co-Founder of Retreat Reinvent Recharge, an international collaboration of practitioners and academics providing professional development for women at different stages in their careers.

Dr. Annette Watkins brings decades of research and corporate experience to her work throughout Asia and Australia. She is the Associate Dean of the University of Notre Dame Business School (Australia) and supervises Ph.D. candidates researching the career paths of women. Annette is an accomplished business owner, higher education academic, and researcher. She is the Co-Founder of Retreat Reinvent Recharge, an international collaboration of practitioners and academics providing professional development services to women at different stages in their careers.

CHAPTER 14
LEADING FROM ANY POSITION: THE IMPACT OF INFLUENCE

by Joy Karavedas, Ed.D.
Division of Teacher Education, School of Education
Azusa Pacific University

Vicki Rosser (2004) called mid-level leaders the "unsung heroes of the academy." I would take that a step further to say mid-level female leaders are the *unseen* heroes of the academy. When I made the move from K-12 administration into higher education, it was immediately clear that my experience was not enough to lead within the halls of the academy; I must have additional letters behind my name to be taken seriously. So, I did that. I went back to school and earned a doctorate in Organizational Leadership. Perhaps, I was foolish to believe an advanced degree would now be enough. It wasn't.

Moving into leadership within higher education has long been a difficult path for women. Although numbers are rising, women still hold only 32% of the full professor positions and only 30% of university presidencies (Johnson, 2017). Like me, you may also find yourself in a position with untapped desires, ambitions, and skills. We aren't alone. There are over 900,000 middle management leaders in higher education, which comprises the largest portion of professional staff (U.S. Department of Education and NCES, 2018). These positions are stressful, usually involve less authority, offer fewer material

175

rewards, are less likely to lead to senior positions, and are often undervalued within the academy (Garcia et al, 2020).

Do not give up hope. The news is not all bad. These middle positions also provide the unique opportunity to influence others and evoke change. Holding the position between decision making and decision implementation means your days consist of essential work that flows between addressing the requests of those in senior leadership above you and leading those down the line who report to you. These middle management positions are literally surrounded by opportunities to influence others. Embracing that influence is the mark of a true leader, with or without the position, title, or direct authority.

Women are especially well qualified to use their influence to impact others because they usually place a high value on the actual experience of the work they are doing. Women are more likely to seek enjoyment by building relationships with others (Helgesen and Goldsmith, 2018), and your relationships are an essential part of your influence. Addressing the rising trends in higher education today requires leaders who recognize their influence and are willing to use it. In the next few paragraphs, I will provide specific steps to help you embrace your influence and shape the future of your institution.

Unfortunately, women sometimes create barriers to the development and use of their influence. They build habits that keep themselves stuck in self-defeating behaviors, unwilling to change (Helgesen and Goldsmith, 2018). You can break the cycle. The following three specific behaviors allow you to live into your influence as a female leader of impact:

1. Cultivate and maintain a broad network of relationships.

2. Interact strategically with senior leaders.

3. Build confidence in your own leadership and influence.

Cultivate and Maintain a Broad Network of Relationships

One of the benefits of holding a position without direct positional authority is the opportunity to engage with a wide variety of people. Your lack of authority actually provides entrance into a network of workers that get things done and move the ball forward—a network that might not be as easily accessed from higher levels within the institution. Through common experiences, shared skills, and professional opportunities, you have likely built a broad network of relationships with a variety of people at varying levels of influence.

Think about your network. Think about your levels of influence. If you are like most women, you probably have personal and professional relationships with others inside and outside your institution. You trust those around you, and you have earned their trust as well. These relationships are direct evidence of your influence. Capitalizing on this influence allows you to do your job well, build into the development of others, and strengthen your institution as a result.

We all have our "go to" people for answers. I have one member of our division that understands the registrar's policies like the back of her hand, while another analyst regularly answers my questions about our complex budget projection system, and I can also call upon a former chief of staff when I simply need to work through navigating higher education. My network of resources is the asset that allows me to be an asset to others. Networking has personal benefits, as well. When I was struggling to get my curriculum vitae in the hands of the right dean for a position I desired, I reached out to a colleague from my doctoral program who was able to make the connection, and I got the interview. Maintaining a variety of relationships is critical to your success both professionally and personally.

Each of us should maintain three types of professional network relationships:

Internal Network

These are the people you see every day and are closest to you. They could be coworkers, friends, or even family. They are the people who will tell you when you have spinach in your teeth and, more importantly, will tell you when your idea is bad or when you shouldn't make that move.

External Network

This is the next layer, and often the one over which you have the most influence. These are the second level of people with whom you interact regularly, including other departments in the university, professional organizations, individuals at other universities, etc. You can call on any of these people when you have a question or need advice about a specific work situation, and they can call you for answers as well.

Strategic Network

These people can take your influence to the next level. Your strategic network may be small, but it should not be ignored. One of the greatest problems with influence is that we forget to nurture its growth. Your strategic network should include individuals who can propel your influence forward into new places. Cultivate this network with care.

Interact Strategically with Senior Leaders

Without direct positional authority, leadership and influence are often developed through other means. Within higher education, leadership skills are often obtained through observation of others, especially those in senior-level positions. Holding a position without direct authority requires a focus on a different skillset than those used in higher leadership roles. Multitasking, organization, and time management—skills that are particularly prevalent among women—will serve you well in middle management roles. By interacting with those in positions greater than your own, you expand your vision outside of the day-to-day work world and avoid the trap of focusing on the minutiae rather than the bigger picture.

Higher education, for the most part, is still very hierarchical. Holding a position that walks between senior leaders and direct support creates a level of influence that is critical to your university. You are the tool for communicating the mission and vision of the university to others in a manner that directly influences their professional lives. Interacting with senior leaders can help you understand the long-term strategic message of the university and provide context beyond the short-term "put out the fire" roles many of us hold (Blackwood and Brown-Welty, 2011). The ability to understand and travel through all levels of the hierarchical ladder is a powerful form of influence uniquely beneficial within the halls of higher education. Walk well in this middle role and you will find your level of influence reaches points you never imagined.

Never have I found this to be truer than in my role as staff council chair for my current university. As chair, I have the opportunity to sit on university leadership teams, to meet with the president and his cabinet, and to be a part of the university's strategic planning team. My level of influence is far greater than I imagined when I accepted the opportunity to be a part of the council three years ago.

One note to those interested in rising through the ranks of higher education into greater leadership roles: As you watch and learn from senior leadership, you will find yourself growing as well. Pay attention to those lessons. Regular interactions with those in positions above you grants you access to role models and professional advice that will be instrumental to your development as a leader. These exchanges with senior leaders will build your own leadership potential, skills, and leadership characteristics to strengthen your influence now and into the future. Finally, never forget your influence on others who want to become leaders—take the time to invest in other leaders who may also be traveling this leadership journey.

Build Confidence in Your Leadership and Influence

John Maxwell said, "leadership is influence." Yet, many of us, especially women, hesitate to identify ourselves as leaders unless someone has given us this label through position or authority. Even at the highest levels of leadership, over-confidence is rarely a female failing (Helgesen and Goldsmith, 2018). Yet, leadership is exercising influence with or without having been told to do so. Leaders understand what is required and have the confidence to show up and engage. Exercising this type of leadership influence requires confidence, but confidence is tricky. Too often, when we are most lacking in confidence is the time when we need it the most. Fortunately, your confidence can grow with practice, and as it grows, you will find it can have significant impact on your influence.

It's often easy to picture yourself as the second-in-command, but could greater confidence in your potential result in a different view? Pulling back the curtain and looking a little deeper, you may realize the wizard isn't as scary as you previously thought. The mere fact that you are reading this book demonstrates that you have great leadership potential. Through experience and action, your confidence grows from knowledge gained by each experience. You can then lean into that confidence to approach new leadership situations. I had to learn this when I earned my doctorate. The degree wasn't enough; I also needed confidence in my expertise to carry me forward.

You can follow two specific practices to build your confidence and your influence—*Practice Vulnerability* and *Act Like a Leader.*

Practice Vulnerability

In her book *Daring Greatly,* Brené Brown, the leading researcher on vulnerability, writes that vulnerability is the cornerstone of confidence (Brown, 2012). To move forward, you must be willing to risk the first step. Leadership and influence always carry some uncertainty, but with each opportunity to lean into a new situation, we grow.

You must get out of your comfort zone. If you are comfortable, you are not learning (Brown, 2012). Your actions may become stuck on autopilot. Waking up to your actions allows you to become self-aware as you try out new actions and monitor the results. With each new success, you develop new skills. Perhaps more importantly, with each failed attempt, you learn something about the situation, other people, and yourself.

Act Like a Leader

This is not a "fake it until you make it" platitude, but an actual research-supported assertion that as we move into areas of greater influence and leadership, our actions will lead our thinking. When you use your influence strategically to make connections, provide resources, and contribute your expertise, people will begin to view you as a leader. The affirmation of this new leadership identity is internalized, and you then confidently step into more leadership opportunities (Ibarra, 2015). Leadership begins on the inside. If you view yourself as a leader and are willing to step up and act in those places, your level of influence and impact will grow regardless of your position or title.

I began this chapter saying I believed mid-level leaders are the *unseen* heroes of the academy. Reluctance to claim achievement is common among women at all levels (Helgesen and Goldsmith, 2018). Yet your influence is greater than you know. You may not yet be in the position of your dreams, but *never* doubt that you have influence. Understanding this influence, embracing it, and acting through it can make the difference in your level of satisfaction at any position. Not only that; it just might make those dreams come true.

QUESTIONS TO PONDER

1. Helgesen and Goldsmith (2018) state that women can create barriers to their own development and influence with self-defeating habits they are hesitant to change. What habits have you "stuck" in your current position?

2. Leadership is exercising your influence regardless of your position. Where do you believe your influence could have the most impact in your institution?

3. Every leader should have three networks with strong relationships in each—an internal network, external network, and a strategic network. How broad is your professional network?

4. As a follow up to question to No. 3, who is in your internal network? Who is in your external network? Your strategic network?

5. We are influenced by the leadership of senior leaders around us. The nice thing is that we don't even have to know those senior leaders to benefit from their influence; sometimes strong observations are enough to influence our growth. Think about those in your sphere of influence. Which individual exhibits leadership and influence in a manner you admire most? Why?

6. Because leadership naturally entails uncertainty, growth occurs when we step out of our comfort zone and embrace that uncertainty. Brené Brown (2012) contends

that a level of vulnerability is required to step into that uncertainty. Where do you feel most vulnerable within your leadership?

7. As female leaders, we tend to dismiss our influence as less important. We often accept the role of an unseen leader within the academy. How do you view your level of influence? Your level of leadership?

8. Recognizing barriers and establishing commitments to break through those barriers is necessary to becoming an influential leader. It all begins with that first step. What three things will you do over the next 6-12 months to grow your influence?

FOR FURTHER CONSIDERATION:

Daring Greatly by Brené Brown

How Women Rise by Sally Helgesen and Marshall Goldsmith

"The Power of Vulnerability," Brené Brown, Ted Talk. www.ted.com

Women's Leadership Development Institute, CCCU.org

Resources

Blackwood, Jothany, and Sharon Brown-Welty. *Diversity in Higher Education. Women of Color in Higher Education: Changing Directions and New Perspectives.* Vol. 10, p. 109-133, 2011.

Brown, Brene. *Daring Greatly: How the Courage to Be Vulnerable Transforms the Way We Live, Love, Parent, and Lead.* New York, NY: Gotham Books, 2018.

Garcia, Hugo A., Kimberly Nehls, Kimberly Florence, Yvonne Harwood, and Tamara McClain. *The Ones Who Move Things Along: How Women Mid-Level Managers Navigate Academic Landscapes. New Directions for Higher Education.* 2020: 25-39. doi: 10.1002/he.20358

Helgesen, Sally, and Marshall Goldsmith. *How Women Rise.* Hatchett Books. New York, NY, 2018.

Ibarra, Herminia. *Act Like a Leader, Think Like a Leader.* Boston, MA: Havard Business Review Press, 2018.

Johnson, Heather L. *Pipelines, Pathways, and Institutional Leadership: An Update on the Status of Women in Higher Education.* Washington, DC: American Council on Education, 2017.

Rosser, Vicki. "A National Study on Midlevel Leaders in Higher Education: The Unsung Professionals in the Academy." *Higher Education.* 48: 317-337. 2004.

U.S. Department of Education. *Enrollment.*
nces.ed.gov/programs/digest/d16/ tables/dt16_303.70.asp.
2018.

About the Author

Dr. Joy Karavedas is an experienced leader and professor with over 25 years of administrative experience in business and educational settings, including her current role in higher education administration. Her research interests focus on leadership and professional development of mid-level leaders in higher education. She has published articles and presented on the topics of the Impact and Influence of Mid-Level Leaders, Building Relationships that Matter through Networking, and Maximizing Your Productivity as a Department Chair.

Joy is currently employed by Azusa Pacific University, where she serves as the Chair of the university's Staff Council, the Strategic Plan Enhancement Team, the Strategic Plan Initiatives Team, and the WSCUS Accreditation Steering Committee. Dr. Karavedas also serves as an adjunct professor for the Brandman University School of Business and Professional Studies and for the Westcliff University School of Education. Joy is married to her husband Nick (a high school teacher and administrator), and together they have two children (both also teachers) and five amazing grandchildren.

PART 5

LEADING AND THRIVING
AS WOMEN OF COLOR

CHAPTER 15
DEAR WOMEN OF COLOR: OUR COMMUNITY IS POWER

by Josephine Gonzalez, M.Ed.

and Angie Kim, M.A.
Associate Director, Inclusive Engagement and Student Life, New York University

Introduction

> *"What is the greatest lesson a woman should learn?*
>
> *that since day one*
> *she's already had everything she needs within herself*
> *it's the world that convinced her she did not"*
>
> — Rupi Kaur, *The Sun and Her Flowers*

At times, our identity as women of color (WOC) at Predominantly White Institutions (PWI) has made us question our self-worth and sense of belonging. When we find ourselves experiencing imposter syndrome as a result of workplace environments that uphold and protect white supremacist culture, we often gain strength from this powerful poem. Rupi's words remind us to look inward when faced with self-doubt as leaders. At the same time, we invite you to reflect on how our own strengths can add to our collective strength as a WOC community. In this chapter, we introduce narratives of WOC who generously have shared lived experiences and advice as they have navigated their roles as leaders in higher education.

Our Inspiration and Framework

In order to sustain our well-being as WOC leaders, we have turned toward each other and other WOC leaders in the field for inspiration and guidance. We are indebted to the activist work of WOC such as Angela Davis, Gloria Anzaldúa, and Audre Lorde, who have paved the way for WOC, particularly those who are trans and queer. From the work of the Third World Feminist Movements in the late 1960's and 1970's to intersectional feminist movements now, we learn that there is power when women of color gather together to uplift one another. We believe solidarity work is a daily practice in our roles as leaders within higher education and within our communities. We must strive towards the liberation of all WOC to create just and inclusive higher education institutions, where future generations of WOC can thrive.

One of the elements of Critical Race Theory is Counter Storytelling (2017). It is a strategy we use as WOC that moves us towards collective liberation. Counter Storytelling allows us to analyze and challenge the stories that are often considered "the majoritarian story." Here, we uplift the narratives of WOC navigating the field of Higher Education. We welcomed perspectives from WOC of varying cultures, gender expressions, religions, spiritualities, sexual orientations, and backgrounds. Here are some of the tools and tips we and our very own community of WOC have cultivated and utilized to navigate the field of higher education, particularly in PWIs.

1. Practice Authentic Leadership

We describe authentic leadership as letting go of who you think you're supposed to be and embracing who you are. We acknowledge that embracing your authenticity comes with risk. WOC are constantly taking on the burden to act, look, and talk in a way that upholds practices rooted in white supremacy, sexism, and heteronormativity.

Shaquana Gadsen shared the following:

> "I was faced with my tone and assertiveness being a problem. A colleague once said higher education is not for me since I didn't have a more bubbly and enthusiastic voice when I spoke to staff and students. I have a very assertive tone and presence, which was deemed intimidating by countless colleagues, staff members, supervisors, and students. Just being who I was without the "fluff" of cheer was a difficult battle for me to face, and it caused me to question whether this profession was for me. I thought maybe I didn't have the personality for it, or I just didn't belong. All of which were absolutely not true."

Lack of ability to exercise your authentic voice is crippling and disastrous to our wellbeing and to those around us. It does not promote social change or allow us to bring our whole selves to work. Danielle Berkman, as a white-passing Latina woman, shared the importance of overcoming imposter feelings. She said: "Do not let other people's perception of your identities invalidate your sense of self or your lived experiences." We want to remind our fellow WOC that authenticity is the catalyst for transformational leadership. We invite you to reflect on how your race, ethnicity, and culture can be used as tools to enhance how you lead yourself and in turn lead others. One of the ways to do this is to determine if your personal and professional values align with your role and institution.

Sarah Childs provides the following advice to WOC seeking to bring authenticity to their leadership:

> "You really need to make sure to define yourself as a professional in the field and on your campus by your own standards. Be who you are and who you want to be. Know your moral and ethical compass. Know your values. Know what you bring to the table. Always learn and challenge yourself so that you are consistently growing and expanding your perspective. Seek to be excellent without trying to be perfect. Show up authentically. Bring your cultures with you too and let them live in how you show up."

Authentic leadership allows you to determine how to show up in times of adversity and how and when to speak up in meetings. The goal is to have your professional intentions align with your authentic self. Though this takes practice and can be met with challenges, we encourage you to be patient with yourself and don't be afraid to ask for help. We recommend reading books, articles, listening to podcasts, attending professional development opportunities, joining affinity-based spaces that are made by and for WOC. It's important for us to see our narratives and experiences represented so that we can find the courage to fully live authentically in our personal and professional lives.

2. Honor Self-Preservation

As WOC, it's imperative that we remember leading in higher education is a marathon, not a sprint. We are often asked or told to take on roles that require us to use our emotional and cultural capital to repair and address campus harm that's rooted in institutional oppression. Cultural taxation, a term coined by Amado Padilla (as cited in Joseph and Hirshfield, 2011) refers to the additional labor the faculty and staff of color take on as "unofficial" diversity consultants on campus. Considering how often we take on this type of leadership role, we look to Audre Lorde for advice on self-preservation. She shares, "Caring for myself is not self-indulgence, it is self-preservation, and that is an act of political warfare." In order for us to practice self-preservation for ourselves, it is dire that we create and communicate our boundaries to others both for accountability and support. When possible, say "no," so that you can say yes to things you really want to do. As WOC, we have to periodically ask ourselves: "What kind of professional environment do I need to be at my best?" Finding answers to this will not be an overnight journey, but rather, something you will need to prioritize and revisit throughout your career. We urge you to use your vacation days unapologetically, take your lunch break, flex your time when working late or on the weekends, and advocate for your needs (discussed later).

We invite you to think of at least two habits that you can incorporate into your current routine that will aid in your self-preservation journey. Habiba Braimah shares, "You do not need to overextend yourself to prove that you are worthy. This is the quickest way to burn out. Instead, invest your energy into finding your people." One of the biggest parts of self-preservation is finding a community who are deeply committed to your wellbeing.

3. Nurture Your Support System

Almost every single WOC who shared their narratives said "finding your people" is one of the biggest challenges, yet is critical for WOC. Allying yourself with other WOC and nurturing the community you build is essential to your leadership journey. For Leiry Santos, cultivating a strong intergenerational community of WOC is an integral part of her values in higher education. She said,

> "Oftentimes, we are the role model for our siblings when we are growing up. Unknowingly, we become role models for our students and peers. This becomes an opportunity

> for our students, who experienced similar hardships as I
> did, [and who now have] direct access to connect and be
> mentored by people that look like them. It is an immense
> honor to be able to inspire the next generation and watch
> them pave their own paths. I always say, 'Become better
> than me... We didn't forge this path for you not to surpass
> it.'"

It is one step to build a community, but it is another to lift the next generation as you climb. Visible representation is one of the first steps to building a legacy of WOC leaders in higher education. E.D. highlights another aspect of how we can nurture our support system She shared that "you will need spaces to vent and process the aggression you will face. It is most helpful to have friends within your department and out of your department." In particular, we invite you to create WOC-based spaces. When intentionally cultivated, these spaces can be both transformational and healing. It has provided us a safe space to share, strategize, and support one another. We recognize that an institution's location, demographic make-up, budget, and workplace culture are all factors that contribute to the possibility of this space, so we want to provide you with an array of platforms you can use. Once you take the initial step to find the WOC who uplift, validate, or share similar experiences as you, then we invite you to organize. It's important to note that these WOC don't need to be from your institution or in the field of higher education. You can plan a virtual meet-up, lunch date, retreat, Facebook group, potluck, book club, or plan an event—any platform that will provide a space of belonging for WOC. It's important to treat our WOC community like a plant. You have to water it and give it nourishment to grow. We encourage you to seek meaningful WOC relationships and to actively support the work of WOC in and outside of your institution. This is how we thrive.

4. Embrace Mentorship

For WOC, mentorship can feel scarce due to the lack of representation of WOC in higher education leadership roles. However, we must not be discouraged, as mentorship is a critical part of our professional development and trajectory. K. Sosa shared: "As a Latina, some of the challenges I've faced working at a PWI is finding mentors who are Latinx or even a Latinx community in general, continuously fighting to be at 'the table' and making my knowledge heard and respected, and navigating university politics while being my authentic self." Mentors can often be the person who can invite you to have a seat at the table. We ourselves had several WOC mentors who both championed and challenged us throughout our careers and personal lives, where they unapologetically equipped us with transparency, care, and tough love. However, mentorship is not "one size fits all." It is important to understand that mentorship is a spectrum and having mentors for different needs and goals allows you to have a holistic support system. Successful mentorship includes investment in mutual collaboration when supporting each other's needs, while understanding boundaries around time and capacity. For example, our mentors invited us to present alongside them at conferences, co-write articles, and served as sounding boards when we were going through tough situations at work. Taking time to cultivate your relationship with your mentor based on your shared interests and background will allow for meaningful story sharing, identifying opportunities for growth, and tangible goal setting. We also challenge you to give back to the WOC community by mentoring the younger generation of WOC. This helps you to reflect on your own journey and pass along the generational wisdom. Impactful mentor/mentee relationships can lead to tremendous professional as well as personal growth.

5. Identify your Needs

The majority of the women described self-worth and advocacy as skills they needed to cultivate as WOC in leadership. Arianna Deans shared the following advice, "Don't be afraid to leave a position that doesn't serve you. Your talents, your voice, your skills, and your blackness will all be great qualities your next role is looking for and WILL respect. Don't compromise your wellbeing for the benefit of someone else or an institution." Her words speak truth to the challenges women of color may face in a workplace environment—especially when the work environment lacks an inclusive and racially-conscious framework. Utilizing reflective practices such as journaling and meditation can be a powerful tool as we explore our leadership style and best work environment. For example, what kind of support do you want and need from your supervisor? If your answer does not align with your current work situation, it may be time to re-evaluate your role.

It's important to acknowledge how our identities become hypervisible and how our needs shift over time as we navigate various leadership contexts. Eena Singh shares the following when considering her needs in the workplace:

> "I never understood what it meant to be a WOC in our field until I moved up and started finding myself as a part of committees, working groups, and various settings where I was often one of the only women of color, especially one of the only South Asian women administrators in those spaces. You begin to notice how people might talk to you, how you are included or not included in certain spaces, how you have to prove your worth differently."

Eena reminds us of the importance of asking good questions when interviewing with a potential employer. These may include but are not limited to:

- How are professionals of color supported at the institution?

- How is the institution responding to bias incidents occurring on campus and in the greater community?

- What are some ways non-professionals of color are trained in equity and inclusion?

- How would you describe your student culture towards social justice work?

The answers to these questions will give you insight into whether or not this institution has the ability to meet your professional needs.

Conclusion

Being a WOC leader in PWI requires tactfulness, boldness, and a strong community behind us. We cannot be on this professional journey alone. In the end, we hope this chapter provides you with the courage and tools to shine in your position as a WOC leader. With that, we leave you with a quote by Shaquana Gadsen: "Reclaim your time professionally with love and logic—you are not an imposter but a beacon of home to the next women of color who can't be who they can't see. Sis, shine on and I hope to see you soon, Queen."

QUESTIONS FOR REFLECTION

What does being a woman of color mean to you?

What were the earliest messages you received about women of color in leadership roles?

What challenges have you faced as a woman of color in higher education?

Who's part of your support system? *Or:* What does your ideal support system look like? What steps can you take to create this support system?

> What advice would you give other women of color entering/navigating the field of higher education? *Or:* What advice would you give your younger self?

Resources

Delgado, Richard, and Jean Stefancic. *Critical Race Theory: An Introduction* (3rd ed.). NYU Press, 2017.

Joseph, Tiffany, and Laura Hirshfield. "'Why Don't You Get Somebody New to Do It?': Race and Cultural Taxation in the Academy." *Ethnic and Racial Studies, 34*(1), 121-141. 2011.

About the Authors

Josephine Gonzalez was born and raised in Brooklyn, New York. She earned her B.A. in Gender & Women's Studies from the State University of New York at Plattsburgh (SUNY Plattsburgh) and her M.Ed. in Higher Education and Student Affairs at the University of Vermont (UVM). She's currently pursuing her Juris Doctorate (J.D.) at City University of New York School of Law. Josephine has extensive experience with developing programs that engage the community in conversations about inclusion, diversity, belonging, and equity. In her spare time, she enjoys cooking, going for a bike ride, and playing board games with loved ones.

Angie Kim (she/her) is the Associate Director of Inclusive Engagement and Student Life at Silver School of Social Work at New York University. Angie formerly served as Residence Hall Assistant Director at New York University. Angie is passionate about examining DEI initiatives through the lens of neoliberalism and racial capitalism. Angie graduated with a B.A. in Cognitive Science from the University of Southern California and M.A. in Higher Education and Student Affairs at New York University.

CHAPTER 16
RISING BY LIFTING OTHERS: STEPS TO TAKE IN BUILDING COMMUNITY FOR WOMEN OF COLOR

by Thanh Nguyen
Interim Director, Center for Multicultural Engagement and Inclusion
Metropolitan State University of Denver

and Ally Garcia, Ed.D.,
Director, TRIO Student Support Services
Metropolitan State University of Denver

Reflecting on our own experiences as women of color who work in the realm of higher education, we are reminded that institutions need leaders who look like us, who care about us, and who are committed to guiding us as we grow in leadership. As we face and dismantle systems that were not structurally created for our success and advancement, it is imperative for women of color to band together in community and sisterhood. The wisdom and bravery unearthed in our collective stories and shared experiences of truth and vulnerability encourages other women of color to lead authentically even when faced with adversity and possible consequences within the academy (Faircloth, 2017).

We understand the power, responsibility, and humility of representing our communities in higher education. bell hooks, an accomplished writer, professor, and feminist activist, when exploring her own experiences, shared that many higher education programs tend to focus on white women, as though they are a representation of all women. The experiences of women are unique, multifaceted, and complex. Grouping women together does not allow for all women to be heard. By representing white women exclusively, higher education disregards women of color. hooks (1989) further encouraged higher education leaders to center their programs on the narratives and experiences of women of color in order to challenge race and racism and to include the voices of all women.

Due to historic injustices, patriarchal values, and systems entrenched with white and racist views, women of color often feel isolated and unwelcomed. Because senior leadership at institutions of higher learning often lacks representation of women of color, breaking into this arena seems daunting. The road women of color take to leadership is not without its intellectual and emotional landmines. Not only do we need to become proficient in navigating our paths around systemic and political potholes, we must often deal with offences from other women of color.

Rare enough are the opportunities for higher education career advancement for women of color. When women of color are selected for leadership positions, they often find themselves justifying the selection, as questioning behaviors and resentment surface from others, including other women of color. Resentment is often directed to the person chosen, rather than the system that has limited the growth potential of so many women of color. Those who have felt the misdirected pain and jealousy from other women of color, may be wary of initiating actions toward building community and self-love. We understand the reluctance. We, too, have often been resistant to the idea of engaging in collaborations with those who have hurt us rather than lent support. Instead, we have chosen to find meaningful ways to connect with one another through stories, expressions of kindness, and compassion.

We ask that women of color who have reinforced the idea of competition consider the alternate course of building authentic and ego-free relationships for their growth and the growth of the women of color who follow. We hope this chapter offers ideas on how to actively resist the cycle of competition against other women of color through community building, self-love, and healing. Members of a strong sisterhood can uplift themselves while dismantling a system never meant for them.

Critical Skill: Learn to Build Community Early

In some cultures, informal or formal women's circles are created to allow women to bond, share stories, create ceremonies and rituals, and set goals. The concept behind women's circles emphasizes the notion that we are more powerful together than alone. By intentionally creating space and community, we are developing self-recognition that we are a force. As women of color in higher education, we too are stronger when we come together in our academic, professional, and personal lives.

By creating women-of-color circles within our institutions, we can come together to hold vulnerable and courageous dialogues, share our stories, knowledge, and experiences, and gain inspiration and healing. Such gatherings can be organized broadly throughout the university, involving all women of color from all organizational ranks, or they can be more intimate, with only two or three colleagues of color participating.

Mentorship is a valuable tool in building community. Women of color who have leadership roles on campus can help guide others in their professional development. The mentor can serve as a "navigator" and can share knowledge of the political nuances at the top levels, which ultimately dictate institutional action. The mentor's knowledge can help other women of color in the navigation and understanding of the intricacies and complexities of leadership. Developing the mentor/mentee relationship affords the mentors the opportunity to promote the knowledge and skills of the mentee. Having a mentor/advocate in one's corner can have a significant impact on whether someone is for committee work and other leadership opportunities.

The mentee should also understand that the role of mentor often requires navigating highly political, colonized, and male-dominated space, which often limits information sharing for self-preservation. Women of color in senior leadership positions may feel a need to be methodical and strategic about what and when they challenge ideas. It is important that community building experiences include an understanding of all spaces and the roles the participants occupy on campus. We encourage participants to enter all conversations with grace, humility, and loyalty.

Learned Experiences: We Have Too Many

As women of color in higher education, the field has not always been kind to us. We have had to prove our worth in a field dominated with ideologies of whiteness. We have been challenged academically, professionally, and personally as we work and fight for racial justice for ourselves and those who aspire to be in our profession, but more importantly for the students of color whose voices are often silenced. Racism, patriarchy, heterosexism, and capitalism are embedded into our professional lives on a daily basis. They often challenge our daily activity through dominant rhetoric that forces its way into our conversations and actions. We recognize the power structures in play and realize how the ideas of whiteness and privilege oppress others because we, ourselves, have been demoralized, dehumanized, and made to feel insignificant in our field. Nonetheless, we continue our ventures into higher education because, as hard as this work is, we wake up each morning with purpose, to assist students in changing their lives through education.

Some of our strongest bonds with other women of color have been through the building of community. In sharing authentic truths, we can understand each other, offer advice, and lend a listening ear. Historically, communities of color have strategized and organized by banding together as one. Our families have passed down the value of community, and those powerful lessons should not stop in institutions of higher learning. In community, we share meals, traditions, and stories that make us laugh, cry, and remember. In community, we offer other ways of thinking, celebrate victories, and learn about ambitions and dreams. For the community to be working at its fullest, we must let go of our egos and let them dissolve into the collective good.

Steps to Take in Building that Community

Be the first!

You may have to be the first person on your campus to start building and reinforcing the power of women of color in community. Start small and invite women of color together for a lunch or potluck. Make sure you are clear about your expectations and sincere in your convictions. Ask yourself, "How many women of color have I lifted up today?" Celebrate women of color in their successes and wins. Make it a point to be loud and unapologetic when it comes to sharing your successes as a woman of color. Applaud the accomplishments of others.

Ask for support

Let your supervisor know how important gathering together with other women of color would be for you, your work, your colleagues, and your students of color. Ask to see if she/he/they will advocate for funding to support women of color on campus. Funding a luncheon, a guest speaker, certificates or awards, or a professional conference for group members would speak volumes about the institution's commitment to diversity and inclusion. Be transparent about your needs and be courageous when asking for support.

Embrace different places

Unfortunately, not all women of color will be onboard, and some may even continue to hurt you. They may not have had the opportunity to learn how their behavior is harmful. They may also not want to learn. As hard as it is, neither of these should be a reason for you to stop trying to build community with other of women of color. Your resistance to continue allows the status quo to continue.

Invite faculty

Women faculty of color also know what it feels like to be fighting a white, male-dominated system. By inviting faculty women of color to join in the community building, you could be making needed connections on campus and offering more spaces for women of color to be heard and valued. It could also provide space to remind tenured women of color of their power on campus for pushing and radicalizing change.

Take the time to heal and be healed

Practice self-love and healing in the very spaces that have denied you love and health. Be kind to yourself and know that you will have days that are emotionally and mentally difficult. Even in these moments, you can find knowledge and value. Healing is a different process and a journey for everyone. Where you are right now is enough and valid. Keep reconnecting to yourself, learn to listen, and truly see yourself for who you are.

Take care of yourself first, before you take care of others

Remember to nourish yourself physically and mentally before serving others. Most importantly, learn to let the things that do not serve you well, go. Embrace who you are and be comfortable with the uncomfortable, so that you are whole and complete with yourself. Then, you can begin to help others begin the process of feeling complete. Never forget your importance and purpose. Whether you find that truth, define it, or ignore it, at the end of the day, it is your life and your story. Care for yourself first before you take care of others in your community.

Know your worth

Take the time to love yourself. Realize that you deserve all the great things that life has to offer. Frame your thoughts that count yourself as deserving, that you hold value. You will appreciate yourself when you start to acknowledge and recognize your self-worth.

So what does an empowering sisterhood and community look like for women of color in higher education? There is no exact formula in developing an authentic and empowering sisterhood and community. Rather, the creation of sisterhood should be driven by the women of color who are seeking out community.

For us, our sisterhood and community have been created in the following ways. We intentionally seek out mentorship and schedule times to connect over meals in order to share our accomplishments and struggles, as well as validate each other's feelings and experiences. We look to one another's wisdom and expertise in guiding our career paths. For those in positions of power, there is relentless advocacy of others in our group for career advancement opportunities. In larger group meetings, we validate our sisters' courage in speaking their truths and sharing their knowledge, through praise and encouragement. We then follow-up with emails to our sisters when we learn they are navigating challenges or resistance.

We lean on each other for growth by offering constructive feedback rooted in social justice and equity. Because our relationship is built on love and trust, we are able to offer our honest and candid suggestions for continued and professional growth absent the fear of reprimand or retaliation. This commitment includes challenging each other when we become envious of the accomplishments of other women of color. This is paramount in dismantling the destructive cycle and stopping its reproduction of competition, oppression, and jealousy. Our experience in this arena is not a definitive prescription on the embodiment of an authentic sisterhood or community, but an example from which we hope the reader can render their own creation.

The significance of community has strong and powerful implications to the work that we do in serving others. To lead culturally in a way that is responsive to the community is not for the faint of heart. Community-based cultural work is at the very center of the work we do and asks us to acknowledge our vulnerabilities and tap into our voices, so that our stories can be heard. Many of us have been called to perform within the walls of higher education and we have graciously embarked on the journey of serving our communities, while maintaining our authenticity and sense of identity. We hope you will join us on this purposeful adventure.

Resources

Bordas, Juana. *Salsa, Soul, and Spirit: Leadership for a Multicultural Age.* Berrett-Koehler Publishers, Inc. 2012.

Brown, Brene. *The Gifts of Imperfection: Let Go of Who You Think You're Supposed to Be and Embrace Who You Are.* Hazelden Publishing. 2010.

Duckworth, Angela. *Grit: The Power of Passion and Perseverance.* Simon and Schuster, Inc. 2016.

Faircloth, Susan C. "Reflections on the Concept of Authentic Leadership: From an Indigenous Scholar/Leader Perspective." *Advances in Developing Human Resources, 19*(4), 407-419. 2017. https://doi.org/10.1177/1523422317728935

Freiere, Paulo. *Pedagogy of the Oppressed*. Penguin Education, 1972.

hooks, bell. "Feminism and Black Women's Studies." Sage: *A Scholarly Journal on Black Women*, 6(1), 54-56. 1989.

Kaur, Rupi. *The Sun and Her Flowers*. Andrews McMeel Publishing, 2017.

Matias, Cheryl E. *Feeling White: Whiteness, Emotionality, and Education*. Sense Publishers, 2016.

Ruiz, Don Miguel. *The Four Agreements: A Practical Guide to Personal Freedom*. Amber-Allen Publishing, Inc, 1997.

Saad, Layla F. *Me and White Supremacy: Combat Racism, Change the World, and Become a Good Ancestor*. Napreville, IL: Sourcebooks, 2020.

Steele, Cassie P. *We Heal from Memory: Sexton, Lorde, Anzaldúa, and the Poetry of Witness*. Houndmills, Basingstoke, Hampshire: Palgrave, 2000.

About the Authors

Thanh Nguyen is a third-year doctoral student in the Higher Education Program at the University of Denver. She currently serves as the interim Director for the Center for Multicultural Engagement and Inclusion at the Metropolitan State University of Denver. Her research interests include racial equity for communities of color, women of color's higher education experience in leadership and organization, and the racialization experiences of students of color in higher education, as well as their postsecondary access and success.

Dr. Ally Garcia received her Doctor of Education Degree from the University of Denver. She currently serves as Assistant Dean/Director of TRIO Student Support Services at Metropolitan State University-Denver. In addition, Dr. Garcia is a research assistant for Alliance for PROS, teaches a course on race and racism at the University of Denver and has facilitated numerous workshops on diversity and equity issues. She is currently engaged in research regarding policy in higher education. Her Doctoral Research Project is entitled, *A Policy Discourse Analysis of Disciplinary Transcript Notation in Cases of Sexual Assault on College Campuses.*

CHAPTER 17
STILL TOO FEW BREWERS, BURNS, AND HOBSONS IN THE HIGHER EDUCATION SPACE

by Wendy Wilson, Ed.D.
Vice President of University Relations
and Chief of Staff, Albany State University

As we develop professionally, quite often we become students of, or admirers of, prominent post-secondary education leaders, trailblazers, or titans of industry. The study of their professional experiences and expertise relative to their fields provides insight and guidance as we design and navigate our own professional paths. Thanks to technology, we can readily experience the writings and teachings foundational to the domains they expertly represent or exist within. As most executives within higher education, I regularly consume information relevant to the industry, but also avidly study corporate C-suite influencers and the environments that have shaped their development and professional ascension. Although they worked outside of the realm of post-secondary education, there have been three exemplary C-suite trailblazers that I continue to study with great intensity and admiration. Rosalind Brewer, Ursula Burns, and Mellody Hobson are acclaimed executives whose triumphant, transformative leadership continues to impact a cross-spectrum of systems and industries. All three have leadership stories that encompass great achievement and prominent industry contributions. Unfortunately, their career journeys are not absent of challenges. Not unlike many women of color within both higher-ed and corporate spaces, their stories include experiences of ill treatment, of bias, systematic inequity, and disparity. Specific to the higher-ed space, there are legions of women exceedingly capable of leading at the executive level, but themselves stagnated by the perils of disparate systems and practices. As a result, there are still too few Brewers, Burns, and Hobsons in the higher-ed space. Fortunately, their stories provide insight into the range of inequity and disparity that exist—and introduce practices that can be implemented to shift the culture and conditions that hinder the advancement of women of color in the academe.

As stated, I am an avid student of Brewer, Burns, and Hobson. Each have taught me time-treasured lessons, including the value of considering diversity when selecting mentors, the importance of being a respected thought leader, and the steps to becoming a subject-matter expert.

Specifically, it was Rosalind Brewer who taught me the significance of this quote from the famed comedian Steve Martin: *"Be so good they can't ignore you."* Brewer is the first woman and African American to serve as CEO of Sam's Club, a division of Walmart. As a result of her impressive body of work at Sam's Club, she was highly sought to lend her expertise as chief operational officer of Starbucks in 2017. Brewer is also the first African American to serve on the board of Amazon. In March of 2021, Brewer will assume the role of CEO of Wallgreens Boots Alliance, making her the only

African American woman to serve currently as the lead executive of a Fortune 500 company. Her rare air status was recently heightened, as she will be the only and first African American woman to serve as board chair of a Fortune 500 company—Starbucks—beginning March 2021. To describe her as good is an understatement. She is beyond exceptional!

Ursula Burns reigns as the first African American woman to lead a Fortune 500 company, Xerox. One of her greatest points of instruction is that knowledge and expertise are foundational to one's ability to speak bravely and boldly. Burns' unabashed brilliance led to an invitation to serve as the executive assistant to former vice president Wayland Hicks. After years of exposure and development within the C-suite, Burns became president of Xerox in 2007 and in 2009, the Chief Executive Officer. Burns reigns as a first among firsts!

And then there is Mellody Hobson, co-CEO and President of Ariel Investments. Ariel has an asset portfolio in excess of $10.2 billion. Hobson has been dubbed the "Beyoncé" of the world of finance. Notwithstanding her acumen and respectability factor, she exists in rare air. Hobson is one of the few, if not the sole African American woman to lead a major investment firm in the United States. Due in part to her unique status, Mellody's wealth of expertise and knowledge spans beyond the realm of finance. She is also recognized as a diversity and inclusion subject matter expert. Her heralded 2014 TED Talk, "Color Blind or Color Brave," has over 4 million views. Since that time, she has been sought around the world to educate on the value and importance of intentional equity practices and the relative impact of these practices on the bottom line, regardless of the enterprise, company, or institution.

Without a doubt, all three have contributed to their individual and collective successes as women in the C-suite. In addition, they demonstrate the yields of diversity and inclusion within the executive leadership space. However, their examples also bring to light an unfortunate and continued reality—they remain a minority within a minority. Few women of color lead at the C-suite/executive level in either the public or private sector. This is particularly true when you consider the landscape of colleges and universities. Based on a 2016 study conducted by American Council on Education (ACE), only three out of ten college presidents were women. Congruent to this representation, women of color comprise an even smaller number. Specifically, only 8% were African American women, and these represented the largest number of minority women serving in presidency roles. This data offers a sobering reminder that there are still too few Brewers, Burns, and Hobsons throughout post-secondary education.

It was during my daughter's 2018 Spelman College commencement ceremony that I learned details of Rosalind Brewer's experiences of inequity and associated micro-aggressions. I was honored to hear Brewer share her academic and career path. However, I was deeply struck that despite impressive academic credentials and a stellar corporate career trajectory, she is often profiled and questioned by peers and observers about her authenticity as a leading corporate executive. Her resonating message: As long as the glass ceiling exists, the pervasive assumption is that if and when women of color ascend to an executive-leadership level, they are anomalies and can be questioned about their legitimacy to serve and lead in the role.

Ever present on my professional wish list, is my desire to one day meet trailblazer Ursula Burns. Her existence within the hallowed halls of the Fortune 500 C-suite messages possibilities for other minorities. It also serves as a reminder of the need to normalize and expand the presence of women of color in the executive ranks. Burns served as CEO of Xerox from 2009-2016. Prior to the January 2021 announcement of Brewer's CEO appointment, Burns remained the only woman of color to lead a Fortune 500 company.

Thanks to a higher-ed colleague, in 2017 I did meet and converse briefly with the amazingly brilliant and charming Mellody Hobson. This remains one of my favorite professional experiences. If you're wondering if I went into "fan girl" mode, I did not—but in full transparency, it was difficult to contain. Our exchange was followed by an interview, observed by hundreds attending the Chicago Urban League's 2017 Summit Luncheon. In typical fashion, Hobson dispensed a range of knowledge, always underscoring the need for equity throughout each facet of society.

Although enlightening and enjoyable, the interview was reminiscent of Brewer's Spelman College commencement address. Hobson discussed her personal and many experiences of being the sole African American woman navigating C-suite circles. She noted that it was not uncommon for her to encounter industry peers and colleagues who were confused and perplexed by her professional role and stature. To emphasize the ill effects of sparse diversity and inclusion, Hobson shared a story in which she was assumed to be a member of the dining wait staff instead of the keynote speaker at a national political event. Brewer recounted a similar experience during her speech, as well, in which a newly-met peer could not fathom the idea that she was a member of the elite C-suite group, initially assuming she was only a guest of one of the attendees. Like Hobson, Brewer was in fact the keynote speaker at an annual retreat for C-suite executives.

Just as Brewer's, Burns', and Hobson's careers highlight achievement and possibility, they also highlight the need to address the consequential barriers of inequity that impede opportunities for growth and advancement, for women of color in particular. In the world of higher education and depending upon the institution, these barriers either exist as "haunting shadows" or "glaring neon signs." Regardless of the manner of their existence, the impediments of inequity have and continue to thwart and halt the trajectory for many who desire leadership roles as vice president, provost, or president. Just as the three powerhouses discussed in this chapter possess well-developed acumens, talent, and expertise, so, too, do thousands of women of color who traverse the halls of the academe. Despite comparable preparation, institutionalized systems continue to hinder opportunity and stymie traction for many.

As an African American woman who continues to serve proudly as a higher education professional, with over 17 years of experience, I am acutely aware of the practices and behaviors that maintain inequities, impacting diversity and inclusion. In full transparency, I have lost count of the number of women who are post-secondary education's version of Brewer, Burns, and Hobson combined, and who, despite effort, never advance. At best, they are assigned to lateral positions while simultaneously observing male colleagues with limited acumen and experience ascend to more advanced roles.

For those women of color who have achieved statuses of executive leadership, their ascension occurred at high premiums—sexism, racism, flagrant or subtle acts of disparate treatment, and temporary residence at the proverbial glass cliff. For those unfamiliar with the term, University of Exeter's Dr. Michelle Ryan and Professor Alex Haslam coined the phrase "glass cliff"; with emphasis placed on leadership challenges experienced by women and other minorities, their research and study concluded that women are more often extended opportunities to lead at the C-suite level only when a college or university is at a point of major disarray or in impending peril. The study also concluded, through observations and responses, that the women serving in these roles were often met with harsher expectation and criticism. In contrast, male counterparts more often receive leadership positions when a college or university's organizational health is favorable and fiscally sound. Both scenarios underscore that gender inequity is common throughout the higher-ed landscape, replicating systematic behaviors and practices found in the greater society.

When post-secondary education systems mimic practices that marginalize underrepresented populations, their intended purpose and mission—to academically prepare and develop individuals, positioning them for acquisition and fulfillment of social and economic opportunities—suffers. Integral to the educational process is the implementation and management of systems and practices that demonstrate equitable social and economic opportunity for all who desire to lead and for those who currently serve in executive roles.

A standalone force, Mellody Hobson is married to a fellow standalone force—film industry titan, George Lucas. Lucas is the creator of the fabled Star Wars franchise. Earlier movies within the franchise showcase the very loveable and perceptively wise character, Yoda. Often known to reference their similarities, Hobson affectionately identifies her husband as Yoda's dad. The character's presence throughout various storylines offers a breathing directory of great and profound intellect. One of Yoda's most heralded philosophical statements is, "Do or do not. There is no try." As mentioned, Hobson is recognized as and celebrated as a diversity and inclusion educator. When lecturing on the topic, she uses the "Do or do not…" statement to emphasize the implications of disparate practices and systems.

Specific to higher education, studies and data indicate whether current practices align with Yoda's philosophy. In fact, there is evidence that we in higher ed are guilty of "do not" practices. At best, we *try*, as it pertains to women landing and leading in executive roles. To minimize the strides and gains made regarding diversity, inclusion, and equity is never my intent; my sole intent is to emphasize that there is still much work to be done, particularly for women of color.

Case in point:

- In 2016, only 33% of public college and university presidents were women.

- In 2017, only 36% of community colleges were led by women.

- In 2017, only 17% of university and college presidents were racial minorities.

- In 2018, only 5% were women of color.

The sobering reality is that these statistics are representative of over 4,200 degree-granting institutions within the United States. To paraphrase Yoda, there is no try, and if the assumption is that we are "doing," then we aren't "doing" enough. Clearly, matters of diversity, inclusion, and equity are not being fully considered or addressed throughout the higher-ed space.

In 2017, the American Council on Education (ACE) conducted a diversity and inclusion study. Of the university and college presidents polled, 89% indicated they deem it important to ensure *periodic review* of institutional policies to eliminate gender bias. 92% of the presidents polled thought it important to make *public statements* about the status of racial minorities on campus. 45% stated they have initiatives in place to *attract* women and other minority faculty. Informative, but certainly not applause-worthy. To simply periodically review institutional policies is an exercise in futility. Periodic reviews lack specificity. Reviews should be regularly scheduled, coupled with assessments to determine effectiveness, and there need to stated, desired outcomes in addition to a review. If polices are determined ineffective, corrective and actionable measures should be implemented.

Public status statements cause pause and attention, but it is equally important to discuss the experiences of minorities on campus. If challenged experiences are presented, in particular those influencing advancement, retention, and promotion, correction measures should be designed and implemented. Such actions not only serve the employees responsible for the students they educate but provide students with examples of what is achievable post-degree completion. In a 2017 *Atlantic* article, Alana Semuels noted, "Across socioeconomic classes, women are increasingly enrolling and completing post-secondary education, while, even as opportunities for people without a college education shrink, men's rates of graduation remain relatively stagnant." However, women within the employee ranks, particularly faculty and administrative leadership, don't reflect the large number of students who are women. Female students can easily see their mirror reflection in the adjacent classroom seat, but their vision fails when seeking their mirror reflection in the form of a faculty member or executive administrator. This is acutely problematic for women of color.

The impact is broad and fluid throughout the college or university's organizational environment. Education is commonly referenced as the great equalizer. Yet students, faculty, and staff often express that this equalization occurs only in theory within the hallowed halls. Gender gaps and inequity are identifiable in academic major segregation, hiring practices, institutional and departmental behavior and culture, and in employee compensation. As Mellody Hobson astutely explains, when educating, failure to enact diversity and inclusion throughout all levels of an organization can ultimately harm sustainability, longevity, and the bottom line. To further expound Hobson's point, and specific to post-secondary education, employee morale and student recruitment are also easily harmed when inequity is intrinsic to the college or university culture.

Is there a magical elixir to remedy issues of disparity and inequity within higher education's leadership ranks? Perhaps not; however, corrective action can begin through acts of intentionality. To fellow colleagues, specifically vice presidents and sitting presidents: It is incumbent that we support and align ourselves with the underrepresented and marginalized groups of the academe by:

1. Creating succession plans targeting diverse populations.

2. Identifying and supporting those who express a desire to advance in the faculty or administration ranks.

3. Grooming, mentoring, and sponsoring women of color.

4. Holding individuals and collective bodies accountable for inequitable and disparate treatment of others.

5. Incorporating diversity and inclusion planning into departmental, division, and institutional planning.

6. Threading diversity and inclusion measures throughout an institution's strategic plan.

7. Developing and implementing diversity and inclusion initiatives that are measurable.

Intentional and targeted programming not only benefits aspiring leaders but serves the institution as a whole. Critical to the postsecondary education process is the demonstration of actions and behaviors that promote and align equity, diversity, and inclusion. Through intentionality, institutions of higher learning can teach and be an example to the greater society, as opposed to mirroring its historically poor posture regarding the underrepresented leading in executive, C-suite positions.

In addition to intentional actions, college and university C-suite planners must also broaden the definition and application of diversity and inclusion. Upon initial consideration, diversity typically encompasses race, gender, and/or sexual orientation. In theory, the definition should incorporate diversity of thought, perspective, experience, and background. Furthermore, diversity should not be viewed as an independent function, but to ensure effectiveness, it should be coupled with inclusion. Diversity becomes actionable when inclusion is attached. The amalgamation and application improve institutional practices and systems and creates equitable opportunity for those traditionally stricken by disparate treatment.

As emphasized throughout, postsecondary education should display practices that improve opportunities for those who aspire to C-suite opportunities but who are often excluded or marginalized due to systematic inequities. Legions of future Brewers, Burns, and Hobsons walk the halls of the academe daily, seeking the opportunity to lead as dean, vice president/provost, or president. In preparation, they continue to expand their base of knowledge, develop and hone their expertise, and demonstrate commitment to the execution of their respective academic institution's mission. With anticipation, they await the dismantling of systems that thwart and impede their advancement. These ambitious and driven marginalized women seek gender equity while rebuffing microaggressions in the form of actions and words. They desire to be tapped to lead healthy and viable divisions and institutions and not only ones in need of great repair and teetering on the brink of disaster. The future Brewers, Burns, and Hobsons wish to be acknowledged and judged on their merit, acumen, and track records, as opposed to biases and stereotypes. Lastly, legions await their ascension opportunity; however, this ascension can only occur when higher-education systems take intentional and actionable steps to address diversity and inclusion, ultimately shifting the narrative from too few Brewers, Burns, and Hobsons to Brewers, Burns, and Hobsons leading exponentially in the higher education space.

Resources

Caprino, Kathy. "The 'Glass Cliff' Phenomenon That Senior Female Leaders Face Today And How To Avoid It." *Forbes*. 20 Oct. 2015.
www.forbes.com/sites/kathycaprino/2015/10/20/the-glass-cliff-phenomenon-that-senior-female-leaders-face-today-and-how-to-avoid-it/.

Forbes Profile: "Rosalind Brewer."
https://www.forbes.com/profile/rosalind-
brewer/#4aae33fc31d1

Lapan, Julia C. "Equal Opportunity, Unequal Outcomes:
Exploring Gender Inequality in Post-College Career
Outcomes." *National Association of Colleges & Employers*, 1
Nov. 2018, www.naceweb.org/job-
market/compensation/equal-opportunity-unequal-outcomes-
exploring-gender-inequality-in-post-college-career-
outcomes/.

Lanum, Mackenzie. "Ursula Burns (1958-)." *Black Past*, 6
Feb. 2020, www.blackpast.org/african-american-
history/burns-ursula-1958/.

Loebs, Walter. "Roz Brewer is the new CEO of Walgreens."
Forbes, Jan 29, 2021.
https://www.forbes.com/sites/walterloeb/2021/01/29/roz-
brewer-is-new-ceo-of-walgreens/?sh=372648be1bb0

Marcus, Jon. "The Degrees of Separation between the
Genders in College Keep Growing." *The Washington Post*, WP
Company, 27 Oct. 2019,
www.washingtonpost.com/local/education/the-degrees-of-
separation-between-the-genders-in-college-keeps-
growing/2019/10/25/8b2e5094-f2ab-11e9-89eb-
ec56cd414732_story.html.

Semuels, Alana. "Poor Girls Are Leaving Their Brothers
Behind." *The Atlantic*, Atlantic Media Company, 27 Nov.
2017,

www.theatlantic.com/business/archive/2017/11/gender-education-gap/546677/.

Wiener-Bronner, Danielle. "Starbucks Names Mellody Hobson Board Chair—The First Black Woman in the Role." *CNN Business*, December 9, 2020, https://www.cnn.com/2020/12/09/business/starbucks-mellody-hobson/index.html

About the Author

Dr. Wendy M. Wilson currently serves as Albany State University's (ASU) Vice President of University Relations and Chief of Staff. Wilson facilitates strategic management processes and interacts with members at all levels of the internal and external university community. This macro level of engagement has proven successful in defining, advancing and assessing the work of the Office of the President in support of effective institutional alignment and synergy. Recognized as a leading diversity and inclusion expert within the public and private sector, Wilson was selected to develop and implement the inaugural Centers for Diversity, Inclusion and Social Equity at Albany State University. With regard to the current public unrest and call for social equity in 2020-21, the Centers' mission is to provide students a learning community to promote cultural pluralism and develop acumens that create and support social justice.

Wilson's civic and community engagement is equally distinctive. She is noted in the southwest Georgia region as the host of *Realizing Potential*, a decades-long television show highlighting the accomplishments of state and regional leadership. Wilson expanded the region's platform to feature notable conversations with UNICEF Ambassador and film star Danny Glover and trained dancer and actor, Jasmine Guy. She additionally serves her community as a board member for Partnership for Excellence in Education, the Sowega Council on Aging, and as a past president of Girls Inc. of Albany.

Wendy Wilson is a native of Detroit, Michigan. She holds a Doctorate (Ed.D.) in Curriculum Leadership from Columbus State University, a Master of Science in Human Resource Management from Central Michigan University, and a Bachelor of Science in Organizational Management from Bluefield College.

CHAPTER 18
SURVIVAL STRATEGIES FOR AFRICAN AMERICAN WOMEN CURRENTLY EMPLOYED, NEWLY EMPLOYED, OR CONTEMPLATING EMPLOYMENT AT A PWI

by Rochelle Bornett Lee, Ed.D.
Associate Professor, Nuclear Medicine Technology
Georgia Southern University – Armstrong Campus

I didn't come to the academic table with a burning desire to teach in academe. I entered the academy as a seasoned professional by way of the healthcare system. I spent more years than I am willing to share in this space as a practicing nuclear medicine technologist. I answered the call to teach after a fatiguing career as a staff technologist, lead technologist, manager of a private physician's office, and assistant manager of a free-standing imaging center. I wasn't a novice to professional life; however, I was a novice to academe. I began my career at the academy without a terminal degree. I was hired to be the founding director of a new program offering in nuclear medicine.

There is a different skillset required to teach, serve, and perform scholarship in the academy. The communication skills I acquired in healthcare were woefully inadequate in the academy. In healthcare, communication filled with vital information delivered in a succinct manner is the accepted communication style. In academe there is an unspoken requirement for polite delivery of information and statements presented as theses backed by copious research. There is also the requirement of pedigree that includes the possession of a doctoral degree, preferably a Ph.D.

The 10 Commandments

After seven years of frustration and a stagnant career in the academy because I did not possess a doctoral degree, I returned to school to acquire the proper credentials to legitimize my existence. What follows are the lessons I learned during my time in the hallowed halls of academe. I have labeled these lessons *The Ten Commandments for African American Women Faculty Teaching, Serving, and Performing Research at PWIs in the Deep South*. Although written from the perspective of an African American woman teaching at a PWI, these strategies are applicable to all women who choose to work as faculty members in higher education.

Commandment 1: Survey Your Surroundings

African American women must become fully aware of the academic environment and campus climate prior to the inception of employment. During the interview process or the campus visit, take the opportunity to interview as well as be interviewed. It is important to ascertain if the commitment to diversity, equity, and inclusion is a marketing ploy or an actual commitment supported by policies, procedures, training, and actions taken by the stakeholders of the college or university. Inquire as to whether there are college or university-sanctioned affinity groups for minority faculty organizations or other marginalized groups, and ask to speak with the membership as part of the interview process. Speak with minority students while on campus. Assess their perception of the campus climate or the comfort level of members of each group.

I know you want the teaching position; however, what is your "gut" saying to you about the feel of this space/place? Do you have the courage to listen to, trust, and act on what you are feeling/hearing? Can you trust yourself to do the right thing for you? Are you willing to walk away from the offer in hope of a better "fit" for you?

Commandment 2: Negotiate, Negotiate, Negotiate

Negotiate position, negotiate presence, and negotiate prosperity. *Negotiate position* speaks to a clear and concise plan and procedure for tenure and promotion by ascertaining what the institution considers valuable for tenure and promotion. The literature illustrates that faculty of color spend copious amounts of their time and energy in service to higher education through advising minority and non-minority students, committee work, and search committee work. *Negotiate presence* addresses becoming full participants in academic departments, colleges, the university-at-large, and the surrounding community. This need not be a formal process; however, the prospective employee should assess the measures taken or the resources provided by the search committee or other administrative representatives to assure the individual fits into the academy and the surrounding community. These measures or resources might include a map of the city, as well as a list of retailers, pharmacies, churches, sororities and fraternities, and popular eateries of the local population. *Negotiate prosperity* speaks to self-evaluation of the talents that you as the prospective employee bring to the institution. Appraise the worth of your contributions to the university and negotiate a salary commensurate with your experience, accomplishments, and talents.

What is your professional value? Have you evaluated what you bring to the professional table, your worth, your work, your talents, and your scholarship? Are you prepared to negotiate your position, your presence, and your prosperity? Does what you are being offered meet or exceed your professional value?

Commandment 3: Be Authentic— Identify and Name Yourself

Faculty report that they are identified by the majority culture on campus as the social categories they represent (gender, race, ethnicity, nationality, sexual orientation, religion, culture, and socioeconomic status). Often, faculty women of color are not given the opportunity to define their own identities in the environment of the academy. Therefore, it is imperative that African American women faculty introduce themselves to the academy and self-identify, so there is no confusion regarding how they should be referred to and addressed. We are more than our social categories and possess greater depth than what can be seen on the surface. We come to the academic table with a rich history, academically prepared, and with a wealth of experience outside of and within the academy.

Who are you? Have you identified and named yourself? Are you able to stand in the truth of who you are? How do you convey who you are to others? Are you willing to make compromises for the position?

Commandment 4: Establish Your Voice

We bring to our work a critical self-consciousness about our positionality, defined as it is by race, gender, class, and ideology. The position or place we are assigned on the margins of the academy informs but does not determine the positions or stances we take.

Whether a new employee or an established employee of the academy, be silenced no more by members of the academy who choose volume of voice over substance of what is being uttered. Be silenced no more by those who would demean and consider unimportant the words that you speak in open forum or in classrooms. Be silenced no more by those who would debase your research because it is based on race, gender, and/or class, topics not considered mainstream research desired by A-list journals. Elevate the volume of your voice, elevate your arguments, and elevate the relevance of your research.

Can you identify your voice? Is your voice quiet and intimidated, or is it loud and confident? Does your voice speak with authority regarding your research and professional position? Is your voice capable of defending your position on subjects being discussed?

Commandment 5: Mentoring, Networking, and Research Support

The professional and scholarly conversation is filled with examples of the need for mentors for African American women faculty. However, formal networks to establish these professional mentor-mentee relationships are virtually non-existent on the campuses of PWIs. Mentors do not need to be a minority or female; however, it is important that they be aware of the politics of difference. Therefore, it is necessary for African American women faculty to seek likeminded faculty as mentors (inside or outside of their discipline or the academy) and/or to establish or become part of a network of faculty who are willing to serve as a support system for the research agendas of the members of the network.

Do you really need a mentor? Is your mentor knowledgeable in the politics of difference? Do they recognize your marginalized position in the academy? Do they advocate for you and your research?

Commandment 6: Get Involved and be Mindful not to Become the Token Black

Seek opportunities for exposure. Make yourself known. Because African American women are few in number, there is a tendency for the majority to view these women as spokespersons for all Blacks instead of seeing them as individuals with other qualifications. Oftentimes the academy wants them to serve in the capacity of being an expert on all things Black or to serve in the capacity of solving problems or handling situations having to do with racial difficulty. It seems the most helpful place for this to be addressed is from the administrative level. If, however, these issues are not addressed from the top, consider educating those making the request by stating your individual opinion about the situation or seeking assistance from the Office of Multicultural Affairs or the Office of Diversity, Inclusion, and Equity if it exists on the campus. Additionally, there is often no reward for this extra work. In fact, this service may be discounted during the tenure and promotion process. African American faculty women should seek opportunities of service that support their tenure and promotion success and that do not detract from the time allotted for research.

Are you being strategic regarding where you serve and donate your professional talents? Are you involved with organizations that feed your passion? Are you serving the University, College, and community in visible positions? Does your service meet the guidelines for tenure and promotion?

Commandment 7: Produce Excellence Always

Yes, it is exhausting to constantly prove the worth of your presence and place in the academy. Yet, not to do so spreads the marginalization, alienation, and isolation that so many African American women faculty report. African American women faculty should inquire regarding how the academy defines excellence or "exceeds expectations," and then go about the work of achieving this distinction. Produce excellence in teaching as evidenced not only by student evaluations but produce excellence in teaching by reporting classroom or programmatic outcomes. Produce excellence in service by documenting requests for service from administrators and the academic community and presenting these requests in the creation of the tenure and promotion portfolio. Produce excellence in research by establishing a research agenda that supports tenure and promotion success. Publish, speak, write grants, and push your research agenda. Assist the academy in understanding the politics of difference if your research includes race, gender, class, or other minoritized social categories.

How is excellence in teaching, service, and scholarship defined by the institution? Have you researched the current promotion and tenure guidelines? Are you meeting/exceeding the standards and timeline defined in those guidelines?

Commandment 8: Self-Promote Without Arrogance

African American women are not good at self-promotion. We tend to wait for others to acknowledge our contributions, accomplishments, talents, skills, and academic achievements. However, this recognition may be long in coming, or it may not come at all. African American women must become accustomed to publicizing their professional triumphs without feelings of conceit or self-aggrandizement. This self-advocacy goes a long way in proving to the academic community that African American women faculty possess the ability to produce credible research.

Has your research been published? Have you been asked to speak during a professional meeting? Have you been recognized for your teaching or service excellence? If so, tell your dean, department chair, or mentor. Ask to have an announcement placed in the University or College newsletter. Have you updated your professional webpage with your accomplishments?

Commandment 9: Seek "Atta" Girls Outside of the Academy

Compliments, encouragement, and confidence building rarely come from within the academic environment. African American women faculty should rely on family, friends, or spiritual communities to fill the void created by members of the academic environment. Furthermore, these external communities can sound the alarm and warn the faculty member when work begins to supersede self or community.

Do you have a person in your life that is your cheerleader? Does this person speak truth to you? Are you listening when they sound the alarm? Can you sit in your truth in their presence?

Commandment 10: Self-Care, the Balance within the Selfish-Selfless Continuum

The academy is oftentimes a fatiguing environment for African American women faculty. To overcome the exhaustion created by the demands of teaching, service, and scholarship, it is necessary for African American women faculty to identify or create ways in which they step away from the pressures of the academy to rest, reflect, and refresh. Many of us think it is selfish to take time for ourselves. We instead continue to push forward in selfless ways to meet the needs of others (students, colleagues, and administrators). Conversely, within this selfish-selfless continuum is a place of balance, called self-care. Self-care requires that we remove ourselves from the source of fatigue and engage in activities that promote self-renewal. Once the self has healed from the wounds of selfless acts, we can re-enter the academic environment with renewed spirit, mind, and body.

While checking items off on your to-do list, are you making time for you? When your worlds collide (family, work, deadlines, appointments, etc.), how do you respond? What do you do to rest, reflect, and refresh? You would prioritize yourself if…

Resources

Books and articles

Britton, Dana M. "Beyond the Chilly Climate." *Gender & Society*, vol. 31, no. 1, 2016, pp. 5–27., doi:10.1177/0891243216681494.

Cheeks, Maura. "How Black Women Describe Navigating Race and Gender in the Workplace." *Harvard Business Review*, 26 Mar. 2018, hbr.org/2018/03/how-black-women-describe-navigating-race-and-gender-in-the-workplace.

Gutierrez y Muhs, Gabriella, Yolanda Flores Niemann, Carmen G. Gonzalez, and Angela P. Harris (Eds.) *Presumed Incompetent: The Intersections of Race and Class for Women in Academia.* Utah State University Press, Boulder, CO. 2012.

Lynn, Marvin, and Adrienne Dixson (Eds). *Handbook of Critical Race Theory in Education.* Routledge, New York, NY. 2013.

Phillips, Layli. (Ed.). *The Womanist Reader.* Routledge, New York, NY. 2006.

Conferences

NADOHE (National Association of Diversity Officers in Higher Education)

NatDC (National Diversity Congress)

About the Author

Rochelle Bornett Lee, Ed.D., MBA, RT (N) is an educator and registered Nuclear Medicine technologist. She is an Associate Professor and founding Program Director of Nuclear Medicine at Georgia Southern University-Armstrong Campus located in Savannah, Georgia. She has served at Georgia Southern University in these capacities since 2004. She continues to be involved in the Nuclear Medicine profession as well as other pursuits in higher education. Her research and scholarship interests include Critical Race Theory, Womanism, Portraiture, and issues of diversity in higher education. You may contact Dr. Lee via her professional email rblee@georgiasouthern.edu.

CHAPTER 19
NAVIGATING LEADERSHIP
ROLES AS WOMEN OF COLOR

by Dr. Nicole Caridad Ralston
Director of Education and Programming,
Beloved Community

Many of us in higher education are aware that there is a lot of work to be done in regard to diversity, equity, and inclusion on campus—particularly in the hiring and retaining of Black, Indigenous, and People of Color in upper leadership roles in higher education. My own field, Student Affairs, is often leaned on as the division that supports students of color and multicultural initiatives; yet even in Student Affairs, there is a lack of equitable representation of women of color as Chief Student Affairs Officers (CSAO). Student Affairs is defined as the "co-curricular higher education division responsible for the student's personal development and holistic growth" (Waltrip, 2012, p. 13). Black and Latinx women Chief Student Affairs Officers represent only 9.4% of all CSAOs, even though 47% of CSAOs are women (Wesaw and Sponsler, 2014). Now more than ever, it is crucial to have leaders who represent the racial diversity of our students, particularly when it is becoming more evident that issues of race and gender are deeply embedded systems that higher education needs to address.

As a mixed-race Latina, it was important for me to learn about the shared experiences of fellow women of color who have navigated careers in leadership, particularly in Student Affairs. I dedicated my doctoral research to this topic by studying how women of color who serve as CSAOs navigated both their racial and gender identities in their professional role (Ralston, 2019). My study utilized Kimberle Crenshaw's intersectionality as a theoretical framework to reveal the multiple layers of marginalization that influenced the experiences of these women. Intersectionality is a term that is used often in higher education, but I have found that many professionals are not aware of the full definition, or of the origins of intersectionality. So, what is it, you ask? The theory of intersectionality is the study of overlapping or intersecting social identities and their related systems of oppression, domination, and discrimination. Intersectionality is specifically rooted in how the experiences of Black women and other women of color differ from those of White women. All of the women of color in my study identified as either Black or Latina, and all of them served as CSAOs at predominantly white, four-year colleges or universities. The data from this study provided rich examples of ways that women of color can successfully navigate careers in Student Affairs while also advocating for marginalized student populations and staff on campus. Interviewing these women and spending countless hours in the rich data they provided gave me hope and practical advice. This chapter will share with you the advice and wisdom that these leaders offered to fellow Student Affairs professionals, and some steps you can take to put their advice into practice.

The main skill that all of the leaders utilized and leaned on the most, was their ability to use their own identities and positional power to advocate for underrepresented populations on their campuses. Being that all of the women identified as women of color, and that many held additional marginalized identities, including a disability, growing up in a low socioeconomic-status household, or being the child of immigrants, these leaders knew intimately what it felt like to be underrepresented on campus. Their sense of duty in giving back to their communities and leaning into their identities as women of color were bonds that tied the leaders together. This skill directly assisted the leaders in overcoming the barrier of being the only one with their social identities who sat on the president's cabinet.

The compounded stress of "being the only one in the room" and having to "prove one's worth" is a common theme in studies about the experiences of women of color leaders who advance their careers in higher education (Dowdy and Hamilton, 2012; Ngunjiri and Hernandez, 2017; Scott, 2016; Turner, 2007; Turner, Gonzalez and Wong; 2011). Many of the leaders in this study shared that by leaning into their own experiences with marginalization and discrimination, paired with their academic knowledge of the issues, they were able to have a seat at the table and advocate for marginalized and underrepresented populations on campus. We will review how you can put this skill into practice at the end of the chapter.

Some of the most compelling implications for practice come from the advice that the women shared while answering the question, "Is there something you wish you knew as a younger woman of color, earlier in your career?" The leaders all shared a desire and commitment to mentor women and other underrepresented professionals in the field. In the table below, you can review one piece of advice that each of the women offered up to fellow Student Affairs professionals. Their advice and learned experiences can also assist campus departments in envisioning new ways to create more equity-centered practices for their most marginalized community members. Hopefully, you will find their wisdom to be both practical and inspiring for wherever you may be in your career.

EVA: LEARN HOW TO NAVIGATE MICROAGGRESSIONS.

"Not to say that I haven't dealt with microaggressions in that direct way, but I can see how sometimes micro-aggressions come out of direct racism and sometimes they come out of ignorance and misunderstanding, and sometimes you have to take a step back and recognize where someone is at and change your approach to them if you really want to understand who is in the room. So, I have seen other women of color and other people of color and it has put them in some bad situations—whether they burned a bridge, messed up a relationship, got fired from a job—so just having that information (how to handle microaggressions) would have been helpful."

BUG: DON'T TAKE YOURSELF TOO SERIOUSLY.

"I don't know, probably not to take myself so personally or so seriously... but also not taking things so personally and maybe not having such thin skin. I wish (some) sort of things wouldn't bother me so much, or I wish they didn't take up so much unnecessary energy."

ROSE: UNDERSTAND THAT SOME PEOPLE DO NOT WANT TO DO WHAT IS RIGHT.

"I wish I had understood politics more, you know, my personality, glass full, everybody's in here because we all want to do what's right and learning. No, some people want to do what's right for them and/or their unit and could care less about anybody else. And so, I've had some hard knocks that way, because I'm too open and too forgiving sometimes, and can be taken advantage of, and so I've learned to be more strategic in my thinking and also, listening more."

TAYA: THERE IS A NEED FOR MORE WOMEN OF COLOR IN THESE ROLES.

"I wish I had known women of color, like when I was in law school even, and other, you know, in earlier career paths, there were just very few women of color in the roles that I was seeking. So, I wish had known more when I was coming up through the ranks."

LANA: WEIGH THE COSTS OF FOCUSING TOO MUCH ON YOUR CAREER.

"I wish I had more time to think about how hard I go and what that can cost me personally because I put so much of my life focused on my career that other important things that I wanted to do or have—have kind of gone to the wayside."

RIA: EMOTIONAL INTELLIGENCE IS CRUCIAL TO SUCCESS.

"I've learned as an older—as a person who has been through a lot and seen a lot... I have seen brilliant, brilliant, people crash, because although you might be brilliant—which, I don't consider myself brilliant, I consider myself smart, but I don't consider myself brilliant—but if you do not have compassion and if you do not have strong interpersonal skills that show emotional intelligence, you're ultimately not going to do well. And so, I really believe that treating people well and with respect is really so, so, fundamental, no matter how brilliant you are."

ALMA: DO NOT FEEL THE NEED TO BE THE FACE FOR EVERYTHING IN THE UNIT.

"I have associate VPs, I have directors—they're leaders of their units, they are getting paid to do this work. I don't have to be at everything, so I told the director, 'you tell me what your signature event is that you would like me to come to, and I will come.' I am not coming to everything!"

VIRGINIA: KNOW WHERE YOU WORK.

"Understand the culture of where you're gonna work and be comfortable with that, because if—sometimes, there's things you just can't overcome. But you have to be able to get a sense of what you're walking into, as best you can. But also understand that at some point if, you know, if you feel like, from an ethical standpoint, from a philosophical standpoint, something's not working—I mean just, this isn't the place for you, you need to be ok about looking and making that change, and being open to make that move."

VIOLA: GATHER YOUR CREDENTIALS.

"I mean, it's important to be a strong Student Affairs professional too, but (make sure) you write, that you're publishing something, even if it's just in a journal; make sure that you present, always, at a national conference or a regional conference, and get an MBA! An MBA doesn't really help you any better but it's a credential that you can pull out of your back pocket, like 'Back up! I have a degree... I'm credentialed!'"

ZARA: GET INVOLVED IN THE FIELD, OUTSIDE OF YOUR CAMPUS.

"If I could give advice to my younger self, I would have accepted the idea that this was a valid career path and one that would be worth dedicating a decade or more of life to so that I would have approached it a little bit differently. I would have gotten involved more in professional organizations and made more contacts."

OLIVIA: PREPARE TO BE UNDER CONSTANT SCRUTINY.

"I wish I'd known, like, how much you will be constantly under the microscope in this type of role, and it's no—it's like nuts. Like, I can go to a town hall. Let's say there's, like, four or five hundred staff, and I'm doing a presentation, and it's—we're starting to run out of a little bit of time, and I go a little bit faster on the slides. If I don't say this is why

> I'm gonna go faster on the slides, at least three or four times, people will then make an assumption and gossip will start that I went through them fast because I didn't want anyone to see them."

It is clear from the advice that these women of color shared, that they are often met with obstacles in their leadership role, which include navigating microaggressions on campus and existing under constant scrutiny, just to name a few. Despite those barriers, the leaders remained dedicated to the field of Student Affairs and felt immense pride in being a role model to other campus members who shared experiences of marginalization or underrepresentation.

3 Ways to Practice This Skill

As promised at the beginning of the chapter, I will now outline what you can do to practice that common, necessary skill to which these leaders attributed their success: leaning into your own identities as a tool to advocate for marginalized and underrepresented campus populations.

1. In order to begin reflecting on your social identities, and how they affect your perceptions, biases, and experiences, begin by taking an inventory of who you are. Start by building an identities map that includes categories like race, gender, socioeconomic status, sexuality, religion, education level, language spoken, and any other identities that are important to you.

Reflect on how these identities have impacted your childhood, adulthood, career path, and how you lead and advocate for certain topics or populations.

2. Next, reflect on the systems of privilege or oppression that are historically and socially attached to your identities. Ask yourself: how can I begin to learn more about how my identities afford me power, privilege, or marginalization?

3. Third, practice getting comfortable with naming how your identities influence your leadership style and how you advocate for certain topics or populations. You might consider attending workshops on equity and inclusion, discussing your identities with those who share your identities and with those who do not, and journaling on how your identities can be a tool to unlocking advocacy skills in your position. The more comfortable you can be with naming how your identities influence your perspectives, the easier it will be for you to lean in to your identities and advocate for underrepresented populations.

In conclusion, it is imperative for higher education professionals to dismantle the barriers that women of color face as leaders in higher education, and for their words of wisdom to be shared with others who are navigating careers in higher education. I hope that this chapter will assist underrepresented professionals to thrive and persist in leadership roles in Student Affairs and more broadly in higher education.

Resources

If you are looking for ways to lean in to your identities, advocate for underrepresented populations, and put into action any of the pieces of advice that resonated with you, consider these additional resources for your journey.

Read the full dissertation study, *Navigating the Intersections of Identity: The Shared Experiences of Women of Color Chief Student Affairs Officers:* https://scholarworks.uno.edu/td/2635/

Attend:

- The Social Justice Training Institute (www.sjti.org).

- The National Conference on Race and Ethnicity: www.ncore.ou.edu/en/

- A women of color leadership institute.

Read these books to dive deeper into topics of identity:

- *Asian American Feminisms and Women of Color Politics* by Lynn Fujiwara and Shireen Roshanravan.

- *So You Want to Talk About Race* by Ijeoma Oluo.

- *Caste* by Isabel Wilkerson.

Listen to *The 1619 Project*, a podcast by Nikole Hannah-Jones, which outlines how anti-blackness is foundational to how the United States was formed.

https://www.nytimes.com/interactive/2019/08/14
/magazine/1619-america-slavery.html

References

Crenshaw, Kimberle. "Demarginalizing the Intersection of Race and Sex: A Black Feminist Critique of Antidiscrimination Doctrine, Feminist Theory and Antiracist Politics." *The University of Chicago Legal Forum* 140:139-167. 1989.

Ralston, Nicole Caridad, "Navigating the Intersections of Identity: The Shared Experiences of Women of Color Chief Student Affairs Officers." *University of New Orleans Theses and Researches*. 2635. 2019. https://scholarworks.uno.edu/td/2635

Waltrip, Laura. *Voices from The Field: Stories of Women Who Chose to Leave Their Careers as Student Affairs Professionals.* Unpublished doctoral dissertation. The University of Florida, Gainesville, Florida, 2012.

Wesaw, Alexis, and Brian Sponsler. *The Chief Student Affairs Officer: Responsibilities, Opinions, and Professional Pathways of Leaders in Student Affairs.* NASPA Research and Policy Institute, 1-23, 2014.

About the Author

Dr. Nicole Caridad Ralston is the Director of Education and Programming at Beloved Community, where she develops and facilitates core content on diversity, equity, and inclusion for a wide variety of audiences. She is an award-winning higher education student affairs professional and is devoted to creating communities that center and uplift the most marginalized populations. In her career in higher education, she developed retention and community engagement initiatives, built social justice education programs, taught courses on the white savior complex, and led the undocumented student support committee. Nicole's doctoral research focused on how women of color in senior leadership roles in higher education navigated multiple intersections of identity and systems of oppression on predominantly white campuses. Additionally, she is an adjunct professor at The University of New Orleans, where she teaches, "Diversity in Higher Education" in the Educational Leadership graduate program. She is also a graduate of the Social Justice Training Institute, 4.0 Schools Essentials, and the Progressive Change Campaign's Candidate Training. As a volunteer, she serves on the board of directors for the ACLU of Louisiana, and Success Preparatory Academy at Thurgood Marshall. Nicole also chairs various committees for the New Orleans Hispanic Heritage Foundation's Azucar Ball. In her free time, she enjoys sharing her New Orleans food adventures on her Instagram food blog, @eatenpathnola, and serving as a doula to local moms.

CHAPTER 20
THRIVING THROUGH A TEACHING CIRCLE: CREATING SPACES FOR THE SUPPORT AND CULTIVATION OF FACULTY WOMEN OF COLOR

by Annmarie Jackson, Ph.D.; Holley Johnson, Ed.D.; Lauren C. Johnson, Ph.D.; Winnifred Namatovu, Ph.D.; Richelle Oakley, Ph.D.; Chantelle Renaud-Grant, Ph.D.; Emilia Solá Gracia, Ph.D.; Wendy Walker, Ph.D.; & Cristina Washell, Ed.D.

This chapter provides insight into the development and maintenance of our Teaching Circle for faculty women of color at a predominantly white university located in the rural southeastern United States. This Teaching Circle, developed by a faculty member in the College of Education in 2017, has received annual stipends from the institution's Center for Teaching, Learning, and Leadership initiative to promote productive dialogue and foster academic excellence. Our group has regular meetings focused on readings and discussions relevant to our experiences as women of color, a number of whom fill leadership positions, as we navigate the complex hierarchical system of academia while maintaining our identities. Our contributions to the group and to this chapter stem from the challenges, successes, uncertainties, and capabilities that we have faced in higher education. Here, we hope to illustrate the importance of creating spaces for the cultivation and liberation of underrepresented faculty. The

Teaching Circle itself has provided an access point for junior and senior faculty to benefit from the mentorship, shared experiences, and bond that we create each semester. Informed by the work of Gutiérrez y Muhs, Niemann, González, and Harris (2012), Berry and Mizelle (2005), and Moraga and Anzaldúa (2015), the development of this particular circle demonstrates our efforts toward belongingness within the academy, the university system, and the physical and conceptual spaces of our institution.

Learned Experience

Navigating academic environments and contending with the cultural dissonance these experiences often engender can be stressful for underrepresented individuals. As faculty women of color, we are rarely part of the dominant group in the room. At times, female faculty feel like our ideas are insignificant (Jones, Hwang, and Bustamante, 2015). Many of us have left faculty meetings feeling frustrated and undervalued. We also struggle with the gender dynamics that impact interactions between female faculty and students. For example, we have had the common experiences of witnessing male faculty glorified or given a pass, as they are often not held to the same scrutiny as female faculty. Our realities reflect the data that point to disparities between the treatment of women and men in academia; women tend to be more involved in service work than men and are generally held to different standards by university leadership (Flaherty, 2018). Similarly, there are clear gender disparities as related to students' perceptions and treatment of female instructors (Stanley, 2006). During

Teaching Circle meetings, we have delved into the challenges of internalizing biased student evaluations and feeling pressure from students to go above and beyond as compared with the experiences of our male counterparts. Here, we find that issues specific to our identities as women of color in academia are reflected in research on minoritized faculty in higher education. These issues include perceived discrimination, the effects of the imposter syndrome, difficulty finding adequate mentorship within our institutions, and the added burden of proving our worth to colleagues, students, and administrators (Berry and Mizelle, 2005; Boring, Ottoboni, and Stark, 2016; Gutiérrez y Muhs, Niemann, González, and Harris, 2012; Stanley, 2006).

Being a faculty woman of color can feel akin to a minefield, as we work to manage different biases and recognize which struggles to take on. In working through these realities, we grapple with negotiating between our values and beliefs, which are influenced by our identities as women of color, as well as the values and beliefs of our colleagues, students, and the wider institution. Through this experience of disequilibrium, it can sometimes feel like we have to give up aspects of our identities in order to fit into the academic space. During this process, the academic space we occupy can feel unwelcoming, cold, and restrictive (Marbley et al, 2011). At times, it seems clear that our knowledge and skills are undervalued by our colleagues and students. We have learned that the stress of navigating academia can be eased by seeking out and relating to other individuals who have similar lived experiences. However, this is much easier said than done. Thus, many of us are left to work through the process of owning our place in the space of academia without losing a piece of our identity, in isolation.

Unfortunately, working in isolation can become debilitating to our ability to steadily progress in our fields (Frazier, 2011). We are no longer "in the know," finding ourselves excluded from faculty gatherings as our peers and students comfortably distance themselves from us because of perceptions that faculty women of color are "angry" (Jones, Hwang, and Bustamante, 2015). As we work to maintain our identities and claim our space in academia, humility can take us a long way in accomplishing our goals. It sometimes has to begin with us all leaving our egos behind. Following the norms of white colleagues, we can easily get caught up in allowing our degrees and publication agendas to define us (Edwards, 2011). Combating this egocentrism can involve steps as simple as admitting that we do not know everything in our field and accepting the support of others. This type of mindset shows that we are human and not afraid to allow others to see the "real" us. In doing so, we find common ground among our peers and students, which reveals that our experiences and insecurities are quite similar.

Through the Teaching Circle for faculty women of color, we find mutual support in navigating our realities and challenges from colleagues with similarly intersecting identities. Being able to talk freely about troubling issues and knowing that some of the issues are not unique to us has allowed us a space to understand the commonality of our experiences. The results are beneficial for us and for our students. Increasingly, we feel more empowered and better equipped as we learn tools for interacting with colleagues, successfully addressing issues with students, and positioning ourselves to succeed as faculty members and rising leaders at our institution. Over time, we have had to learn to trust ourselves and our ideas more. By affirming ourselves and each other, we are able to recognize our own value and thus find our place in the meeting room. We have quickly learned how to speak up and strategically bring our sister peers into the conversation, while letting our male peers know that their thoughts and opinions are equally valued, thus, building each other up. Moreover, we have found ourselves and each other as sources of power and support. We now know that we are not alone in our experiences and thoughts.

The Skill of Networking

Networking can be a tool to help contribute to career success, as making connections in one's field can broaden access to resources and opportunities. For women, building deeper professional relationships in addition to typical networking activities can be particularly beneficial (Yang, Chawla, Uzzi, 2019). Participation in a close-knit group of women as part of a professional network helps women discuss common concerns and barriers we face as part of our careers. On top of providing access to resources and opportunities, such groups can provide emotional support to women as we navigate the uncertainties of an academic career path. This can help us to share our experiences with issues like discrimination, harassment, and ethical issues that can be more difficult to address in a broader network (Allen and Joseph,

2018). This type of affinity group can be especially helpful for women who are minoritized for identities that are often Othered in higher education, including non-white, LGBTQ+, and individuals with disabilities. Faculty who are part of underrepresented groups generally have higher attrition rates than other faculty and are less likely than their dominant-group colleagues to achieve leadership positions within academia (Benitez, James, Joshua, Perfetti, and Vick, 2017; Blackwood and Brown-Welty, 2011).

Structural barriers are not uncommon in higher education and often impede faculty women of color from attaining positions of leadership (Garrison-Wade, Diggs, Estrada and Galindo, 2012; Gupton, 2012). Minority women often struggle to find a place of belonging in academia due to the prevalence of deeply embedded racism and sexism in our institutional cultures. We often find ourselves professionally and socially neglected by our colleagues and excluded from participating in social networks that can support the development of belongingness (Mertz 2011). A group of faculty women of color are likely to have similar concerns that are unique to the intersections of gender and ethnicity. As such, learning to develop supportive professional relationships that facilitate inclusion is a crucial skill that can bolster women's success in academic careers. Collegial relationship building and participation in close-knit groups empower and support underrepresented women faculty as we challenge structural barriers and create systems of support within institutions. Building relationships with others who have a collective purpose and shared goals fosters emotional reciprocity, supports belongingness, the development of agency, and a more impactful collective voice in the institutional community (Nganga and Beck, 2017).

Putting It into Action

Being comfortable expressing our ethnic and gender identities is not only critical to our personal and professional wellbeing as faculty, but also assists us in solidifying our places in academia. As such, this chapter discusses how our Teaching Circle for faculty women of color has facilitated the bonding and mentorship of the participating members.

We offer the following action steps for the development of similar spaces for women of color and other underrepresented populations in higher education:

1. Support for faculty-led initiatives

Higher education initiatives related to diversity and inclusion are typically student-focused. However, there is a great need for faculty of color to have safe, preferably off-campus spaces to gather for authentic self-expression and guidance. The conversations that begin with discussions of issues related to teaching and learning eventually support faculty on a variety of topics, such as research and publication, tenure and promotion, access to resources, and significant aspects of institutional culture.

At our university, the Center for Teaching, Learning, and Leadership provides annual mini-grants to fund informal conversations among colleagues with a common interest relevant to their educational practice. While this institutional support is not a requirement for the development of similar groups, this type of support demonstrates the extent to which faculty are encouraged to engage in productive dialogues on education. An important consideration is how institutions can provide the structure for faculty to meet and discuss concerns, issues, and ways to manage issues. Faculty should explore institutional opportunities for funding and relevant resources that will support similar programs.

2. Identification of Teaching Circle participants

The development and maintenance of groups similar to our Teaching Circle requires annual applications for institutional funding and the recruitment of new faculty participants. Aside from faculty contacts within the coordinator's department, many of the members learn about the group through word-of-mouth. The benefits of participation in the Teaching Circle can be explained and rationalized in terms of the support offered, in addition to the inclusion of group membership in faculty evaluations and promotion and tenure portfolios. For institutions that provide credit to faculty for diversity and inclusion related activities, programs such as this demonstrate a relevant affiliation. Within the groups themselves, it is critical to have a leadership structure for managing the logistical aspects and to ensure group continuity.

3. Expansion of the Teaching Circle

As the Teaching Circle evolves over time, members will inevitably add to the materials utilized, modify the topics addressed, and explore opportunities for scholarly presentations and publications. Our particular Teaching Circle involves in-person meetings in various locations in the general geographical area where most participants reside. During the onset of the COVID-19 pandemic, our Teaching Circle was able to transcend physical constraints by meeting in a virtual video chat. The video chat has provided a sense of community and allowed members to share the effects of the pandemic on their academic work. Online spaces provide a more convenient way to conduct these meetings that was adaptable to our hectic schedules. Having this type of flexible structure and sharing this virtual space from our own homes has also contributed to the intimate nature of this circle. Our support and empathy for each other is probably needed more now than ever.

Resources

Allen, Evette L., and Nicole M. Joseph. "The Sistah Network: Enhancing the Educational and Social Experiences of Black Women in the Academy." *Journal About Women in Higher Education,* 11(2), p. 151-170, 2019.

Benitez, Michael, Mary James, Kazi Joshua, Lisa Perfetti, and Brooke S. Vick. "'Someone Who Looks Like Me': Promoting the Success of Students of Color by Promoting the Success of Faculty of Color." *Liberal Education,* 103(2), 2017.

Berry, Theodorea Regina, and Nathalie D. Mizelle. *From Oppression to Grace: Women of Color and Their Dilemmas in the Academy.* Stylus Pub, 2005.

Blackwood, Jothany, and Sharon Brown-Welty. "Mentoring and Interim Positions: Pathways to Leadership for Women of Color." In Gaetane, Jean-Marie, and Brenda Lloyd-Jones (Eds.). *Women of Color in Higher Education: Changing Directions and New Perspectives* p. 109-134. Emerald Group Publishing, 2011.

Boring, Anne, Kellie Ottoboni, and Phillip B. Stark. "Student Evaluations of Teaching (Mostly) Do Not Measure Teaching Effectiveness." *ScienceOpen Research,* 2016.

Edwards, Nivischi N., Monifa Green Beverly, and Mia Alexander-Snow. "Troubling Success: Interviews with Black Female Faculty. *Florida Journal of Educational Administration & Policy,* 5(1): p. 14-27, 2011.

Flaherty, Colleen. "Study Finds Female Professors Experience More Work Demands and Special Favor Requests, Particularly from Academically Entitled Students." *Inside Higher Ed,* 10 Jan. 2018. www.insidehighered.com/news/2018/01/10/study-finds-female-professors-experience-more-work-demands-and-special-favor.

Frazier, Kimberly N. "Academic Bullying: A Barrier to Tenure and Promotion for African American Faculty." *Florida Journal of Educational Administration & Policy* 5(1): 1-13, 2011.

Garrison-Wade, Dorothy F., Gregory A. Diggs, Diane Estrada, and Rene Galindo. "Lift Every Voice and Sing: Faculty of Color Face the Challenges of the Tenure Track." *The Urban Review,* 44(1), 90–112, 2012.

Gupton, Stephanie L. "Leadership Role of Academic Chairpersons in Higher Education: Issues and Recommendations." In Brown, Genevieve, Beverly J. Irby, and Shirley A. Jackson (Eds.), *Women Leaders: Advancing Careers* (pp. 51-68). Information Age Publishing, 2012.

Huston, Therese A. "Race and Gender Bias in Higher Education: Could Faculty Course Evaluations Impede Further Progress Toward Parity?" *Seattle Journal of Social Justice,* 4, 591, 2005.

Jones, Brandolyn, Eunjin Hwang, and Rebecca M. Bustamante. "African American Female Professors' Strategies for Successful Attainment of Tenure and Promotion at Predominately White Institutions: It Can Happen." *Education, Citizenship, and Social Justice,* 10(2), 133-151, 2015).

Marbley, Aretha Faye, Aliza Wong, Sheryl L. Santos-Hatchett, Comfort Pratt, and Lahib Jaddo. "Women Faculty of Color: Voices, Gender, and the Expression of Our Multiple Identities within Academia." *Advancing Women in Leadership,* 31(1), 166-174, (2011).

Mertz, Norma. "Women of Color Faculty: Recruitment, Hiring, and Retention." In Gaetane, Jean-Marie, and Brenda Lloyd-Jones (Eds.). *Women of Color in Higher Education: Changing Directions and New Perspectives* (pp. 41-71). Emerald Group Publishing, 2011.

Moraga, Cherrie, and Gloria Anzaldúa (Eds.) *This Bridge Called My Back: Writings by Radical Women of Color.* State University of New York Press, 2015.

Muhs, Gabriella Gutierrez, Yolanda Flores Niemann, Carmen G. González, and Angela P. Harris (Eds.). *Presumed Incompetent: The Intersections of Race and Class for Women in Academia.* University Press of Colorado, 2012.

Nganga, Christine W., and Makini Beck. "The Power of Dialogue and Meaningful Connectedness: Conversations Between Two Female Scholars." *Urban Review,* 49(4), 551-567, 2017.

Stanley, Christine A. "Coloring the Academic Landscape: Faculty of Color Breaking the Silence in Predominantly White Colleges and Universities." *American Educational Research Journal,* 43(4), 701-736, 2006.

Yang, Yang, Nitesh V. Chawla, and Brian Uzzi. "A Network's Gender Composition and Communication Pattern Predict Women's Leadership Success." P*NAS Proceedings of the National Academy of Sciences of the United States of America,* 116(6), 2033-2038, 2019.

About the Authors

Annmarie Jackson is an assistant professor in the Elementary and Special Education department and coordinator for the ESOL Endorsement program in the College of Education.

Holley Johnson is an assistant professor in the Middle, Secondary, & Science Education department in the College of Education.

Lauren C. Johnson is an associate professor and currently serves as assistant dean for the UNG College of Education as well as research associate at the University of Johannesburg, South Africa.

Winnifred Namatovu is an assistant professor in the Middle, Secondary, & Science Education department in the College of Education.

Richelle L. Oakley is an associate professor of Information Systems in the Computer Science and Information Systems department in the Mike Cottrell College of Business.

Emilia Solá Gracia is a Biology lecturer in the College of Science & Mathematics.

Chantelle Renaud-Grant is an associate professor of education currently serving as department head of Middle, Secondary, & Science Education in the College of Education.

Cristina Roque Washell is an associate professor and the current department head for the department of Elementary and Special Education in the College of Education.

Wendy J. Walker is a professor of Management and serves as the associate dean for faculty and graduate programs in the Mike Cottrell College of Business at the University of North Georgia.

FACULTY OF THE UNIVERSITY OF NORTH GEORGIA

PART 6

RELATIONSHIP BUILDING AND OPENING THE DOOR FOR OTHERS

CHAPTER 21
THE IMPORTANCE OF HOLDING THE DOOR OPEN

by Selvi Bunce
Advancement Program Coordinator
University of Wisconsin Foundation and Alumni Association

When I was an intern at a big State agency, I was invited to attend a party with the Commissioner in Beijing, China. I felt so out of place—I'm talking serious imposter syndrome. The lights were bright in the three-story old embassy building with a garden rooftop, and I felt small—not only because of the grandeur, but also because of the numerous NBA stars in attendance. In spite of all that, the commissioner interacted with me with such grace—she treated me as an equal, and she leaned over to tell me things about people she chatted with. Most memorably, as we entered the VIP area she turned around, reached for my hand, and made sure I made it in.

I had only spent a few days with the Commissioner, but this act of physically turning around to bring me through the door, showed me how something so simple can make a great impact. I will never forget the experience of walking through that door, and I will have the connections I made in that room for a lifetime.

It is no secret that in academia and higher education, like many industries, it's a man's world. We all know it and many of us want to change it. But most of us don't know how—how to get women through the door and how to hold the door open.

The most valuable skill I have learned in higher education is how to hold that door open and open others at the same time.

If your goal is to help other women succeed in higher education, this chapter is for you. While I am still building my career in higher education, I have seen leadership (both good and bad) that has shown me exactly what to do to empower fellow women. If you are able to encourage other women to the point of success—to hire them, to provide feedback, to push them—you will eventually see more women in leadership. You will see a change in workplace culture, family leave, and dress code. Goals will be changed, and giving will be realigned. I would not be where I am today had the woman in front of me not held the door open.

I believe there is an odd feeling amongst many women that if we try to hire women, if we favor women, we will be seen as sexist. That if we address the elephant in the room, if we push for more diversity, we will be seen as ungrateful for the strides the institution has already made. This is untrue. If we are not intentional about encouraging, pushing, and hiring our female coworkers, we will simply be women working in a man's world. And I do not intend to make it a woman's world, but we do deserve an equal share of it. If we want to work in a place that feels like home—free of wage gaps and misogyny—we must lead the pack.

You may be thinking, *How will holding the door open for someone else help me in my professional growth?*

First, learning how to look out for others will make you a better leader. If you are able to recognize when someone needs help, when they are not meeting their potential due to societal barriers, or when they could use a push in the right direction— you will gain both trust and respect. And the best leaders are trusted leaders. Knowing that your leader has your back, and wants the best for you, can change how you work by providing greater motivation and a deeper connection with your organization.

Second, companies with more women in leadership are more successful (Turban et al.). A diverse workplace leads to greater creativity, innovation, and attracts talent. By lifting up other women, you are lifting up your entire institution. And, as Malala Yousafzai said, "we cannot all succeed when half of us are held back."

There are two examples that come to mind when I think of leaders who know how to hold the door. The first is that party in Beijing I mentioned earlier. Second, I started my current position last year, and as you know, a new job is always a little awkward. But my supervisor has been a superhero. She is the first one to copy me in on emails she thinks I should be included in. She is constantly reminding people to copy me in, introducing me to her supervisor and her supervisor's supervisor. And she is always ready to bring some awareness to projects I am working on, especially if she sees that I am receiving unfair pushback. To some people this might sound pushy, but this is how to build women up! You need to know your colleagues, know where they can be effective, and put them there. You need to make sure people know their name (and say it correctly). How many times have you met a male intern because someone said he has great "potential" (Player et al.)? Women are judged off achievements, not potential, but what if we started seeing our potential too? We cannot wait for anyone else to give us that power; we must give it to ourselves.

But what does this mean for us, as women? If we can't change perception, what can we do?

First, it is imperative to meet yourself where you are. Are you confident enough to support other women in your workplace? Are you asking for what you need? Do you have a female mentor at work? If you don't think you're ready to empower your coworkers, that's okay. But reflect on why. Is it your work environment, or a habit of complacency? Who in your workplace can help guide you?

A good place to start is by connecting with colleagues like you. This doesn't have to be formal, and you don't need to have an official book club. A casual (virtual) happy hour can do the trick. Be intentional—ask about their experience as a woman in the workplace; odds are, they have faced the same challenges you have. If you are more of an introvert and don't like the idea of calling people up for what could be an awkward chat, treat this like a research project. Write down a list of questions that will help you understand their experience better and go from there. And as always, don't forget to end the conversation with, "Who should I talk to next?" They may know someone you don't, and you could gain further insight.

If you are ready to take empowerment into your own hands, who in your direct circle can you have a positive impact on? Who can you reach out to? Who can you connect? What can you share about yourself, and how can you be more vulnerable in order to foster deep and honest relationships with colleagues? What is toxic in your work environment? How can you address it? Who can help you address it?

When it comes to empowerment, the little things matter. If you are a director, let the coordinator send the proposal email, with you copied in. Let them act as liaison for cross-departmental meetings. Let them know you have their back and trust them to come to you with questions when they arise. Though it may be cliché, it truly is the little things that can make a difference.

Vulnerability is not everyone's strong suit, and that's okay. If you believe that the workplace is only for work, make sure your colleagues know that if they have a work-related problem, they can come to you. A safe work environment will lead to greater confidence, which makes one feel empowered.

If you are ready to do the work, look around and see the opportunities that already exist near you. A friend of mine was a site manager at a counseling center and was complaining about the lack of women of color in the office. I asked her who did the hiring (other than HR). She did. She had the power to hire the people she wanted to see in the workplace; she just hadn't realized it. It is easy for us to get lost in the expectations and patterns that exist. But it is imperative for us to acknowledge our power, and, as Maxine Waters would say, reclaim your time (Emba, 2019)!

This goes for "inviting yourself" to meetings as well. Often, I find myself curious about a certain topic of discussion, but I have not been invited to the table. There is certainly a time for confidential meetings, but that doesn't mean every meeting is on a "need to know" basis. So, if you are interested in learning more, ask to attend! Email the coordinator; the worst they can do is say no. And if you do attend, you could learn a new facet of your institution that will make you a better, well-rounded leader and employee. The same goes for inviting people you supervise—push them to go on your behalf, so they can learn and grow.

Lastly, how can you, on a daily basis, keep an eye out for women? How are women and non-binary folks being represented in your institution's content? Who is your workplace hiring? Where are jobs being posted? Have you checked the Black Business Bureau, the Hispanic Chamber of Commerce, your local YWCA, and the League of Women Voters? Post it there!

If this sounds like a lot of work to do on top of your already hectic schedule, know that you are not alone! If each woman lifts up one woman a day we will feel on top of the world in no time. The power of women is limitless.

Resources

Emba, Christine. "Opinion | 'Reclaiming My Time' Is Bigger than Maxine Waters." *The Washington Post*. WP Company, 6 Apr. 2019, www.washingtonpost.com/blogs/post-partisan/wp/2017/08/01/reclaiming-my-time-is-bigger-than-maxine-waters/

Player, Abigail, et al. "Overlooked Leadership Potential: The Preference for Leadership Potential in Job Candidates Who Are Men vs. Women." *Frontiers*. 19 Mar. 2019, www.frontiersin.org/articles/10.3389/fpsyg.2019.00755/full

Turban, Stephen, et al. "Research: When Gender Diversity Makes Firms More Productive." *Harvard Business Review*. 12 Feb. 2019, hbr.org/2019/02/research-when-gender-diversity-makes-firms-more-productive

If you are interested in learning more about lifting up women in your workplace, including women that don't look like you, check out these articles:

Elting, Liz. "4 Ways Women Mentoring Women Can Change the World." *Forbes*. November 26, 2018. https://www.forbes.com/sites/lizelting/2018/11/26/4-ways-women-mentoring-women-can-change-the-world/#7db22dc93813

Goldin, Kara. "7 Impactful Ways to Support Women in the Workplace." *Thrive Global*. September 24, 2019. https://thriveglobal.com/stories/impactful-ways-to-support-women-in-the-workplace/

Jain-Link, Pooja, Julia Taylor Kennedy, and Trudy Bourgeois. "5 Strategies for Creating an Inclusive Workplace." *Harvard Business Review*. January 13, 2020. https://hbr.org/2020/01/5-strategies-for-creating-an-inclusive-workplace

About the Author

Selvi Bunce is relatively new to the world of Alumni Relations. After graduating from Calvin University in 2019, where she founded the Women in Action conference, she went to work on a vineyard in Greece. She soon realized she missed the rush of the workplace and connecting with others, and she joined the Wisconsin Foundation and Alumni Association (WFAA) in 2020. A Minnesota native, she is pleased to be back in the Midwest as the Advancement Program Coordinator at WFAA. She is passionate about connecting people and making all spaces as inclusive as possible—from alumni events to the office cafeteria. She looks forward to a long career in higher education and believes that leadership is not about your position; it's about how you use it. Selvi has spoken at the Gustavus Adolphus Women of Color Summit and TEDx. She currently sits on the Associate Board for the Boys and Girls Club of Dane County. In her spare time, she reads and writes poetry. Her first book, *NAKED: The Honest Musings of Two Brown Women*, will be published in Fall 2021 by Black Spring Press Group.

CHAPTER 22
RELATIONSHIP BUILDING

by Tes Mehring, Ph.D.
previously Interim Provost, Baker University

A president has cookies delivered to every employee on his or her birthday. A faculty member is surprised to receive a handwritten card from the dean congratulating her on a recent publication. The provost invites three faculty members to lunch asking them to share their thoughts about a proposal for creating a new academic program. Members of the Executive Cabinet host a bi-monthly campus meeting providing an update about the impact of Covid-19 on campus, enrollment, how instruction will be delivered, the budget, and any important issues affecting the campus. What do each of these examples have in common? Relationship building.

Having served as an administrator for 36 of the 40 years I have worked in higher education, *many* skills and actions for thriving as a woman leader in higher education come to mind: know your personal values and principles and never vary from them; demonstrate integrity; always be truthful; be as transparent as the situation allows; respect others; recognize that the imposter phenomenon is alive and active, so don't be afraid to follow what you know is the right direction to proceed with action; be confident but not cocky in decision making; know your strengths and use them; know your weaknesses and surround yourself with others who possess strengths in those areas; be loyal to the institution; be visible on campus at fine arts, athletic, academic department, and donor events; be honest; and make sure to spend time focused on personal mental, socio-emotional, and spiritual growth, as well as physical health. All of these are important leadership skills for all individuals in a leadership role in higher education, but especially female leaders! However, the skill I have found to be the *most* important throughout my career is relationship building.

The Skill of Relationship Building

Fostering relationships with others provides a foundation for almost all of the other essential leadership skills. Early in my career I had the opportunity to participate in professional development that focused on Covey's *7 Habits of Highly Effective People*. All seven of the habits focus on some element of relationship building. Covey described the importance of focusing on expanding the 'circle of influence' through the 'emotional bank account.' He used the metaphor of a bank account to explain how 'deposits' with others (courtesy, kindness, honesty, keeping commitments, empathic listening, employing win-win problem solving, and valuing differences of opinions) foster relationships that lead to mutual trust. Continuing the metaphor, Covey described how withdrawals or actions which are the opposite of deposits—including discourtesy, disrespect, overreacting, and ignoring others—lead to distrust and increased friction with others.

Almost all authors of leadership theories and books focus on the importance of relationship building and its connection to growing trust with constituents. Northouse (2019) described authentic leadership, indicating that "authentic leaders have the capacity to open themselves up and establish a *connection* with others." According to Northouse, authentic leaders are willing to share their own story with others and listen to others' stories, as well. Through mutual disclosure, leaders and followers develop a sense of trust and closeness (p. 201). Su (2019) stressed the importance of 'presence' in relationship building and the need to be grounded, centered, and calm in our interactions with others. Brown (2018), in *Dare to Lead*, discussed the importance of leaders being vulnerable, giving permission to others to share honest feelings, and living with an "unarmored heart" (p. 77) as strategies to build relationships and trust with constituents. Gordon (2017) suggested in *The Power of Positive Leadership* that to build relationships with others, leaders must demonstrate caring about constituents. "When you care about someone, they know it and feel it. And when they know you care about them, they will care about you and follow you with loyalty and passion" (p. 128). According to Gordon, positive leaders build great relationships with others. Van Hooser (2013) suggested that leaders who practice universal principles of respect (fairness, honesty, interest in others and what they have to offer, willingness to lend a helping hand, and consistency) build relationships with others and earn their trust. Blanchard and Miller (2009) in *The Secret* emphasized listening, investing time, caring deeply, and accentuating positive influence in building relationships with others. Cashman (2008) in *Leadership from the Inside Out* described relationship building as the foundation for building bridges. He stated, "Unfortunately, many driven leaders fail to comprehend how nothing is accomplished without engaging in relationships and appreciating the unique contribution of many, many people." Good leaders demonstrate "good people competencies" (Cashman, 2008, p. 83-4).

One of the oddities of pursuing leadership roles in higher education is the chasm that grows wider and deeper between leaders and the constituents they serve. The higher one climbs up the leadership ladder, the easier it is to become more isolated—both because your calendar is imposing and because individuals who were personal friends and colleagues often want to distance themselves from you because in their eyes you've 'gone to the dark side'! While relationship building will likely not alter that perception that you're on the dark side, it will promote others seeing that you genuinely respect them and have an authentic interest in them.

Learned Experience

When I served as a department chair, the colleagues in my department dropped by my office regularly just to chat, share a story about their family, tell me about something fun they did over the weekend, or just to ask a question about some procedural process to accomplish a task within the department. However, these informal visits dwindled during my early days as a dean—and even more so when I became a provost.

Continuing to be intentional with relationship building with the wider bodies of faculty and staff I was leading at each successive step of leadership made a significant difference in how constituents viewed me as a person and as a leader. Instead of waiting for others to set up an appointment, I reached out by informal walks into every building on campus, dropping by offices just to say 'hi' or asking about a recent publication or presentation, sharing a compliment I may have heard about them from a student or peer, or just visiting about what a nice day it was after many days of cold or rainy weather. Being visible at department-sponsored guest speakers, attending athletic events, concerts, plays, or even student presentations or performances, were other ways of letting faculty know I was genuinely interested in their department and in the faculty, staff, and students who were part of those department 'families.' Empathic listening is another strategy that helped build and sustain relationships. Being mindful of body language (especially in situations where conflict might have existed), listening first to understand all points of view, being attentive when interacting with others—especially when a cell phone was vibrating almost continually in my pocket—are behaviors that indicated to others that they had my full attention. Handwriting a note of congratulations, sympathy, or complimenting an exhibition or performance was also a way to build relationships with others. Having an open office hour every day for any student, faculty, or staff member who wanted to visit about a concern or even share an accomplishment provided an opportunity for individuals who wanted the ear of a campus leader to have access. Keeping commitments was another important action that promoted relationship building. I tried to arrive early to events, to have the opportunity to interact informally with others before the event officially began. Keeping confidential information confidential was another important element of relationship building. Having my actions match my words and having both of these demonstrate personal and professional integrity on a daily basis (even during 'off' hours and while on vacation) was critical. As a president who served as one of my mentors was known to say many times, "Don't do anything you don't want to see in the newspaper or on someone's Facebook page!"

Putting It Into Action

Here are 20 suggestions for actions that can demonstrate relationship building.

1. Be visible!

Walk the halls at least once a day, stopping briefly to chat with faculty, students, and other administrators. Ask about their day, or their kids, or the grant they are working on, or the article they just published, or how their classes are going. One president I know spends two hours each day walking the campus. Sometimes she stops to chat with faculty or staff members who are in their offices. Some days, she is visible in the quad during change of classes on campus and stops to chat with students or faculty. Other days, she has lunch in the 'caf' and joins students and faculty.

2. Visit every department or unit that is part of your responsibilities at least once a year.

No agenda—just to listen to their accomplishments, challenges, and what they would like administration to know about their department. When I was a provost, the president, the vice president for student affairs, and I visited every academic department, student affairs area, and residence hall every year. Mostly we listened. Sometimes we were asked challenging questions about resources or the future of the university. It was important during these meetings to demonstrate genuine interest through our body language and the questions we asked. Sometimes requests for additional information emerged in these conversations. One of the three administrators would take responsibility for obtaining information and reporting back in a timely fashion. While there were always skeptics wondering what the 'real' reason was for our visit, most appreciated the effort to hear what was on their minds.

3. Write notes or send cards to others.

Send an electronic birthday card to those you are leading or jot them a note of congratulations or sympathy or... Handwritten notes are always best and most appreciated! As a dean and provost, I wrote five to ten cards a day to faculty and staff. Although it has been almost a decade since I was at a particular institution, upon occasion I run into someone from that institution. Invariably, the person will bring up a time when they received a note from me. Often the person will comment that they still have one or more of my notes posted on a bulletin board or in that 'special drawer' for those days when reading a positive message can provide comfort.

4. Actively seek input about potential policy changes or traditions some may hold sacred.

Make sure the skeptics have an opportunity to voice opinions. An institution's budget received a 33% reduction in state funding during recent state budget cuts. As a result, significant belt tightening had to occur. After conversations with faculty leaders, the provost announced there would be a reduction in reassigned time. The institution had the equivalent of 33 full-time faculty lines being used in reassigned time. The initial step the provost took was to share an initial draft of where reductions were being proposed. The provost held open forum meetings—at multiple hours during the day, to promote attendance and feedback. After only a couple of drafts that incorporated feedback from the open meetings, faculty approved the reductions in reassigned time, and some even volunteered to continue assignments for which no reductions in teaching would continue. Genuinely seeking input and incorporating ideas into the final draft was key to buy-in.

5. Have an open office hour each week...

...for anyone who has a question or wants to provide feedback to administration. No appointments needed; they can just drop by your office during the open time. As an administrator, I always had an 'open door' policy. If I was in the office and someone wanted to see me, they were welcomed as long as I wasn't already visiting with another person. There were times when I would have a scheduled appointment in ten or fifteen minutes. In these situations, I would alert the individual about the time I had available, but I indicated I could either visit with them then for a specific amount of time or I could find a time later in the day when we could chat for a longer period. Valuing the time of others and the importance of their topic was essential to relationship building.

6. Ask small groups of constituents to join you for a brown bag lunch.

The lunch could be broadly topical (e.g., *What challenges are faculty experiencing with student behavior? How is mental health in the residence halls? etc.*) or more focused (e.g., *Budget cuts have recently been announced at the state level. What are your ideas for where we can tighten the belt and what is essential to preserve from the faculty, student affairs, etc., perspective?*). This works well for some leaders to do once a week—for others, maybe once a month. At one institution where I served as a consultant there was a large table set aside in the cafeteria where faculty and staff were encouraged to share lunch if they did not have plans to join others already. This was often where some of the most important conversations in the university took place. The president, provost, and vice president for student affairs joined this table for lunch regularly, as a group or as individuals. As this was a more informal setting, faculty and staff felt comfortable chatting about things happening on campus or with the Board of Regents. Conversations in this setting often led to opportunities for these leaders to seek input or clarify actions taking place on the campus or at the state level. All who joined the table for conversation knew there would be 'straight talk' from administrators if they were present.

7. If you say you will do something, follow through!

Sometimes tracking down information you promise to get for someone can take time. In that situation, send a quick email indicating that you haven't forgotten but are just waiting for additional information about the topic from another source.

8. Provide regular updates about issues on campus.

These can be written, provided via Zoom, or shared through an open forum on campus. Transparency is key. Constituents may not like a message but will be grateful for accurate information. A president of a small private university holds weekly meetings to provide updates about actions taken by the Board of Trustees, the budget, athletics, or new academic programs being considered. More recently, updates about Covid-19 and the almost daily changes to how the campus operates have been added to these updates.

9. Be consistent.

It will only take one variation in your actions for you to be labeled as having favorites or as not applying rules in a consistent manner across individual situations. Many of us have been in settings where administrators speak with different groups about the same topic but share a different message with each group. Consistency, transparency, and honesty should be the guiding principles when discussing issues or actions with constituents—even if it is news one or more groups may not want to hear. The same information needs to be shared with each group of constituents!

10. Apologize sincerely when you have made a withdrawal!

Administrators are human—we all periodically make mistakes! In a small university town, there was a private organization that regularly solicited funding proposals that met their priorities. One of the deans at a university submitted a grant proposal (jumping through all of the hoops within the university to gain the stamp of approval before submitting it) after being asked directly by the chair of the funding organization to submit a request to fund a project within the college. When the president of the university found out the dean had submitted the proposal, the dean was called on the carpet. The president was upset that there might be other more important proposals to the funding agency and that the dean's proposal might result in other potential proposals not being considered. The dean explained to the president that the chair of the foundation had personally invited a proposal and sent the president the email from the chair inviting a proposal. The president walked to the dean's office to extend an apology in person.

11. Keep confidential information confidential.

Every administrator will have to handle situations that may be covered by FERPA, HIPAA, or the Human Resources division at the university. While some details may be public knowledge and shared, the request for other information should always have a response indicating that additional information must be kept confidential. Most constituents will respect keeping confidential information confidential.

12. Mentor others...

...especially other women who have the potential to be in leadership roles and those who are actively engaged in leadership roles. Mentoring is exceptionally powerful! As women in leadership roles, it is critical that we actively seek out other women (and men) who have the potential to become dynamic leaders. Providing encouragement through conversations, introducing aspirants to other women leaders who can serve as mentors, and promoting opportunities for leadership growth is the responsibility of every female leader. Some campuses have created leadership development programs for aspiring leaders. If you aren't already doing something to actively promote the growth of aspiring leaders, develop a plan now.

13. Be a role model in all that you do.

If you are in a position to evaluate teaching, scholarly activity, and service activities of faculty, be actively engaged in all of these yourself. Your academic productivity will both allow you to serve as a role model who 'walks the talk' but will also give you grounding to be able to empathize with faculty about the expectations they must fulfill as they are engaged in annual evaluations and as they are considered for tenure and promotion.

14. Never be complicit!

Talking about others behind their backs almost always gets back to the person, resulting not only in a damaged relationship with that individual, but also with others who are their friends and acquaintances. It is so easy to engage in gossip. As an administrator, it is critical, even with those you consider to be close associates, to distance yourself from negative conversations about others. It's a pretty good bet that your name will be used in the next conversation these individuals have with others: "Just yesterday, Provost Sally said…"

15. Be *present* when meeting with others.

Turn your cell phone to silent. Try to position yourself so that you aren't behind your desk. Be conscious about your body language. It's not unusual for the phones of administrators to be continually buzzing with notifications of text messages, emails, or calls. Early in her presidency, the talk around campus at one university centered on how frequently she would be in a 1:1 meeting with someone or involved in a meeting where many were in attendance and would take out her phone to read and respond to emails or text messages. One of her vice presidents took her aside and shared the negative view developing on campus related to this behavior. Immediately, the president started keeping her phone in her pocket and gave full attention to those she was meeting with. Another example is a dean who has a small couch and two end chairs in her office. Whenever the dean has someone come to her office for a meeting, she gets up from her desk and invites others to join her in the more informal setting. *Presence* communicates the importance you place on what others have to say.

16. Be respectful of others.

Make sure your words, voice level, and actions demonstrate respect. We have all read about the importance of nonverbal communication—eye contact, neutral positions for our arms and legs (not crossed), respecting distance between ourselves and who we are communicating with, etc. In addition to what we say, the tone and volume of our voice is also important. Many of us tend to speak louder and faster if we become angry or when we want to make sure *our* point of view is expressed. Especially in conflict situations, make sure to monitor body language and voice level.

17. Take the blame when things under your purview don't go well. Give others the praise when things do go well!

Often, administrators have to push, pull, drag, or sometimes even dictate the way a task will be completed. A dean had an academic department that was experimenting with how instruction was provided. The faculty were divided and had become somewhat entrenched in whichever 'side' supported their point of view. The dean finally entered the brouhaha and told the faculty how things would be done in the future. Within a year, the program had received numerous state and national awards and recognitions. When the dean was contacted to talk about the program, she would always invite faculty to be the speakers. When awards were presented, the dean invited faculty to represent the department in receiving the award. When news articles congratulated the dean for the program, she was consistently quoted giving credit to the faculty.

Here is a second example, this time illustrating taking blame. As a first-year dean I inherited the oversight of a summer academy for high school students funded by an external source. The faculty committee met to select participants, and I sent a note to the representative of the funding source, updating him about the candidates selected to participate in the academy. About three days later, I received a very irate phone call from the representative. He raked me over the coals for about twenty minutes, indicating that he should have been a member of the selection committee and that if this is how we were going to run things, the funding source would just put their money elsewhere. When I could finally interrupt his tirade, I indicated that not including him in selection activities was my fault and that somehow as a new dean I must not have attended to the requirement that he was to be involved as a member of the committee. It didn't matter that there were no written guidelines indicating his involvement. After about two minutes of silence, he kind of chuckled and then he apologized for perhaps coming on a little too strong. I assured him that in the future we would schedule the selection process at a time when he could be actively involved. We became good friends, and we received funding for several additional projects over subsequent years.

18. Be overt in developing connections with others.

Do this through seeking out others, through quick emails or phone calls, or by exchanging greetings while walking across campus or in the cafeteria or even at the grocery store. Every campus has at least a handful of 'Achilles heel' faculty members. These are the loud voices who don't like technology, or who believe their department is the only one on campus that has standards, or who think new policies recently implemented by the Board of Regents that have lowered admissions standards are out of line, or… As a provost, I made a point of scheduling time with these faculty or staff, inviting them to chat about a topic I knew they had strong opinions about. Sometimes I would invite one or two for coffee or lunch. Other times, I might run into the person in the grocery store or in the university cafeteria, and I would ask if we could chat about a topic sometime the following week. Then I would follow up with a phone call or email asking what time would be good for them to meet. Often, I gained valuable insight about their point of view that resulted in adjustments in planning. Other times, our informal chats expanded their thinking a degree or two!

19. Leadership can be exhausting! Take time to renew and reinvest in yourself.

This will ensure that you will have the energy to engage in positive actions that promote relationship building. Leadership roles can be 24/7, leaving little time to renew and regenerate. However, it is critical to make time for a spouse or significant other and family members. One president I know has a special date night with her spouse. Sometimes, date night is bringing home takeout to eat together. Sometimes, it is going out to eat or to a movie.

Renewal also means finding an hour or two for relaxing each week—taking a walk, reading a book for pleasure, going to a concert or play (not at the university), or having Zoom or phone conversations with family and friends. One president mandates that her senior administrators take at least two weeks off every summer for a vacation. She expects a full report with pictures after vacations are completed! She also shares pictures from her two weeks with her staff so that they know she is following her own advice.

20. Apply the Golden Rule in interactions with others.

Treat them as you hope they will treat you.

Resources

Nearly every book about leadership focuses on relationship building! Some you might enjoy are listed below.

Blanchard, Ken, and Sheldon Bowles. *Gung ho: Turn on the People in Any Organization.* New York: William Morrow & Company, Inc., 1998.

Blanchard, Ken, and Mark Miller. *The Secret.* San Francisco: Berrett-Koehler Publishers, Inc., 2009.

Brown, Brene. *Dare to Lead: Brave Work. Tough Conversations. Whole Hearts.* Random House Publishing Group, 2018.

Cashman, Kevin. *Leadership From the Inside Out: Becoming a Leader for Life.* San Francisco: Berrett-Koehler Publishers, Inc., 2008.

Covey, Stephen R. *The 7 Habits of Highly Effective People.* New York: Free Press, 2004.

George, Bill, and Peter Eagle Sims. *True North: Discover Your Authentic Leadership.* San Francisco: John Wiley Sons, 2007.

Gordon, John. *The Power of Positive Leadership.* Hoboken: John Wiley and Sons, 2017.

Kouzes, James M., and Barry Z. Posner. *The Leadership Challenge* (6th ed.) Hoboken: Jossey-Bass, 2017.

Maxwell, John C. *The 21 Irrefutable Laws of Leadership.* Nashville: Thomas Nelson, 2007.

Miller, Mark. *The Heart of Leadership: Becoming a Leader People Want to Follow.* San Francisco: Berrett-Koehler Publishers, Inc., 2013.

Northouse, Peter. "Authentic Leadership." In P. G. Northouse (Ed.), *Leadership: Theory and Practice* (8th ed.) Los Angeles: Sage Publications, 2019.

Sanborn, Mark. *The Fred Factor.* New York: Doubleday, 2004.

Su, Amy Jen. *The Leader You Want to Be.* Boston: Harvard Business Review Press, 2019.

Van Hooser, Phillip. *Leaders Ought to Know: 11 Ground Rules for Common Sense Leadership.* Hoboken: John Wiley & Sons, Inc., 2013.

Wooden, John, and Steve Jamison. *Wooden on Leadership.* New York: McGraw-Hill, 2005.

About the Author

Dr. Tes Mehring received undergraduate degrees in Applied Music, Music Education, and Psychology in 1974 from St. Mary College in Leavenworth, KS. She has an M.S. degree in Counseling Psychology from Southwest Missouri State University, and an M.S. degree and Ph.D. in Special Education from the University of Kansas. Just completing her 46th year as an educator, Dr. Mehring has been a school psychologist in Montana, Kansas, and Missouri, and has taught and served as Dean of Schools of Education and as Provost at Emporia State University and Baker University. Tes has served as President of the National Teachers Hall of Fame, the Teacher Education Council of State Colleges and Universities, Kansas Council for Learning Disabilities, and the Kansas Association for Colleges of Teacher Education. She has been a member of the Board of Directors and Executive Councils for the American Association for Colleges of Teacher Education, the Renaissance Group, Kansas Council for Exceptional Children, and Olathe Youth Symphony. She has published five books and 40 chapters in professional books, has presented at more than 70 national and international professional conferences, and has written 22 grants totaling two million dollars in funding. She has received numerous national awards, including the Renaissance Group Leadership Award, the American Association for Colleges of Teacher Education Edward C. Pomeroy Award for Outstanding Contributions in Teacher Education, the Distinguished Professor of the Year Award from the International Council for Learning Disabilities, and numerous Who's Who in America, Who's Who in American Education, and Who's Who of American Women recognitions. At ESU Dr. Mehring received the highest honor given to one professor each year recognizing excellence in teaching and scholarly activity—the Roe R. Cross Award. For the past nine years, Dr. Mehring has worked at Baker University, serving as the major advisor to 46 doctoral students and as a professor in the Leadership in Higher Education doctoral program.

PART 7

MAKING THE CASE
FOR YOURSELF
AND YOUR INITIATIVES

CHAPTER 23
VOICE AND VALUES IN LEADERSHIP

by Susan Gano-Phillips, Ph.D.
Dean, College of Arts and Sciences, University of Michigan-Flint

When I became dean nearly five years ago, I assumed the position in an institution where I had already worked for 20 years, after moving through the tenure ranks and serving in a couple of other administrative roles. As such, you would assume that I was a familiar and well-known figure to the colleagues I was now charged to lead. I made that assumption too, but I found that my colleagues were immediately skeptical of my intentions, and many perceived our long-standing relationships to have suddenly changed when my title changed. It was as if I was perceived to have completely changed my values, personality, and approach to interactions, simply because I occupied the Office of the Dean. The age-old "administrative-faculty divide" had struck again.

Leaders who join an institution from outside are obviously subject to the same sort of skepticism and uncertainty that I encountered. Who is this new administrator? What is her *modus operandi*? What drives her thinking and decision-making? Can she be trusted to support faculty, staff, or students when needed?

When you assume a leadership position, it is critical that colleagues develop an understanding of you as a person, your values, and how they guide your decision making. *While a multitude of skills are required for 21ˢᵗ century academic leaders, this chapter focuses on the importance of values-based decision making and communication as a critical factor in leadership success.*

The Importance of Values in Decision Making and Communication

Academic leaders face a deluge of decisions on a daily basis. Our organizations are complex, and our work requires collaboration with student affairs, development, facilities and operations, registrar's and admissions offices, and alumni relations, among others. Academic leaders must decide how they will organize their work, what structures and reporting lines make sense for the supervision of their staff, and how much time to allocate to various activities. Leaders make decisions about all of these matters, and more, on a daily basis—but without a clear sense of one's own values, you could easily mistake urgent matters for important ones and lose focus toward strategic priorities. Often referred to as the Eisenhower Decision Matrix, popularized by Stephen Covey in his best seller, *The Seven Habits of Highly Effective People* (2013), this matrix requires users to know their own values in order to define "importance." Our values give us purpose, prevent us from making poor choices, and give us confidence and courage in making difficult choices. The matrix below demonstrates how individuals who do not have a clear sense of values, as defined by what is important, may end up spending a lot of time on activities which are not truly important and which contribute little to their effectiveness as a leader.

DECISION MATRIX	*Low Importance*	*High Importance*
Low urgency	**LIMIT** the trivial and wasteful	**FOCUS** on opportunity and planning
High urgency	**AVOID** interruptions and busy work	**MANAGE** crises and pressing problems

Further, academic leaders who use their values to make decisions but do not communicate the values underlying those decisions risk leaving their colleagues confused and disengaged, because their colleagues cannot understand why particular issues are being focused upon or why specific decisions are being made. Instead, leaders who communicate not only their decisions but the values behind them help their colleagues to gain insight as to the leader's focus and form a more cohesive picture of their leader and her actions. Rather than seeing the leader engage in a variety of decisions which may appear unrelated to one another, colleagues come to see the patterns and values underlying the leader's energy, efforts, and decisions. Values serve as a catalyst in clarifying and crystallizing your vision for your team, while communicating those values allows you and others to unite and weave a shared vision for future success (HERS Leadership Institute). You can preserve momentum toward a shared vision by using internal communications, social media, recognition programs, and speaking engagements, to reinforce and clarify the values and vision which you hold for your unit.

Examples of this Skill in Action

In my first address to the governing faculty of my college after being named dean, I took the opportunity to lay out three goals for the future of the college:

1. To position the college for stability and long-term success.

2. To support ongoing professional development for faculty and staff.

3. To improve diversity, equity, and inclusion across the college's faculty, staff, and students.

These goals were developed throughout the interview process for the position, as a result of reflections on my experiences as a faculty member, and as a result of conversations with the provost. While these goals have served me (and, I believe, the college) well, they did not provide an explicit statement of my values and therefore may have been received as decontextualized pieces of information.

As I continued in my first year, I realized how important the explicit communication of my values would be to the college's constituents, as I was repeatedly surprised by their skepticism of my thinking or motives. Toward the end of my first year, I recall a moment in a faculty meeting where we were discussing our plans to implement a system of professional staff advisors in the college, and questions shifted to "administrative bloat." I turned to my colleagues and said, "Folks, you *know* me. I am the same person today that you have known as a colleague or committee member for the past couple of decades. I have always worked tirelessly to support our students and to ensure their success, and I will continue to do so as your dean. This is an issue of student success and a moral one—I cannot lay my head on my pillow at night, knowing our current retention numbers, without feeling we are failing far too many of our students." This very real moment, where I was willing to be vulnerable, to explicitly state my values, and to express my core beliefs as the reason for my decision to support a professional advising program was a turning point for me, professionally and for my work in the college.

So, in the following weeks, I spent some time clarifying and defining what I truly value as an academic leader and how those values inform my actions and decisions. There are literally thousands of values you might hold, and none are better than others. After taking some time to think about and prioritize those values, I decided it was important to communicate those values in my ongoing work. Among the most important values I hold are: diversity of thought and social justice, continuous learning and professional develop-ment, collaboration and consultation, an unwavering commitment to student success, honesty, and fairness. I also deeply value openness to change and innovation in the work that we do together.

Equity and social justice issues presented themselves regularly in my activities. My first year of tenure-track hiring demonstrated gaps in faculty awareness of conditions to optimize diverse hiring. So, I decided to require all members of search committees to participate in training to understand implicit bias and to ensure inclusive practices for review of candidates and campus visits. And when I provided this training, *I was sure to explicitly tie the rationale for this training to both my value that diverse groups are most effective, and to my stated goal of improving diversity in the college.* In a subsequent year, I further introduced the concept of faculty search advocates as a mechanism to improve diverse hires (based on research in STEM disciplines to increase the success of female candidates in searches), and again *I tied this decision to my value of ensuring diversity of thought and social justice* among our faculty, staff, and students.

To communicate and demonstrate my value of collaboration and consultation, I started hosting "Coffee with the Deans," where I and my associate deans routinely sought input from faculty and staff through informal interaction over coffee and doughnuts. And in each of these gatherings, *I tied the activity back to an explanation of why these activities are important—to a statement of the value of collaboration, consultation, and honest communication.* Over time, my open-door policy and my routine visits to all 18 of our academic departments have come to be synonymous with my values of collaboration, consultation, and honest communication.

VOICE AND VALUES IN LEADERSHIP

I have become very intentional in sharing both my values and our goals in a wide variety of routine communications within and beyond the college. My monthly newsletter always has an introductory segment where I tie a value, such as continuous learning and professional development or innovation, to a success story from within the college, thereby contextualizing the importance of the success story for our strategic progress as a college. These values are also infused in prospective student communications, in alumni newsletters, in social media posts, and in addresses that I deliver to various groups on campus.

Clearly defining and communicating my values has proven invaluable when I have faced particularly challenging times in the college as well. In one case, where the challenge was a deeply personal one, communicating in an honest and direct way allowed me and the college to face the situation collectively and with great support for one another. I had to inform the college of the untimely death of a beloved young staff member and find ways for us to support one another in our grief. In other institutionally challenging circumstances, such as needing to limit faculty hiring due to budget constraints or to reorganize the administrative staff to better serve our students, tying those communications and decisions to the values of honesty, collaboration, innovation, and student-centeredness helped others to understand the decisions, even if they did not agree with them.

Over time, the explicit communication of my values to the college as the basis for my interactions and decision making has become routine, and this communication has led the college to explore and adopt a shared set of values through our strategic planning process. These shared values guide our collective activities, efforts, and decision making every day.

Practical Steps Toward Defining and Communicating Your Values

If you are ready to advance your leadership by clarifying and communicating your values in your decision making, take some time to answer these questions:

- If you had to state your professional values in one or two sentences, what would they be? At your core, what matters the most to you as an academic leader?

- Would your colleagues be able to describe your administrative values? If not, how can you make your values more explicit to your team?

- How do you demonstrate those values through your actions? Is your allocation of time aligned to your values? Consider monitoring your time using the decision matrix presented above. Log how you spent each 30-minute increment of your workday in one of the four boxes. Is the distribution of time satisfactory or do you need to adjust it to better reflect your values?

- Daily, ask yourself: Are my values explicit in my:

- o Interactions with faculty and staff?

- o Formal presentations at meetings?

- o Written communications (emails, newsletters, policy documents)?

- o Social media posts?

- o Websites?

Resources

Buller, Jeffrey L. *The Essential Academic Dean or Provost: A Comprehensive Desk Reference*. San Francisco: Jossey-Bass, 2015. (See chapters 1, 3, and 4.)

Bolman, Lee G., and Deal, Terrence E. *Reframing Organizations: Artistry, Choice and Leadership*. Hoboken: Jossey-Bass, 2017.

Covey, Stephen R. *The Seven Habits of Highly Effective People*. New York: Simon & Schuster, 2013.

About the Author

Susan Gano-Phillips is Dean of the College of Arts and Sciences and a Professor of Psychology at the University of Michigan-Flint, where she has worked for 28 years. She joined UM-Flint in 1993 as a lecturer cum assistant professor, was tenured and promoted as an associate professor in 2000, and was promoted to professor in 2011. Gano-Phillips served as director of the Center for Learning and Teaching, faculty liaison for the Center for Civic Engagement, Interim Assistant Dean, Department Chair in Psychology, and Associate Dean, prior to being named interim dean in 2015. She was a Fulbright Fellow at City University of Hong Kong during the 2008-2009 academic year.

Her publications examine gender roles and cognition in married couples and, more recently, cultural change and leadership in higher education. She has co-edited a book, *A Process Approach to General Education Reform: Transforming Institutional Culture in Higher Education* (2010), has published in the *Journal of General Education and Liberal Education*, has presented at more than 30 professional conferences, and has delivered over 50 professional development workshops in Hong Kong, India, China, and throughout the United States. Gano-Phillips is a licensed psychologist in Michigan. She earned her B.S. from the University of Michigan, and her M.A. and Ph.D. from the University of Illinois at Urbana-Champaign.

CHAPTER 24
HOW TO MAKE THE CASE FOR YOUR INITIATIVE AND YOUR ORGANIZATION

by Michelle Wieser, Ph.D.
Dean of the School of Business and Technology,
Saint Mary's University of Minnesota

It is widely known that women are less likely than men to advocate for themselves and for the needs of their department or organization. A quick online search on "women and self-promotion" or "women and self-advocacy" reveals many articles and blogs on the subject. The challenge here is two-fold: women are often uncomfortable with self-advocacy or self-promotion, and therefore, they are less likely than men to advocate for themselves. This becomes a self-fulfilling prophecy; because women are less likely to advocate for themselves, we have less practice and lower confidence. It is easy to see how this phenomenon extends into advocating for organizational needs. If women are more hesitant to advocate for themselves, advocating for their department or school—which often has more far-reaching impact on an institution—may seem like a truly daunting task.

Within higher education, there is a clear example of this presented in research conducted by Janoff-Bulman and Wade. The example concerns two equally qualified, newly hired assistant professors—one man and one woman. The two individuals were offered the same starting salary; however, the man negotiated and was ultimately offered higher pay. Essentially, the man was rewarded for his willingness to advocate for himself, whereas the woman was penalized by her lack of advocacy. This could have been due to her inexperience, lack of confidence, low self-esteem, or potentially all of these, but the result was a discrepancy in pay between two individuals with equally strong credentials. I cringe when I hear stories like this. I am not a psychologist, but I do know that there have been many research studies examining the motives behind this lack of self-advocacy. Regardless of the reasons, there are things we, as women leaders in higher education, can do to raise our confidence, preparation, and ability to advocate for what we need.

I have held a variety of roles within higher education—starting in staff leadership within career development, then moving into faculty and program administration, and now serving as the dean of the School of Business and Technology at Saint Mary's University of Minnesota. I have worked for four unique types of institutions: a prestigious private, a large RI public, a private all-women's, and a private co-educational with multiple locations and modalities. Before entering higher education, I had a 15-year corporate career with some very well-known organizations including General Mills, Purina, and Ernst and Young. Throughout all of this experience, I have gathered a toolkit to utilize when I advocate for myself and for what I need in order to run a successful program, organization, or school. In this chapter, I share my "strategic seven" tools that have served as my guide. My hope is that you find one or more of these to be helpful as you navigate your career in higher education.

When I reflect on the many times throughout my career when I have been an advocate for my career or my organizational needs, the tools I have called upon group into four categories: systems, structures, support, and self. I have built business cases for new technology *systems* to streamline the work of my organization. I have advocated for new organizational *structures* or processes that create efficiency and opportunity. I have convinced my leaders of the need for *support* in the form of financial or human resources. And finally, I've realized that the quality of my work alone is not enough to move up in the organization. *Self*-advocacy has been an essential part of my career advancement in higher education. Below, I have interspersed stories and experiences which fall under each of these types of advocacy in order to bring the following tools to life.

7 Rules for Advocating for Yourself and Your Organization

1. Offer a solution

We know that presenting a problem without a solution is rarely a good idea. The same holds true when it comes to putting forth new ideas. In my experience, positioning an idea in terms of a solution to a problem often presents a clearer path to "yes." In some cases, upper-level leaders may not even know there is a problem in need of solution. Painting the picture can help show how your idea is not just a smart one, but one that will address that existing or potential problem. As a new dean at Saint Mary's University of Minnesota, I entered higher education at a time when declining enrollments were a challenge present in most traditional institutions. As one solution to this problem, I led a team to look at new "pathway" programs in the School of Business. This resulted in an entirely new stackable credentials strategy and a slew of new master's level certificates. Most university leaders were on board from the beginning, but the strategy did involve many new policies, changes to existing programs, and new structures. Because I presented this as a solution to a challenging enrollment problem, people were less reluctant to jump onboard, change policies, and create a smooth path to launching our new "accelerators" program in about seven months.

2. Collaborate across departments or organizations

As an academic director of a new MBA program at St. Catherine University, I needed to hire new faculty to support our growth. Like most smaller institutions, it was challenging to find the budget to hire three new faculty across three unique disciplines. I decided the best approach would be to join forces with other program leaders in the School of Business as well as the School of Health. The result was three fantastic new faculty who split their time between the MBA program and other business and health programs. This provided a rich teaching experience for the new faculty, while also ensuring that students from multiple programs learned from their deep expertise. By joining together across schools and programs, we were easily able to build the business case for these new hires. Now I actively seek out opportunities to work across traditional academic "silos" to more easily build the case for what is needed and find solutions that benefit everyone.

3. Rally support and bring people along

Shortly after joining Saint Mary's as a new dean, I realized that the organizational structure I inherited was not working for me. I had well over 20 direct reports—far too many to effectively manage while balancing the other elements of my role! I identified an ideal structure that involved significant changes to some roles, elimination of one role, and the addition of a handful of other roles. In order to advocate for this change, I first positioned everything in a way that highlighted both the financial and the people benefit of this new structure. Then, I met with my peers, my supervisor, and key individuals within my organization to walk them through my plans. By garnering support from all of these individuals in advance, I was able to advocate more effectively for this change when presenting it to the senior leaders of the organization. The result was a streamlined and highly effective organization.

4. Leverage the facts and the data

While I was an associate dean at St. Catherine University, the university president had a priority to find new academic pathways for our traditional undergraduate students to pursue graduate work. I knew our MBA was not the right fit for this, so I did some research and identified an up-and-coming new program that was a perfect fit. In order to prove the business case, I conducted significant research from internal and external sources. I was able to weave all the facts I had uncovered into a compelling case for moving in the direction I had suggested. Even in a challenging financial time for the university, I was able to convince the president and her cabinet to invest in this idea. Had I not built the case on the data, I am confident this would not have received such rapid buy-in and approval.

5. Tie it to how it benefits the student

It may seem obvious, but often we overlook the fact that almost everything we do in higher education has an impact on our students. Early on in my career in higher education, I worked as an employer relations manager in a business school career center at Washington University in St. Louis. I adored this role. It was invigorating to go out and build new partnerships with companies who might hire our students. Our organization was structured in such a way that we had one team focused on employer relations and one on student advising. About six months into my new role, I realized that our students were coming directly to me for career advice and interview preparation. They knew I was the one who was interacting with employers on a daily basis, and therefore, the one knew what employers were looking for in our students. My colleagues and I determined that the students would benefit from a more blended structure in which they could receive tailored advice specific to industries or companies they were pursuing. At the same time, we felt a new structure like this would enrich all of our positions. When taking the proposal forward to leadership, we carefully crafted a plan that was centered on the student experience and how this would benefit them. The result was a proposal that was approved immediately. I found my new role to be incredibly fulfilling, and I know with certainty my students' success was in large part because they were able to receive advice that was tailored to their needs. Since then, I have always carefully thought through how anything I am proposing ultimately benefits the students. This has allowed me to advance ideas and proposals with less resistance.

6. Consider a pilot

In my experience, one of the main reasons an idea is not moved forward is because of the heavy investment in financial or human resources. At one point when I was leading an organization at the University of Minnesota, I wanted to implement a new way for our part-time students to access career services. This group of students was not often on campus during the day, and they were busy juggling many aspects of their lives. I had recently been introduced to a new technology that would allow us to serve them virtually. Not only did this require a financial investment, but it was a radically different idea from anything the university had done before. When considering how to move the idea forward, I decided to follow an approach that involved an initial pilot. We could gauge engagement and results during the pilot, which would then allow me to build a fact-based business case for full implementation. The pilot approach was approved with little hesitation. I have learned since then that asking for a pilot is often the best approach when advocating for something. A pilot involves little financial risk from the institution's perspective, while allowing me and my team to gather valuable data that can help build a more compelling case.

7. If at first you don't succeed...

One of the tools that is perhaps the hardest to learn in all of this is how to build resilience if your initial attempt at advocating for yourself or your organization does not go the way you had planned. This can sting a little more, perhaps, when you are advocating for yourself. At one point in my career when I was a director of an organization, I advocated hard to move up to an assistant dean position. I believed I was the right one for this role, and I did not hesitate to throw my hat in the ring when the time was right. I went through the interview process, and felt I performed the best I could. In the end, the position went to a long-time internal candidate who I knew was the heir apparent. Did it sting? Absolutely! However, after receiving some positive feedback and doing a bit of reflection, I realized it was for the best. I did not let this one experience keep me from pursuing my dreams in the future. In the end, had I received that position, I would likely still be an assistant dean. Instead, I continued to advocate for myself and am now a dean of a school of business.

Some Final Thoughts...

There are many more tools and ideas that can help women in higher education advance their proposals for themselves and their organizations, but I have found the seven tips listed above to be especially invaluable throughout my time with four different universities. One additional broad piece of advice is to be sure and communicate clearly and concisely at every step of the process. From garnering initial support, to putting plans in writing, to presenting these plans to a team of senior leaders, to measuring and reporting success... clarity is key! Also, do not be afraid to practice. I have found that saying the words aloud helps increase my comfort. When it comes time to say the same words to even the seniormost leader at the institution, they flow with more finesse and confidence!

Finally, while you are mastering being an advocate for yourself and your organization, do not forget to advocate for others. Raise other women up as well. Be a mentor, a champion, and a trusted colleague. Reach out proactively and find ways to help one another share our accomplishments and advance our careers together. The world of higher education will be changed for the better if we speak up and bring one another along.

Resources

Janoff-Bulman, Ronnie, and Mary Beth Wade. "Viewpoint: The Dilemma of Self-Advocacy for Women: Another Case of Blaming the Victim?" *Journal of Social and Clinical Psychology*, Vol. 15, No. 2. 1996. pp. 143-152. https://guilfordjournals.com/doi/abs/10.1521/jscp.1996.15. 2.143?journalCode=jscp&

About the Author

Dr. Michelle Wieser is the Dean of the School of Business and Technology at Saint Mary's University of Minnesota. In this role, she guides all undergraduate and graduate programs and certificates within the school, providing strategic leadership to ensure academic excellence and sustained success and growth. Before joining Saint Mary's, Dr. Wieser served as Interim Dean, Associate Dean, and Program Director at St. Catherine University. Earlier in her academic career, Dr. Wieser was Director of the Graduate Business Career Center with the University of Minnesota's Carlson School of Management, and she served in a variety of career development roles with the Olin Business School at Washington University in St. Louis. Before entering academia, she held sales, marketing, and consulting roles with General Mills, Ralston (now Nestlé) Purina, and EY Consulting.

Dr. Wieser received a Ph.D. in Organizational Leadership, Policy, and Development from the University of Minnesota, an MBA in Marketing from Washington University in St Louis, and a Bachelor of Journalism degree from the University of Missouri. Her ongoing research focuses on the experience and outcomes of MBA graduates across the U.S.

and Europe, with a particular focus on differences achieved by gender and race.

EMILY O. GRAVETT AND LINDSAY BERNHAGEN

CHAPTER 25
SAYING "NO"
TO GET TO "YES"

by Emily O. Gravett, Ph.D.
Assistant Director, Center for Faculty Innovation; Assistant Professor,
Department of Philosophy & Religion, James Madison University

and Lindsay Bernhagen, Ph.D.
Director, Center for Inclusive Teaching and Learning, University of
Wisconsin-Stevens Point

The Art of Saying "No"

One of the most important skills that all leaders, but especially women, need to nurture is the difficult and delicate art of saying "no." Many of us were never taught to do so at all. We didn't even know we could. Even today, women are often labeled, and sometimes even punished for being perceived, as "bitchy," "bossy," or just plain "not nice," all as the result of saying "no" in various forms. We are socialized, still, to accommodate, to people-please, to be other-oriented, to caretake, to do what needs to be done—all with a smile on our faces.

It is our strong recommendation (and, if we're being honest, our aspiration, as we're still working on this ourselves) that women leaders learn to resist these impulses born out of upbringing, acculturation, peer pressure, and patriarchy. Here is where we can focus on identifying and maintaining healthy boundaries for ourselves, which includes a clear sense of what we want to do and what we don't want to do. This may involve getting comfortable with embracing a healthy "selfishness," a word with many negative connotations that we'd love to leave behind.

The scenarios in which we can employ the skill of "no" are vast. There is no shortage of committees that we *don't* need to steer, projects that we *don't* need to take on, documents that *don't* need our feedback, and meetings that *don't* need our facilitation. Yet what we're offering here is not a comprehensive list of all the things to say "no" to. Rather, we believe saying "no" requires something different. It means letting go of the (possibly self-aggrandizing) idea that, in order for something to be done well, we must be the ones to do it. It means sitting with the guilt or worry we may feel at the possibility of letting others down. It means living with a fear of missing out or of not being asked again. It means going against the "cult of busyness" that can attach our sense of self-worth to how productive and exhausted we are. It means giving up a need to control or a sense of responsibility for others' lives beyond our own. It means refusing to perform the emotional labor that can exact such a toll on us over time. It means having a clearer sense of what our most important values and goals are and bringing our lives into alignment with them.

Before we offer our recommendations (aspirations), it's important to understand *why* we are inclined to say "yes" to so many things. There are several barriers that women commonly face in the academic workplace—higher service expectations, increased demands for emotional labor, lack of recognition for the good work we do, and more. And because we are socialized to be caretaking and other-oriented, our responses to these barriers sometimes become their own problems.

For example, we may have *difficulty delegating*, even when granted the authority to do so. We may feel guilty when we ask a colleague or even a subordinate to take on a task that we are capable of, because we worry about the implication that they are less busy than we are or that we are "too important" to do the work that we've decided to foist onto them.

Another response to the systemic barriers women in academia face is our tendency toward *overworking*. If a certain amount of our work goes unnoticed or is attributed to male colleagues, then it stands to reason that, for the same amount of credit as output, we must have more work to input. But, when we overwork, we can become spread too thin; then, we are not able to give our best to everything. Unfortunately, when others see "less than our best," they may assume that we are less capable or competent, which potentially reinforces the exact gender bias we're trying to combat!

At times, our challenges with delegation and our impulses to overwork combine to create another problematic response: we may find ourselves *doing others' work* for them, reasoning that it is easier or more efficient to just "do it ourselves" than to cajole others into meeting their obligations or stepping up in the first place.

All of which leads us to a final maladaptive response: *doing invisible or underappreciated work*. From emotional labor to service to advising to so-called "administrivia," women leaders in higher ed often take on tasks that somebody has to do, yet that go unrecognized in institutional reward structures. This can prevent women from seeking raises, applying for promotions, or moving up the institutional hierarchy into leadership positions in the first place.

As we've written elsewhere, the consequences of these responses can be myriad, ranging from burnout to derailment. Learning how to say "no" to specific requests or unappreciative people, and to orientations toward work that have us doing too much, at too high a cost—and how to say "yes" to the activities that hold more meaning and promise for us—will go a long way to helping us avoid these potentially disastrous consequences.

Our Own Learned Experiences

Emily: When I first began at my current position as an assistant director in a faculty development center a few years back, I wanted to prove myself; I felt I *needed* to prove myself. I was new, I was young, I have a people-pleasing personality and an aversion to conflict, and so I said "yes" to everything. I agreed to be on committees, I offered to help colleagues, I took on extra projects, I met deadlines that everyone else missed, I said "yes" to things people weren't even asking me to do! And I became totally overwhelmed. There was no way I could do this job in a normal work week. I was working at night, on the weekends, checking email on my phone continuously. In desperation, I turned to the book *Essentialism* and took from it that just because I *can* do something doesn't mean I *should*—or even, that just because I can do something *well* doesn't mean I should. I realized that if I were going to thrive in the way I wanted to over the long term, I needed to learn how to say "no." This was not easy for me. But I made it a goal.

Since then, I've told my coworkers I intend to be saying "no" more. I even wrote saying "no" more often into my annual professional development goals last year—with the knowledge and support of my woman supervisor. I've said "no" to outdated or misaligned programs that it no longer made sense for my team to run. I've said "no" to committees, like the co-curricular transcript committee, that it simply didn't make sense for me to be on. I've said "no" to invitations to collaborate on research projects, even with friends and colleagues whom I respect a great deal. At times, honestly, saying "no" has been hard, but it has gotten easier as I've practiced.

Lindsay: Recently, administrators at my institution decided to adopt a controversial new budget model for our academic departments. Shared governance leadership quickly assembled a working group to make recommendations on the implementation of the model, so we could avoid some of its potential pitfalls. I said "yes" (strategically, for once!) to being on the working group, because I thought it would give me an inside look at an aspect of institutional planning that I was eager to learn more about.

When we met for the first time, our initial task was to pick a chair for the group. Because I was the most neutrally positioned person in the room given my role at the institution, I was immediately "voluntold" to be chair. Before I could reply, another committee member exclaimed, "Let's hurry up and vote so she can't say 'no'!" I was flattered, surprised, and also really nervous. This was a contentious issue. There were a lot of heavy hitters in the room. This was not what I had meant to say "yes" to!

It took me a few meetings to figure out how to manage this critical and high-profile responsibility that emerged from a "yes" I didn't think I was giving. But what worked—though it wasn't my inclination—was saying "no" to doing it all alone (not that anyone asked that of me; that was just my instinct). I was intentional about delegating the work of the committee to other members. I sent out weekly assignments and, when appropriate, attached specific names to specific tasks. I reframed the delegation as collaboration (in fact, a chief value of our shared governance) and not as me shirking duties. When it came time to share the group's recommendations, I assuaged my remaining guilt by giving verbal credit to the other team members who stepped up to the plate to get the work done.

Putting this into Action

This piece is not a call to say "no" merely for the sake of resistance or obstinance. On the contrary, we are encouraging "no" as part and parcel of a larger or more intentional "yes." Rather than the "yes, and..." philosophy that has made its way from improv into countless self-help books, we recommend a strategic "yes, but..." approach, wherein "yes" and "no" are *both* doled out strategically in ways that serve not only the tasks at hand, but also the people doing them. In the following list, we present several strategies that can be used alone or in conjunction to help other women leaders with this skill:

- Pause. Create a bit—just a bit—of space between the time when someone makes a request of you and the time when you respond. Take the time you need. You don't owe anyone answers right away. When you give yourself time to consider and reflect, you are much better situated to make a well-informed decision.

- Pay attention to how your body responds in any given moment. Often the necessity of a "no" will present itself in our physical experience—a quickening of our breath, a tightening in our chest, a flushing of our skin. We may feel, viscerally, what should be a "no" before we even recognize it cognitively.

- As the title of a popular book says, feel the fear and do it anyway. If saying "no" is hard for you, there is no magic formula we can give (we wish we had it!) that will make that discomfort disappear. Rather, you may have to lean into the difficulty and say "no" anyway, knowing that you are doing the right thing and that you are likely to feel some squeamishness as you develop a new skill.

- Be clear; when it's a "no," make sure everyone knows it's a "no." Remember that "no" is a complete sentence. Avoid ambiguous statements like "I will try to do it later." As one of our friends says, "To be clear is to be kind."

- Try saying "I choose not to" or "I don't," instead of "I can't"; the latter almost sounds like an excuse or like you're not in charge of your own life. The former reflects measured consideration and intentional choice.

- Create an "I don't list"; this is a list of all the things you don't do, because we're human and it's not possible to do everything. It can help to frame this list as "I don't do X, so that I can do Y," to allow yourself to see the "yes" behind the instances of "no." It may also be helpful to share this list with other women leaders, so that we aren't assuming everyone else is doing the impossible.

- Let people, especially women, around you know that it is your goal to say "no" more strategically, with the intent of enlisting them in supporting you.

- Practice saying "no" in smaller-stakes situations with projects that don't matter a lot to you or with people you don't worry so much about disappointing. Such practice will help strengthen your "no" muscle, so that you're ready for situations that really matter.

- Look for "no" within a mandatory "yes." Even if you are directed or "voluntold" to do a project, figure out what latitude and autonomy you have to make it your own.

- Continue to champion and clarify what you are saying "yes" to, as a result of strategically saying "no," lest you become known as the person who never does anything.

Briefly, and as a note of encouragement, here are two examples of how some of the above strategies have worked for us.

Lindsay: I have served as chair of our campus's Diversity Council over the last few years. While the work of this group is extremely important to me, I was frustrated to realize that being chair meant attending several additional weekly meetings and investing time in administrative tasks that felt too separate from the real meat of justice, equity, diversity, and inclusion work. I was tempted to take on this responsibility again when no alternatives self-nominated, but I talked through my thinking with a trusted group of women colleagues. They encouraged me to find someone else to be chair and to devote my time to places where I felt I could more easily make change, such as specific task forces and working groups. I followed their advice by recruiting a new chair, and now I feel good about building a leadership pipeline for her, while also giving myself the capacity to do more of the on-the-ground work that I value.

Emily: The global pandemic has provided many distinct opportunities to practice the skill of saying "no," in both large and small ways. I share custody of my five-year old daughter and I'm also still supposed to be working full-time, at home. This situation has felt stressful to me, as I know it has for so many others, especially given my previous pace and levels of productivity. I simply can't provide childcare and work in the same ways as before. This is when saying "no," even to myself, has become essential for me. Can I meet every week for two hours at noon, when I need to be preparing my child's lunch and putting her down for an afternoon rest? No. (And the answer is still "no," even when it butts up against others' strongly stated preferences.) Can I teach on campus twice a week when I will be responsible for watching my daughter at one of those times? No. Can I offer this program I really want to offer when I have literally no more free hours left in the work week? Also no. It is important for me to be present for my daughter on the days she is with me, to fulfill essential work obligations, and to try to cultivate a sense of joy and space amidst a life that feels compromised in so many ways. Retaining a strong sense of my own values and boundaries has gone a long way in this context.

These various, and more recently high-stakes, instances of saying "no" have created room in our lives for better work-life integration, for activities that are aligned with the missions of our teams and units, for time spent living out our own values, and for an increasing sense of self-respect, since we are no longer defaulting to "yes" to justify or convince others of our own worth.

To be clear, neither of us thinks anyone should say "yes" to adopting all of the above strategies! Some will make sense for you, and others will be more difficult or even undesirable to implement. We encourage readers to take stock of their current situation, track it as it constantly changes, and lean on the support of other women, just as we have done with one another.

Resources

Akinola, Modupe, Ashley E. Martin, and Katherine W. Phillips. "To Delegate or Not to Delegate: Gender Differences in Affective Associations and Behavioral Responses to Delegation." *Academy of Management Journal,* 46, no. 1, 2018. Doi: https://doi.org/10.5465/amj.2016.0662

Brown, Brené. *The Gifts of Imperfection: Let Go of Who You Think You're Supposed to Be and Embrace Who You Are.* Center City, Minnesota: Hazelden, 2010.

Gazipura, Aziz. *Not Nice: Stop People Pleasing, Staying Silent, & Feeling Guilty...and Start Speaking Up, Saying No, Asking Boldly, and Unapologetically Being Yourself.* Portland, OR: B.C. Allen, 2017.

Jeffers, Susan. *Feel the Fear...and Do It Anyway.* New York: Ballantine Books, 2007.

Katherine, Anne. *Boundaries: Where You End and I Begin.* Center City, Minnesota: Hazelden, 1991.

McKeown, Greg. *Essentialism: The Disciplined Pursuit of Less.* New York: Crown Business, 2014.

Pinsker, Joe. "'Ugh, I'm So Busy': A Status Symbol for Our Time." *The Atlantic.* Atlantic Media Company, 1 Mar. 2017.

www.theatlantic.com/business/archive/2017/03/busyness-
status-symbol/518178/.

Sandberg, Sheryl. *Lean In: Women, Work, and the Will to Lead.*
New York: Alfred A. Knopf, 2013.

Scott, Kim. *Radical Candor: Be a Kickass Boss without Losing Your
Humanity.* New York: St. Martin's Press., 2017.

Wainwright, Holly. "Every Woman Has an 'I Don't' List.
And It's about Time We Shared Them." *Mamamia.* 12 Aug.
2019. www.mamamia.com.au/i-dont-list/.

Wong, Kristin. "Why You Should Learn to Say 'No' More
Often." *The New York Times.* 8 May 2017.
www.nytimes.com/2017/05/08/smarter-living/why-you-
should-learn-to-say-no-more-often.html.

About the Authors

Emily O. Gravett is an assistant director in the Center for
Faculty Innovation and an assistant professor in the
Department of Philosophy & Religion at James Madison
University (JMU) in Harrisonburg, VA. She earned her B.A.
from Colgate University in English and Religion and her M.A.
and Ph.D. in Religious Studies from the University of Virginia.
She has published widely on topics important to women in
leadership, including pink-collar labor, emotional labor, and
feminist educational development.

Lindsay Bernhagen is the director of the Center for Inclusive Teaching and Learning (CITL) and Diversity Officer for Academic Affairs at the University of Wisconsin-Stevens Point, where she also teaches courses in Women's and Gender Studies, Education, and Sociology. She holds a Ph.D. in Comparative Studies, and M.A.s in Gender Studies and Ethnomusicology. In addition to directing CITL, she serves as the editor of *To Improve the Academy: A Journal of Educational Development* and publishes and speaks regularly on issues of diversity, equity, and inclusion in higher education.

CHAPTER 26
NOT HERE TO TAKE NOTES: LESSONS FROM A YOUNG WOMAN OUTNUMBERED BY MEN AT THE CONFERENCE TABLE

by Anna Horlacher, MBA
recently Associate Director of Alumni Relations, University of Portland

I have the remarkable fortune of working at my alma mater—a community that shaped me, led me to my best friends, led me to my husband, and continues to be a backdrop for many highlights of my life. I am currently employed by the same division where I worked as an undergraduate student. This means that many of my colleagues, and now our division's vice president, all knew me as the shy and smiley student who had a lot of life to learn. Now my role at the university involves stewarding volunteer alumni leaders in various chapter and board capacities, managing alumni events, and assisting with strategic planning efforts for my team in Alumni Relations.

In addition to navigating a career in the same setting where I was once known as a student, it's worth noting that my university is a private, Catholic institution. This institution mirrors the Catholic Church in that there are priests in leadership positions. This system is such that men have run the university for as long as it has existed. Every president of the university has been a male priest. The governing board is

77% male, and 22% of those men are priests. The university's upper administration has three women in leadership positions, out of the thirteen who report directly to the president. And there is only one female dean. Many of the men are of diverse backgrounds and are outstanding at their jobs. Yet the fact remains, women are largely outnumbered in presence and equitable voice. I will clarify that Catholic institutions are not necessarily automatically male-run. My high school experience at a private Catholic high school was an empowering one, grounded in transforming young women into leaders. The high school was founded by Sisters of the Holy Names of Jesus and Mary in 1859 (42 years prior to my university's founding) and maintains female leadership at the administrative level. So, while higher education's history initiated and sustains a disproportionate number of male participants and leaders, my own formative years proved that an institution's Catholicism did not necessitate its male-dominance. The Catholic Church and most specifically, the congregation which founded my university, is to be acknowledged for the incredible sense of community and servant leadership that exists in its community. Yet it is also undoubtedly the systemic source for holding male leaders on a pedestal and perpetuating a hierarchy that leaves women in a severe blind spot.

From the start of my employment, I was committed to earning a seat at the table. Being a female leader in higher education is important to me—and particularly given the environment I described, being a female leader at a Catholic institution is even more important to me. I believe in this community, and I believe that only when we name systemic barriers, can we begin to push through them.

Given these all-too-common work circumstances, I aim to work through feelings of defeat and find motivation every time I sit in a leadership meeting. Here are a few lessons I have learned along the way.

6 Tips

Don't let age define your role.

I found when I first started that I wanted to absorb as much material as possible; I wanted to be a sponge and learn about this new side of higher education. I deferred to more vocal colleagues that I perceived to be older and wiser instead of speaking up and asking questions. I also wanted to show value. I saw my age and experience as a limiting factor, so I provided that value by taking diligent notes and following up promptly with those notes after meetings. Now, while only five years into this role, it is clear that I limited my contributions by assuming the position of the diligent taskmaster. I've learned that the job of note-taker is a task that I can fulfill for myself, but it doesn't need to be a task I fulfill for everyone else around the table. Administrative assistants are brought to meetings to help keep the room on schedule, take notes, or provide printouts, and so much more. Their role is crucial, but it's not my role.

TIP #1

Young voices around the table: Just because you don't know exactly when to speak up or what to say does not

---

mean that you should fill that space by taking notes and keeping track of everyone's tasks. Tell yourself that these moments are when you "teach your colleagues how to treat you." You don't want to be invited to meetings because you're great at capturing the topics discussed and providing detailed follow-up. That is a great skill, but more than that, you want to be invited to the table because of the perspective you bring and the input and value you can provide. Notes are important so that you can be held accountable for your own action items and readily track thoughts you don't want to lose, but that energy is for you. Don't be the group note-taker. Claim your ideas as your own, ask for space at the table, choose your moments to speak up wisely, and let others look out for themselves. In doing so, you'll confirm that however young or new you may be, your spot at the table has grown and shifted beyond the eagerness or reservedness of a new colleague who just wanted to pitch in wherever you could. You are not here to take notes.

Name accidental sexism.

Given that my role involves event production, I am often asked for my opinions on décor, event design, menus, and general aesthetics. Don't get me wrong; I love transforming a space and creating extraordinary experiences. Yet, I can find that skill to be limiting. There are moments when a group of people will physically turn to me when topics related to food or planning surface. Team members will imply my need to step in by saying, "Hey, let's order some lunch in for the meeting this afternoon," followed by silence. I have to stop myself. Am I capable of ordering lunch for the team? Yes. Is everyone else in the room also capable of ordering lunch for the team? Yes. If I pause a beat before responding, I've found colleagues catch themselves in this request and then pitch it as, "Oh, well, you are just so good at picking fun places. You're an expert here, so I thought I'd ask for your help!" That can both be true and be a role I don't need to feel obligated to fill.

> TIP #2
>
> Just because you are capable of completing a task, doesn't mean you should be the first to jump in. If a task doesn't align with your current or desired role or offer you a chance to provide value as an intelligent professional, then sit tight. Let someone else offer first. Whether this is ordering food, decorating the office, purchasing gifts for people, etc., let this be a team effort. I'm not suggesting you take a step back from being a team player; rather, allow space for others to practice being a team player. I'm suggesting you choose to step up in situations that further your place in the working world as a bright, skilled, reliable professional who people lean on for strategic problem-solving and critical thinking.

Share the shoutouts.

Often, in a crowded conference room, I'll hear a woman colleague of mine offer an idea, and then a few moments later, a male colleague will share an almost identical thought, and only *then* will the room nod in agreement and offer kudos. You might experience this as an observer or be the person who can't find footing in a conversation. I have witnessed remarkable female colleagues handle this by looking out for each other and helping the room refocus by acknowledging who shared the original idea. This isn't about credit or ego; this is about valuing everyone's contributions. Own your space—and help deserving colleagues own theirs.

TIP #3

Model the behavior you wish to receive. Find spaces to say, "I really like what ___ said about idea ___. That makes me think...." Or, "That's a great point and is similar to what ___ was getting at when she said ___." When your fellow women professionals feel seen and heard by you, I can almost guarantee that they'll find space to see and hear you as well. Then, the more established colleagues in the room may start to model that behavior too. You can proactively create a culture where people listen actively and absorb information, rather than wait for others to stop speaking so that they can start talking again. This takes time, and you need to remember that it's not about every idea being associated with the originator of the idea. Keep the bigger picture in mind and know that these little interactions and little shout-outs add up. It will make a difference. You'll find people owning their space more naturally because that space is acknowledged and appreciated, including yours.

Own the agenda.

I have been a part of many brainstorm settings, some of which lead to a wonderfully collaborative sharing of ideas and productive next steps, some of which completely devolve towards inaction, and some that are certainly collaborative in nature but after which the output of the meeting doesn't allow for individual ownership. Sometimes, the desire for upper-level management to view what they perceive as ideal teamwork means that the loudest voice in the group (or the most eloquent male) will carry a message. It may feel unnecessary to identify who speaks when, but doing so will be a clear way to ensure equity of voice.

TIP #4

When preparing presentations for upper management, prepping for cross-team meetings, or even presenting goals within your team, clearly identify who will share certain ideas. Take the time to own the agenda. Particularly with the frequency of video meetings, it takes very little time to say, "I'll intro topic x and then I'll kick it to you to talk through topic y," or "I feel like I can deliver this part, and you're really great at speaking to that part. Let's divide and conquer."

This is also an important way to connect to Tip #3. In looking over the outline for a meeting or a conversation with campus partners, look for ways to include others. Perhaps there is a young employee or a fellow female colleague who needs to be intentionally invited to the metaphorical microphone. Operate within reason but provide a chance for your colleague to speak to a specific piece he or she may be passionate about. Not only will this make transitions more seamless; you are also identifying a way to ensure your voice is heard—and doing so in a collaborative and proactive manner.

Be shameless in setting boundaries.

Being a woman carries different roles for each individual. It could mean being a loving daughter, a strong partner, a devoted mother, a loyal friend, or a passionate employee. I find it incredibly important that we allow space for as many of these strengths to exist in one person as that person would like. We can acknowledge that it is perhaps easier to be single without children and rise in the ranks in one's career. It is perhaps easier to be a working mother when one has an empathetic partner. But no one scenario is right or wrong, or more permissible or commendable than the other. Strength in any one area that comes at the cost of strength in another area is not true strength, it's unnecessary sacrifice. It is also important to clarify that perfection in any or all of these categories is impossible. Let's not set ourselves or our peers up for failure by expecting perfection.

When considering a male-led institution like the one I am a part of, this is particularly important. I have experienced numerous instances of late-night calls, Sunday texts, expectations for incredibly short turn-around that involves after-hours work, and the list goes on. These invitations to engage may stem from a lack of boundaries from others or may be an indication of substantive work that legitimately needs to be prioritized. Am I willing to do this work? Absolutely. And I often recognize the importance of doing so. The important thing is to assess whether or not the request truly needs my immediate action; this puts the power in my hands, in choosing how to use my time. A simple, but important step for me has been not responding to emails once I've headed home. I may review my inbox that evening, but I am mindful of not enforcing the habit that I'm constantly and immediately available. Enforcing a habit that work is always top of mind will not lead me to be a strong partner or a devoted mother. I need it to be okay for there to be room for more, and I recognize that I am the source of that being okay.

TIP #5

Boundaries are a critical part of finding success in whatever role you choose to own as a woman. Particularly in a male-driven work environment, there's a popular narrative that time for personal and family life or self-care can be perceived as weakness or lack of commitment to the work. Forget that. Put in the time and energy to succeed in your role and advance your career, but remember to take time to work out, take a lunch break, take a loved one's birthday off—set whatever boundaries you need so that you can thrive in all areas of your life. The perception that self-worth or success is tied to limitless obligations and dizzyingly busy schedules is a false narrative. Try not to let that narrative dictate how you show up at work. Pay your dues and let your work and your passion speak for itself. There will always be another big meeting, another important trip, and a next crisis. Empower yourself to work on mastering the gift of boundaries; how to set them; when to share them; and when you might legitimately need to let work in to attend to something time-sensitive. The more you can showcase the strength that comes from being shameless in setting boundaries, the more others will be motivated to do the same, and the more genuine you can be in owning your unique strengths.

Embrace vulnerability.

Even as I write these tips, I reflect on the fact that if I adhered to them 100% of the time, I should have a healthy relationship with my work and my path at this institution. While I do love my work and my team, I'd describe my relationship with the institution as bruised. And that is okay. One of the most important areas in which I've grown, and in which my nuclear team has grown, is the thoughtful leadership we've experienced through vulnerability. In its most basic sense, vulnerability is key to my work in alumni relations. If we preach that everything at the institution is pristine and sailing smoothly, why would an alum want to help? Why would they give up their valuable free time or their financial resources? Short answer: they wouldn't. At a more intricate level, vulnerability in the professional setting is both incredibly hard and critically important. Further, being vulnerable shouldn't be the hallmark of a strong woman or a strong man; it should be the hallmark of a strong leader. For women, vulnerability can feel too related to emotion to possibly be considered a good thing. Emotion is thought to be perceived as weakness. It can make people feel uncomfortable, it can be distracting, and it can feel like it uproots one's professional respect. Emotion can be difficult to manage and can be especially difficult for women, as the other side of the coin can also be true—lack of emotion can be perceived as cold or careless, while a male exhibiting the same behaviors is perceived as strong and level-headed. A professional's relationship with emotion is complicated, and sometimes raw emotion for emotion's sake is okay. For those instances where emotion can feel like a hindrance, I'd offer that emotion and vulnerability are related, but vulnerability can be the output of internal emotion. It is not a woman's responsibility to be the sole source of vulnerability, but I believe it is an important charge. Modeling this behavior will hopefully inspire others to do the same. Teammates step up for each other in extraordinary ways when another team member asks for help.

TIP #6

Let your emotion fuel vulnerability. Give emotions space to breathe and give your emotions purpose by using them to make your social intelligence stronger. This could look like a short phone call to your boss explaining that you feel frustrated for being talked over in a previous meeting and that you'd like to name that as a pain point you could use help overcoming. It could be a weekly email thread with your team where you share your priorities and areas where you foresee needing help. An important piece in this is owning your own weaknesses and blind spots. Let it be a sign of strength when you say, "Hey, I don't want to be off on this, can I talk through this idea with you?" or "I'm feeling overwhelmed by my workload. Can we talk about priorities so I know where to focus my attention?" Vulnerability can never be an excuse for you not being productive or timely with your work, but it should be a method by which you own the important reality that you don't have everything figured out. Often, when you give yourself space to be real, the emotions will fuel you in a strong way, rather than overpower you. Some people may not respond perfectly. In fact, many may not know what to do at first. But when people feel that there is space to be real, that you aren't posturing in any way, and that you ultimately have the bigger goals of success in mind, guards can begin to come down and likely, hopefully, your collective work will be that much smarter, stronger, and frankly, better.

Moving Forward

Many of these instances could be described as reactionary, as responses to experiences that happened *to* me, to barriers I'm met with, to things I can't control about others' choices. And many people face systemic barriers far more present than those I've described. With the help of others, I am working to own how I choose to move forward. While certain barriers may feel less daunting at other organizations, I find it uniquely empowering to be committed to my seat at my alma mater, to work slowly and persistently toward fewer blind spots for myself, for my peers, for students, and for the community that follows me. I choose to work at owning this reality of mine and at remembering that I am committed to my seat because I believe in investing in progress. If you find yourself walking out of a meeting frustrated or feeling particularly exhausted, reflect on these tips.

It can be daunting and demotivating to feel like you can't change how you're perceived or experienced as a woman in your workplace—particularly in a higher education setting, where leadership positions don't tend to have much turnover. You can also become exhausted quickly if you try to tackle the systemic beast by yourself. Yet there are little things you can do to help change the narrative. I found that when I stopped sharing notes, my peers took their own notes. When I asked to cover a certain topic, I had plenty of time and space to speak. With something like age and experience, I found most of those walls were walls I'd projected on myself. When I focused on not being consistently available to work after hours, I found I was more highly regarded in the situations I actively chose to step into. And the more that vulnerability became the norm, the stronger my team felt, and the higher quality our work became. There is certainly more to learn and unlearn. But this has been a good start.

I encourage you to look out for other marginalized coworkers, look out for yourself, remember that you *do* have a lot of power, and begin to teach your colleagues how to treat you, slowly and with thoughtful persistence. I hope you'll find these tips helpful as you become the woman professional you aspire to be.

About the Author

Anna M. Horlacher is a proud Pacific Northwest resident entering her sixth year of professional experience in the higher education industry. Anna has led her team in growing 15 regional chapters and three affinity chapters, has created and stewards a young alumni board, and serves as creative lead and producer for Alumni Reunion Weekend, as well as local signature events. She graduated in May 2020 with her MBA with an emphasis in strategy and is actively assisting with the office's alumni engagement five-year strategic plan. Anna also leads the Diversity, Equity, and Inclusion task force for Alumni & Parent Relations. She derives joy in facilitating meaningful connection and extraordinary experiences for alumni, parents, and students.

A successful day for Anna involves connecting an inquiring student to a supportive alumnus/a, calling and catching up with an alumni leader, brainstorming goals for the upcoming quarter, having coffee with a colleague to simply check in on one another, walking around the bustling campus, absorbing a thoughtful article or video that pushes her thinking, and ultimately making an alumnus/a feel like they are a valued part of the university community. When she's not heads-down at work creating immersive experiences or connecting with alumni, Anna loves trying new breweries and exploring the world with her husband. Anna firmly believes in people first. "We could produce the best engagement opportunities in the industry, but it wouldn't matter if our team wasn't connected and supportive and felt like they belonged here." Anna aspires to help other women feel like they belong in the world of higher education.

ANNA HORLACHER

PART 8

ADVOCATING FOR EQUITY IN HIRING AND THE ALLOCATION OF WORK

CHAPTER 27
THRIVING AS WOMEN LEADERS
IN HIGHER ED

by Eileen Strempel, Doctor of Music
Inaugural Dean of The Herb Alpert School of Music, UCLA

In this time of numerous unknowns, women are perhaps best positioned to navigate our collective path forward. Women—and anyone living in the intersections of communities and identities—have a lived experience honed through their daily negotiations of power imbalances, calculations of risk assessment and mitigation, and are continually re-discovering the necessity of working across difference. These experiences provide a particular advantage in articulating a transformative path forward. Alongside the anguish of this devastating time, there is also the hope that we might somehow emerge into a better world, with the resolution and collective determination to remain true to a reflective and moral self.

This hope and yearning inspire today's renewed need to call women to assume leadership roles. I believe this emphatically, while I simultaneously bristle over the very concept of "women's leadership," and its implication of a distinctive leadership style or working engagement determined by gender. I stumble over various essentialist arguments: "women are more inclusive" or "men are more commanding." We now acknowledge the vast fluidity of the gender spectrum and its varied expressions, thus further rendering "women's leadership" as an outdated, over-simplified, and limited concept.

Indeed, when I reflect upon my various mentors (both male and female), I believe individuals lead in a manner reflective of their experiences, dispositions, and innate moral character, rather than by the attributes evoked by their gender. The leadership skills and abilities of these role models all center around a particular authenticity and alignment with a rigorously reflective and ethical self. Over the years, a most salient fact that I've become keenly aware of is the power of gentle kindness in both men and women.

As a leader, I have also come to appreciate that the ability to remain aligned with the intrinsic motivations of this kindness and moral character is a refined and elusive skill, one challenged by preconceived expectations. As archaic as gender stereotypes might seem, we must acknowledge that gender is often expressed, assumed, reflected, or evident in our bodies, pronouns, and names. Certainly, my experiences (and those of colleagues) include frequent reminders that gender, racial, class, and other stereotypes and biases are alive and well. While my placement on the gender spectrum is largely irrelevant to how I see myself as a leader, I remain keenly aware that my gender is not irrelevant or unnoticed by others. This interpretive reality underscores that the lived experience of "women's leadership" is actually quite different from that of our cisgender male colleagues. This individual lived experience is perhaps not because our leadership is determined by gender, but because it is received through a gendered lens.

There is, of course, a deep history that underpins the female assumption of a traditionally "male" role. For example, as a scholar of women composers, I've written for years about the various reasons that contribute to the fact that most Americans can't name a female composer, although they are likely to be able to name a female visual artist. If one adds the modifier "living" to "female composer," then even more puzzled looks are generated. The lack of recognition of even the possibility of the female—of the actual existence of composer/creators who identify as women—continues to be the case, and this despite the fact that at most university campuses where music is studied, women dominate the percentages of students. This invisibility was reinforced for hundreds of years; for example, credit for compositions by the women who did manage to compose was generally given to their brothers or husbands (or they "protected" their reputation by publishing under pseudonyms). Of course, women have been historically actively discouraged from many fields, in addition to music. Perhaps it's not surprising that we see a similar absence extended into the leadership of our nation's institutions of higher education.

The absence of female role models in my current role is perhaps revealing. I was thrilled and honored to be selected to serve as the Inaugural Dean of UCLA's Herb Alpert School of Music, the first and only school of music in the University of California System and the first new school at UCLA in decades. After my appointment, I was immediately filled with an urge to reach out to other female leaders of our nation's top music schools, hoping for helpful advice and perhaps insider knowledge and perspective. In those early moments of excitement, I quickly crafted my impromptu, unofficial "top twenty" list of the best music schools across the country and searched for the names of the deans and presidents leading those schools. As my list of leaders grew, I slowly realized that only one woman was on that list, and I stared in disbelief. One? Five percent? In the third decade of the 21st century? Clearly, the well-known lack of STEM (science, technology, engineering and math) gender parity has nothing on music.

What I've experienced as the leader of a music school is emblematic of larger, systemic issues. Despite the best intentions not to discriminate, too many people continue to hold significantly different expectations for women leaders, whether they are aware of this or not. There is no research-based proof of innate differences in women's and men's capabilities; however, there is a preponderance of evidence that identical behavior is evaluated quite differently depending on gender. Why else would 80% (yes, eighty percent) of my tenured music department colleagues be male in 2020? I deeply admire each and every faculty member, but I am reminded (on a daily basis) how challenging it is for even the most "woke" colleague to simply stop lecturing and to leave space for others. It's an occupational hazard for all of us in the professoriate, but I find the consistent exclusion of other voices to be harmful and stifling. Not to mention exhausting.

Especially in the age of the #MeToo movement, we need to have these conversations more than ever. The glacial pace of change concerning women in leadership is a direct consequence of deep-seated, patriarchal, colonialist assumptions, ones that inhibit all of our lives and psyches almost by default. Whether in or outside of the academy, we find ourselves in an inexplicable time. The #MeToo movement that emerged out of the accusations against Harvey Weinstein in 2017 underscored, perhaps more than anything, the problematic nature of power imbalances. Perhaps it is this imbalance, rather than perceived gender roles, that has led women to develop a range of strategies for how to wield power and promote change without being perceived so negatively that they can no longer be effective. As I write today in 2020, the intersection of leadership and power is felt keenly in this new era that we find ourselves suddenly inhabiting, a time further marked by the global COVID-19 pandemic and a time of racial crisis re-illuminated with the murder of George Floyd. In this crisis—and despite the essentialist framework— what might women leaders teach us? Might the skill of remaining aligned with a moral core now be more important than ever? Might the ability to continually reanimate kindness towards everyone, regardless of an individual's status or power, have renewed importance in our current era? How might the more intentional inclusion of all voices help us to foster a sense of community in this new age of social and racial unrest, insolation, and physical distancing?

Let us be clear. Women are capable of extraordinary leadership. The countries that most successfully navigated the pandemic (at least at the time of writing this chapter) are led by women: Germany, Iceland, Finland, and New Zealand. In my home state of California, it was London Breed, the first black woman to ever hold the office of mayor of San Francisco, who issued a "shelter in place" order, before the male mayor of Los Angeles and the governor of California. It was female leaders who made the first brave and unpopular judgement calls to shelter at home in the face of the spread of the novel coronavirus. The fact that the three inspirational co-founders of Black Lives Matter are women—Patrisse Khan-Cullors, Alicia Garza, and Opal Tometi—should not be lost on anyone. All of these inspiring female leaders have displayed a profound ability to protect and advocate for our citizens and to remain true to the intrinsic call to do so. These leaders listened and worked across the table to make decisions and move decisively forward defined by a clear purpose. There is a thrill in this recognition, a celebration of the life-saving leadership and influence of women at the helm.

In this time of our shared pandemic and social and racial unrest, perhaps the COVID-generation will be the one to truly and fully realize that effective leadership takes many forms, colors, and shapes. I believe we are only beginning to articulate the faintest outlines of the depth of our collective entropy, the slow reveal and unveiling of the broad parameters of the impact that COVID-19, intertwined with Black Lives Matter, will forge in our daily lives and in our society. Responding to these vague, emerging contours of pain, anguish, inequality, and unknown catastrophe, all leaders are called to action.

In our global struggle and battle with both COVID-19 and racist, systemic inequality, the urge to engage in an instinctive moment of shared reckoning seems inevitable. We all struggle to make sense of this invisible virus while we simultaneously engage with the painful history and legacy of enslavement. It is humbling that in the relative quiet of "safer at home," our core urges and reduced activities revolve around family and friends, community, identity, and culture.

This fraught time frames a growing recognition of necessity; we must craft a shared pathway forward. A national effort is essential if we are to ever navigate out of a pandemic and, in this complex moment of crisis and opportunity, finally forge an inclusive future grounded in collective responsibility. On various fronts, women are leading our renewed focus on healing, representation, and caring. These inspiring leaders are a salient demonstration of the power of women to inspire and navigate change towards the ethical reimagining of our world for all.

As individual leaders, this is a time to reflect upon intersections of our communities and identities, and to harness the strength of our lived experiences. This is, no doubt, one of the most crucial and transformative confluence of challenges we have faced in higher education, our society, and our culture. The issues raised in this moment will require engagement, conversations, decisions, and actions that will last deep into the future. As female leaders, we bring a lifetime of savvy in successfully navigating power imbalances and working across difference to bring about positive change. In this moment and beyond, these are the skills and experiences that effectively position us to be our country's truthtellers and wayfarers towards a better tomorrow.

Resources

Anderson, Cami. "Why Do Women Make Such Good Leaders During COVID-19?" *Forbes*. April 19, 2020. Accessed at:

https://www.forbes.com/sites/camianderson1/2020/04/19/why-do-women-make-such-good-leaders-during-covid-19/#6cddfdbe42fc

George, Bill. *Discover Your True North.* Hoboken: John Wiley and Sons, Inc., 2015.

About the Author

Dr. Eileen Strempel currently serves as the Inaugural Dean of UCLA's Herb Alpert School of Music. Strempel relishes the joy of founding a "start-up company," as the school is the first and only school of music in the University of California System, and recently formed as a result of a generous $30M donation by trumpeter, producer, and artist Herb Alpert.

Dean Strempel's scholarly interests focus on the music of women composers. Her work includes numerous recordings, commissions, articles, and edited volumes that examine the political, social, and musical contexts of the most influential female composers of our time. As a trained opera singer and a Presidential Scholar in the Arts, Strempel is also a nationally recognized champion for transfer students and views superb public education as one of the principal social justice issues of our time.

Dr. Strempel, with co-author Stephen J. Handel, has completed two books: *Transition and Transformation: Fostering Transfer Student Success* and the follow-up, *Transition and Transformation: New Research Fostering Transfer Student Success*, both with the University of North Georgia Press. Their third book, *Beyond Free College: Making Higher Education Work for 21st Century Students*, was published in January 2021 with Roman and Littlefield Press. Both authors are long-term members of the National Advisory Board for the National Institute for the Study of Transfer Students (NISTS). Articles and essays by Dr. Strempel include "Transfer Matters More than Ever," "Strategic Collaboration in an Increasingly Interconnected World," and "Fostering a Receptive Transfer Student Institutional Ecosystem."

CHAPTER 28
STEPPING AWAY FROM
OUTDATED HIRING PRACTICES

by Umme Mansoory, M.Ed.
Learning Strategist – Mentorship and Leadership
Thompson Rivers University

I identify as a young settler in the hereditary homelands of the Tk'emlúps te Secwépemc within Secwépemc'ulucw and as a racially marginalized Muslim woman of Pakistani decent with an invisible disability. My areas of privilege include my education, my employment, my ability to speak English fluently and unaccented, and I am a cisgender, second-generation British-Canadian. I have navigated my identity my entire life. I have struggled with my religion, my appearance, my language, and my ancestry for as long as I can remember. I am finally in a place in my life where I have accepted who I am, including the advantages and disadvantages I have in society.

I also identify as an emerging leader in higher education. However, I often tussle with reconciling my identity with opportunities in my field. Many racially marginalized individuals habitually question if a job they did not get was because of their name or their identity. As an active member of the Muslim community, I have intentionally hidden my volunteerism with Muslim organizations in an attempt to not be perceived as a Muslim "extremist." Unfortunately, like myself, many Muslims in the Western world do. Why? you ask.

STEPPING AWAY FROM OUTDATED HIRING PRACTICES

We minimize our impact in our communities as a way to modestly advance our careers and make our mark in the world.

My advice for leaders who have the ability to support the careers of women identifying with equity-seeking groups is to re-evaluate your hiring processes and interview practices to address systemic inequalities placed on marginalized candidates.

I once applied for a student-facing administrative position at a post-secondary institution. I was confident that if given this opportunity, I could do the job well. I had experience that was relevant, a passion to support students, and the eagerness to take the next step in my career. I was encouraged by the hiring manager and several others on the team who gave me confidence in my decision to put myself forward as a candidate. Moreover, I was motivated by the realization that, if offered the job, I could serve as a racially marginalized professional, well positioned to support minority students in a system that is dominated by white professionals.

I prepared for this interview for days. I was excited at the prospect of this next stage of my career. My interview passed and I was not offered the job. I was told that I did not speak *enough* about my previous work experiences that would contribute to my ability to fulfill the responsibilities of this role. I was told the successful candidate had far more experience than me.

Admittedly, I was nervous in the interview and may have missed out on small details that could have strengthened my responses. However, the hiring manager was well aware of my abilities to fulfill many aspects of this job. I worked with her directly, she had supervised me in the past, she knew of my previous work experiences, and she was familiar with my work ethic. I was confused because I didn't think I would be disadvantaging myself by not mentioning every detail about my previous work experiences. I spent the next few days kicking myself for not saying more that could have made me shine.

In regard to the successful candidate, I had prayed that whomever they did hire would be another racially marginalized individual who could serve the demographic of our students, with the intercultural competencies needed to deeply understand multi-layered student challenges. An announcement was made that a white woman was hired because of her "years of experience." The irony in all of this was that it was an unsaid expectation that I would help train the new hire for a position I was interviewed for, yet for which I was considered unqualified.

The woman they hired was incredibly lovely and intelligent. We quickly became good friends, and I held no resentment towards her or the hiring manager. I am in no way implying that I did not get the job *because* I am racially marginalized or that the successful candidate was undeserving. I have accepted that there will be times in my life when things will not work out how I plan. I truly believe we are all doing our best to ensure students are being supported. However, that does not mean we cannot do better in intentionally diversifying our teams to ensure fair representation of staff for our students. The system we currently operate within perpetuates *white normativity*, in the sense that white people are considered the standard. Specifically in employment, white people tend to hire white people. This experience highlighted that for me.

I went into the interview confident that despite a perceived lack of "on paper" experience, my lived experiences would count for something. I speak the native language of our largest student population, but this was not viewed as an asset. I grew up as an ethnic and religious minority in Canada. Despite the Canadian multicultural stereotype, I have been bullied, discriminated against, and spat at with racial slurs. Those experiences were not recognized. I have navigated higher education as an ethnic, religious, and disabled minority. The understanding that comes with having lived those experiences was not considered an advantage. What the all-white hiring panel was looking for was experience in technical skills. *Do I have experience drafting professional documents? Can I communicate with stakeholders? Have I attended certain training?* Ultimately, those skills can be taught. The relationships that are formed over common experiences of minorities cannot be taught. The connection with students—ensuring they feel seen, heard, and understood on a more meaningful level—is what is going to impact their success and retention as marginalized students in higher education. When we talk about equitable practices in hiring, the lived experiences of equity-seeking individuals and their ability to relate to other equity-seeking students needs to be given importance and value.

I later had a thoughtful and candid conversation with a superior of mine. We talked about race, equity, and diversity at our institution. I brought forth concerns about how our staff demographic does not represent the diversity we see in our students. At the time of our conversation, all of our student-facing staff, with the exception of myself and very few others, were cisgender, able-bodied, and white, whereas our student body is highly diverse in ethnicity, sexual orientation, and physical and cognitive abilities. I know my superior understood the principle behind my concerns. She has always been a champion of equity and diversity, but she made a comment that struck me. She said that racially marginalized people don't often apply for some of our critical, student-facing jobs. Respectfully, I do not agree with that. I shared my experience with her about how I, and others I know, have applied for positions within our department that needed minority representation and we were not selected because we lacked "on paper" experience. I reminded her that historically, it has been white people who have had opportunities to advance their careers and obtain those sought-after and desirable documented experiences. If we want to sincerely diversify our teams and truly represent minorities in positions of leadership, we must be willing to step away from outdated hiring methods of assessing only a candidate's work experience. We need to assign value and consideration to the lived stories and lessons of minorities. And it is essential that we evaluate an individual's potential to succeed at the job. Ask yourself, *"This person may lack the technical skills needed, but do they have the potential to learn these skills and do this job well?"* If you find yourself leaning towards *yes*, take that leap of faith and give them the opportunity to demonstrate their capabilities. This also becomes an opportunity for you to mentor a young professional who is hungry to learn. A mentoring relationship is a very special one. If you take a chance on a professional who is keen for this opportunity, more often than not, they will prove to be engaged employees. This, in turn, contributes to the greater health of the institution.

Leaders should not view interviews as survival of the fittest: the one with the best interview wins. In post-secondary environments, especially considering that we shape the best practices of future employers and leaders, we need to look at the bigger picture of what our students and society needs, the gaps we need to fill, and identify people who can help us achieve these goals. As with any search for talent, attributing a lack of minority applicants does not absolve you from the responsibility to seek them out. We exist. Just like you may recruit for educational leaders such as deans and chairs, seek out professionals that belong to minority groups, especially for roles where you have identified intercultural understanding as being an essential skill for the job. Embedding your job listings with an equity disclaimer that you are looking for individuals from certain minority groups will generate responses.

Looking back to our roots, North America was colonized by peoples of diverse backgrounds with dreams and aspirations of contributing to the foundation of a better tomorrow. Representation matters if you want to have a society that represents all people. I cannot speak for all minorities, but from the conversations I have had with my peers and colleagues, we are pining for opportunities to demonstrate our potential. We are thirsty to share our ideas and eager to leave behind a meaningful legacy. But, in this cycle of being denied opportunities to grow professionally, many of us wilt in our mid-level jobs, hoping that our children can go one step further than us.

Checklist

Below is a preliminary checklist for engaging in equitable hiring practices. It is my hope that these tips provide guidance for you in diversifying your team, granting opportunities to equity-seeking candidates, and providing representation to your student body.

☐ Include an equity statement in your job listing encouraging diversification of candidates. You may also include an optional self-identification survey in your application to gauge the diversity of candidates prior to shortlisting.

☐ Advertise the position outside of personal connections, using a variety of channels. This can mitigate unfair advantages given to candidates within the same network as the hiring panel and can diversify the applicant pool.

☐ Take time to review your hiring practices, ensuring you are not simply doing what you have done in the past out of convenience. This includes structuring the interview so that all candidates are asked the same questions and creating an objective rubric that is not based on technical skills but rather, on competencies.

☐ Demonstrate commitment to accommodating candidates during the interview process, by including accessible and clear language in your interview invitation and questions, and by reducing barriers in the interview environment.

☐ Promote diversity of perspective and fair representation by ensuring that there is more than one interviewer on the hiring panel and at least one interviewer that belongs to an equity-seeking or racially marginalized group.

☐ Ask interview questions that spark conversation beyond previous work experience and skills. This provides insight into the lived experiences of candidates. Sample questions include:

- What is the toughest situation you have faced as an educator/professional and how have you handled it?

- Describe your post-secondary experience. What would you improve for students based on your experience?

- What life experiences or skills do you bring to this position that could help you relate to and empathize with our students?

- What are you passionate about? How will you showcase your passions in this position?

- Convince me that I should send a student to you for emotional/academic/financial support. (This question can change depending on the position being interviewed for).

   o What is something you have read recently that has impacted you deeply as an educator/professional, and how will you apply it to this position?

☐ Consider your overall student population and the demographic of students the role intends to serve. Are there any gaps that need to be filled in terms of representation? Does the candidate reflect that demographic or need?

☐ If the candidate is lacking desirable technical skills, does the candidate demonstrate the potential to learn quickly and gain the necessary skills?

Resources

Banerjee, Rupa, Jeffree G. Reitz, and Phil Oreopoulos. "Do Large Employers Treat Racial Minorities More Fairly? An Analysis of Canadian Field Experiment Data." *Canadian Public Policy,* 44(1), p. 1-12, 2018.

Burgess, Shelley, and Beth Houf. *Lead Like a Pirate: Make School Amazing for Your Students and Staff.* San Diego: Dave Burgess Consulting, Inc., 2017.

Stovall, Janet. "How to Get Serious About Diversity and Inclusion in the Workplace." Janet Stovall [Video]. TED. September 13, 2018.
https://www.youtube.com/watch?v=kvdHqS3ryw0

Wehde, Mark. "Corporate Culture, Stereotypes, and Discrimination." *IEEE Engineering Management Review,* 46(3), p. 16-19, 2018.

About the Author

Umme Mansoory is a Learning Strategist for Mentorship and Leadership at Thompson Rivers University, a vocational, teaching, and research institution in British Columbia, Canada. She obtained her Bachelor of Arts from Simon Fraser University in 2017 and a Master of Education in Educational Leadership from the University of Calgary in 2020. Umme has over a decade of educational experience in museums, public libraries, children's programming, and post-secondary advising. Umme's areas of interest include equity, diversity, student retention, and student success.

CHAPTER 29
FAIRNESS IN SERVICE

by Martha A. Garcia-Murillo, Ph.D.
Senior Associate Dean
Syracuse University

It is not unusual for female faculty members to be concerned about salaries compared to those of their male colleagues. However, we often fail to recognize that our time is also valuable. Lack of time early in our careers can be the difference between receiving tenure or not. My concern about service allocation came about, in part, because one of my colleagues commented that female assistant professors had significantly higher service loads than their male counterparts. Studies have shown that women often do more work than men. Minority faculty also do more, in part due to the need for diversity on many university committees (Guarino and Borden, 2017). My colleague's claim, though, was difficult for me to confirm. This was because when service was allocated, for the most part it replicated activities the year before and was recorded on multiple pages. The document also did not show how heavy or light a given service activity was.

When trying to determine how to be fair in the allocation of service to my colleagues, I struggled with notions of equality, which means to treat everyone similarly. From my perspective, an equality standard fails to recognize that people differ in circumstances, preferences, and skills (Sun, 2014). Therefore, when making service allocations I decided to focus on equity, which emphasizes treatment and fairness (Raphael, 1946).

There is an important difference between salary and service. Salary is paid in a single currency unit. Service, however, cannot be easily reduced to a single measure because these commitments differ in requirements, resources, and time. There is visible and invisible service, rewarding and tedious, local and remote, short but intense (e.g., faculty searches and admissions), long but light and steady (e.g., curriculum, program committees), and sporadic or single events once a term, to be done by a single person or by a group. Sometimes the same service work can vary from year to year. Some examples are personnel evaluation and search committees which vary depending on the number of candidates to be promoted or hired in a given year. We had instances where our untenured female faculty members were responsible for developing and updating four to seven classes. In contrast, I found, some of our male colleagues rejected the same task. Service duties can also take an emotional toll because they may entail making difficult decisions, such as those on academic integrity committees. Anecdotally, this emotional service appears to be borne by our female faculty. For some faculty, service can be both enjoyable and meaningful, as it may enable greater interaction with colleagues or students.

An equity yardstick you can use is that your action should not result in giving more service to an assistant professor rather than to a tenured professor whose employment is not at risk. We should thus protect faculty members seeking tenure from heavy service obligations. You should also avoid giving an administrative duty to someone who is not good at it or dislikes it when there is a willing and capable colleague. It also may not be fair to assign extra service to someone as punishment for behavior that you do not like. Similarly, I would consider it unjust to give more service to nice people or those who are afraid to say no, which may occur more frequently with untenured faculty, women, and minorities (Mitchell and Hesli, 2013). Finally, it is not fair to frequently assign additional service to women and minorities even when the goal is to bring diversity to a committee.

While service comes in multiple forms, fairness may require developing a comparable unit. My first attempt at finding some sort of equity was to calculate the approximate number of hours that service duties would entail. I did this by asking the chair of each committee to tell me the approximate number and length of meetings, as well as the expected amount of work required. If you were to do this, you would likely find that many are university-level committees, and you may not always know the chair or feel comfortable contacting this person to gather time commitment information. For those, I decided to make an estimate, which was probably inaccurate. Using those estimated times, I then proceeded to calculate the time that the service commitments amounted to for each faculty member. Based on this information, I then determined if these hours were equitably allocated by rank, gender, and type of faculty. Even if the time estimates were accurate, it would take substantial effort to gather such data every year. A third potential problem is that faculty may over- or underestimate the time that the service takes. I thus abandoned time allocations for service.

The approach that I eventually adopted was to categorize and assign numbers to each service duty as heavy (3), medium (2), and light (1). This has worked better because it alleviates time inaccuracies and has allowed me to quantify service and calculate averages. The next step was for me to determine what was heavy, medium, and light service. While it is imprecise, I decided that a committee that meets once a month for one and a half to two hours and often has work outside of that time could be categorized as medium service. Service that is substantially more than that would be a 3 (heavy) and less than that—or infrequent meetings, or with little outside work— would be a 1 (light). I could then use these numbers to help determine if the allocation was fair.

Another piece in the service allocation puzzle is how much service to allocate to each faculty member. I needed to consider the percentage of time that faculty members are expected to dedicate to service and then convert to the equivalent of the H-M-L calculations. I also needed to determine what to count. From total expected service, I only took sixty percent of that total to be allocated to either the university or the academic unit. This is because faculty often take professional service outside of the university that supports their career as well as the mission of the university, such as being a conference chair or a journal editor. It would be difficult to account for that service internally, and it is thus left to each faculty member to manage it with the 40% of their total expected service duties. If a faculty member volunteered for service that does not support the essential operations of the unit, I did not count it.

Normally tenure/tenure track faculty members allocate 20% of their time to service and, assuming a 40-hour work week, this would be equivalent to eight hours of service, of which I allocated five hours (60% of the total) for the university or our academic unit. Thus, there would be a total of 180 hours per academic year, which would be equivalent to eight H-M-L units (e.g., four medium service duties). Your objective should thus be to pay attention to service allocated to female and minority faculty and ensure that they are not overburdened, particularly if they are untenured.

If a faculty member is given a course reduction to take on an administrative position, we then have to convert teaching time to service time. Since a class meets once a week for a least three hours plus meetings, preparation, and grading, it wouldn't be unusual for teaching to take between five and eight hours a week or between 20 and 32 hours a month per class, or approximately 100 hours per course. This would be equivalent to slightly over four H-M-L service units per course.

Up to this point, I presented service allocations as if they were independent of all other responsibilities (research, practice, and teaching), which is not the case in most institutions. You could then modify them to account for individual circumstances depending on the load of other responsibilities, which could include managing large grants, having an active and successful research agenda, or teaching large classes.

If you were to try this method of allocating service among your faculty, there are several things you would need to decide, such as the percentage of service you want to allocate to the school and the university. I would not suggest trying to account for service outside of the university. You also need to determine what counts as service. One of the most difficult service duties to allocate is advising doctoral students, because such service touches all of the pieces of a faculty member's teaching, research, and service. You will thus need to decide what portion of that service to allocate to service alone. In our school we have had female faculty advising four or five doctoral students with no research benefits to these professors, one of whom is untenured. Do you want to protect certain categories of faculty from service obligations? If so, how much less will you give them?

The process is not perfect because some committees may require certain expertise that only one or two of your faculty members have. Some faculty will have personal preferences more aligned with one type of service versus another. If you want your faculty to be engaged, you need to try, to the greatest extent possible, to align their preferences to their service. Regarding this last point, the first time I asked faculty their service preferences, I did it with a form. Most requested their previous committees, which gave me little room for a more equitable allocation. The second time, I talked to each faculty member and got a menu of preferences. I found out in this process that many were not aware of many committees at the school and university. With more options given, I was able to allocate service more easily and equitably.

I began this process of allocating service equitably after taking the position of senior associate dean. The first time I did this I used a spreadsheet, but I quickly realized that to manage the many variables of service required a database. This new tool calculates for me the number of activities and committees a person participates in, as well as their H-M-L loads. It was through this process that I was able to ensure that female assistant professors did not have a higher service load compared to their male colleagues.

I recognize that this process has to be adapted to unique cases and unusual circumstances. As I write this, we are several months into the COVID-19 pandemic, which has added substantial service work for faculty as we try to find solutions. National trends in this area suggest that women were disproportionately negatively affected because of unexpected household responsibilities. You could modify the service allocation to reduce, to an extent, the service of those female colleagues. We need to continue to find ways of treating our colleagues kindly, and part of doing so is to allocate service fairly.

Resources

Curcio, Andrea A., and Mary A. Lynch. "Addressing Social Loafing on Faculty Committees." *Journal of Legal Education*, 67(1), p. 242–262, 2017.

Guarino, Cassandra M., and Victor M. H. Borden. "Faculty Service Loads and Gender: Are Women Taking Care of the Academic Family?" *Research in Higher Education*, vol. 58, no. 6, 2017, pp. 672–694., doi:10.1007/s11162-017-9454-2.

Mitchell, Sara McLaughlin, and Viki L. Hesli. "Women Don't Ask? Women Don't Say No? Bargaining and Service in the

Political Science Profession." *PS: Political Science & Politics*, 46(2), p. 355–369, 2013.

Misra, Joya, Jennifer Hickes Lundquist, Elissa Holmes, and Stephanie Agiomavritis. "The Ivory Ceiling of Service Work." *Academe*, 97(1), p. 22–26, 2011.

O'Meara, KerryAnn. "Ensuring Equity in Service Work (Opinion)." *Inside Higher Ed*, 2018. www.insidehighered.com/advice/2018/05/10/ensuring-equity-service-work-opinion.

Sun, Amy. "Equality Is Not Enough: What the Classroom Has Taught Me About Justice." *Everyday Feminism*, 25 Sept. 2014. everydayfeminism.com/2014/09/equality-is-not-enough/.

UMD. *The Faculty Workload and Rewards Project*, 2019. https://facultyworkloadandrewardsproject.umd.edu

About the Author

Martha Garcia-Murillo is the Senior Associate Dean at the School of Information Studies and previously the Director of the Telecommunications and Network Management (TNM) program. Under her leadership, TNM increased the number of women in a male-dominated field. She also leads the school's efforts on diversity and inclusion, as well as the development of strategic initiatives for the iSchool. She earned a Ph.D. in Political Economy and Public Policy from the

MARTHA A. GARCIA-MURILLO

University of Southern California. She teaches in the area of information policy and has trained regulators from around the world, helping them improve access to information and facilitate investment in the ICT sector.

Dr. Garcia-Murillo's research has been motivated by issues of development and the wellbeing of individuals and nations. Her work has focused on the impact of technology on the private sector, the government, and people such as those displaced by automation and other economic and policy processes.

PART 9

NEGOTIATION

384

CHAPTER 30
WOMEN, POLITICS, AND INTERSECTIONALITY

by Sandra Miles, Ph.D.
Vice President of Student Affairs
Flagler College

Overview

Within higher education there is a very clear glass ceiling that is still evident within the highest ranks of leadership. In 2016 *Forbes* reported that only 30% of college presidents were women. Though women continue to make strides in earning the experience and credentials necessary to be considered for senior leadership, there are still roadblocks in the form of hiring practices, gendered expectations, stereotypes, and the devaluing of women's work and contributions.

While the above-stated roadblocks are formidable and arduous, there are tools that you can employ to overcome some of the stereotypes that can sometimes work against women seeking promotion and advancement. Specifically, women who engage actively, intentionally, and effectively in the politics of higher education are better able to advance further and faster in their career.

Though most people, particularly women, tend to view politics in a negative light, the truth is that whether we realize it or want to, we all engage in politics regularly. The difference for women is that we tend to direct our political activity towards subordinates and/or those within the organization who are not in a position to support and/or influence our advancement. For example, while men will reach out to a dean or vice president to schedule lunch to get to know them and possibly earn a mentor, women will invest that same energy into inviting her direct reports to lunch to get to know them and possibly *become* a mentor.

While there is value in engaging in both types of intentional connections with colleagues, it is important for women to remember that strategic engagement with campus leaders is not inherently disingenuous. Further, when women focus all or most of their energy on developing the next generation of leaders, they do so at the expense of their own development and also limit their exposure to those in a position to get to know them in meaningful ways and help them excel.

Listed below are four recommendations for women to engage in the politics of higher education in meaningful ways. Though the recommendations are generally applicable to all people, specific insight will be offered as it relates to the difference in the way women of different races experience workplace politics. Specifically, in my dissertation study I studied workplace stereotypes and social support of black women in higher education. An unexpected finding revealed that black and white women tend to engage with the environment in different ways, resulting in different professional attainment outcomes. This difference in outcomes can be seen clearly in the percentage of women college presidents. While the

American Council of Education found that 30% of college presidents were women, that number, further broken down by race, indicated that 25% of college presidents were white women and 5% were women of color. Within that study, the woman-of-color category included black, Latina, Middle Eastern, American Indian, Asian, and multi-ethnic. This information indicates that women of color are dramatically underrepresented in senior roles. With this in mind, slight modifications to some approaches will be offered based on relevant cultural considerations. Please note that, while the original data collected only included enough samples from black and white women to be reported, over the past few years when presenting these strategies, I have found that Asian women and Latina women who identify as white relate more closely to the self-identified experiences of white women, and Native American women and Latina women who identify as black or Hispanic/Latina relate more closely to the self-identified experiences of black women.

Tips for Making Politics Work for You

1. Get to know your colleagues.

While this seems simple and straightforward, often women who aspire to leadership tend to feel pressure to follow the "rules" of professionalism. While you may engage in casual conversations around the office Keurig, the extent to which you are willing to engage outside of work hours may vary.

While it is smart to manage others' perceptions of you, letting your guard down gradually and carefully can make a world of difference for the way your colleagues begin to value you as a whole person. Colleagues who value and understand you become critical allies along your leadership journey.

Note: Some white women tend to establish fewer boundaries when developing relationships on campus with other colleagues. Although the desire to be completely open comes from a positive place, the danger in not compartmentalizing relationships and setting clear boundaries for all relationships is that there are some colleagues who will not automatically abide by the expectations of an all-inclusive relationship. Meaning that not all colleagues should be trusted to be friends, but they can be professional colleagues who can assist as sounding boards and strategic partners. Compartmentalizing relationships and expanding your network can be incredibly helpful as you continue to develop your leadership. Further, colleagues who are not "friends" are more likely to give the type of critical and constructive feedback that will help you expand your skill set and learn how to connect with those with diverse backgrounds and perspectives.

2. Invite key players to lunch.

Admittedly, this one is tricky. If you attempt to cold call a leader who you've never spoken to and invite them to lunch, it is very likely that they will decline the invitation. So beyond just inviting someone to lunch, it's important to actually engage key leaders in casual conversations to determine if they are even the kind of person that you would want to sit through an hour of awkward conversation with. So the more complete tip is take some time to get to know key leaders (to the extent that you can) and, if it turns out that the person has a personality you connect with, *then* invite them to lunch. Engage in small talk before the meeting starts, walk back to the office with your boss and discuss hobbies, ask the president about their weekend. As I stated above, politics don't have to be disingenuous, they just need to involve a level of strategy to be meaningful. Personally, I'm an introvert and I loathe one-on-one meetings with people I'm not fully comfortable with, so when I first started pushing myself to try to engage with senior leaders, I would make it a group lunch of 3-4. That way I did not have to feel the pressure of having to carry a conversation, and I also had a wingman who could say nice things about me (and vice versa). Over time, my discomfort started to fade, and eventually I became comfortable having lunch with colleagues whether I knew them well or not.

In addition to offering an invitation, be sure to be straightforward with the agenda. Now that I'm a senior leader, there are times when colleagues invite me out to lunch "just to get to know me" and, honestly, I'm always apprehensive about what that means. When someone says clearly "I want to pick your brain about…" or "I'm hoping you can help me navigate through…," that puts me much more at ease because I know what is expected of me and it's clear that there is no ulterior motive. Senior leaders realize that we represent proximity to power. We don't want to be used, but we absolutely understand that we can be helpful. There are some senior leaders who have no interest in engaging in that way, but you'll learn who those leaders are through your casual conversation, so you'll know not to invite them to lunch.

3. Seek out potential sponsors.

Sponsors are leaders with influence who can speak highly of you and support your advancement. For example, a sponsor may be privy to organizational restructuring well before it is announced publicly. During the planning phase, a sponsor could drop your name as a potential asset in the new role. Further, a sponsor can give you a heads up and tell you when and where to go to position yourself in front of the right people. A sponsor can also help with setting up or inviting you to lunches with other senior leaders so you don't have to take that risk.

A sponsor has to choose you (hence the use of the words "potential" sponsor), but you can do a lot to show those in positions of leadership who may be supportive of you that you are worth the investment. Specifically, you can:

- Volunteer to serve on committees led by the potential sponsor and then contribute in meaningful ways.

- Schedule a meeting to discuss an identified problem and bring a potential solution.

- Identify ways to relieve budget stress and offer well-thought-out recommendations. While others are asking for additional funding, a person who is able to identify cost savings can be a critical asset.

4. Don't settle for letting your hard work get noticed.

Many women are taught to let your hard work speak for you. However, the unfortunate reality is that our employers will notice and even appreciate our hard work, but when the time comes to offer a promotion, the person who is chosen is usually the person that people want to be around, not the person who works the hardest. While that may seem unfair, in truth, senior administrators spend a lot of time together and often engage in tough negotiations with each other. When making a decision about who you want to engage in difficult conversations with, a person will choose the person they think they can communicate with over the person who does a good job but who is untested in difficult conversations.

If you want to be considered to be a trusted leader, then *you* need to get noticed for the right reasons. Your colleagues need to see you speaking up in meetings, being diplomatic, offering great ideas, and contributing to the overall success of the institution. Producing an impressive report from behind your closed office door will get you a reputation for being great at delivering reports, not leading.

Note: For black women, this advice is critical. Often, when trust is broken, some black women will withdraw from the social aspect of being engaged in the workplace. As a result, finding sponsors or creating allies among colleagues becomes almost impossible. Further, when black women are not able to show their full selves at work, your colleagues, rather than making an effort, tend to default to workplace stereotypes that are usually more negative than positive.

Conclusion

Women experience a variety of barriers, stereotypes, and threats to their success. The above tips are not presented to minimize or dismiss the legitimate experiences that we have all faced. Additionally, it is possible that, despite our best intentions, we may still interact with colleagues who lack integrity and who make it impossible to engage with them in meaningful ways. Over my career I have certainly experienced my fair share of colleagues that I didn't trust or desire to get to know in any way. I am not suggesting that you ignore your intuition or attempt to befriend anyone whose values do not align with your own. I am suggesting that most of our colleagues can be incredibly helpful in supporting our professional and personal development if we give them a chance.

Are there risks to putting yourself out there? Absolutely! I have been burned twice while engaging in what I thought were legitimate colleague relationships. One resulted in a severed friendship and the other resulted in me leaving the campus altogether. Both of those situations, though painful at the time, have turned out to be meaningful, because I now know my limits for vulnerability as well as where my values lie. Since I have never engaged in insincere attempts to get to know colleagues, I have no regrets—only lessons learned.

In contrast, as it relates to being promoted, securing references, and/or having colleagues in my corner, I have benefitted overwhelmingly from putting myself out there and actually getting to know my peers in meaningful ways. My hope is that this information will help you make meaningful connections that can propel you forward in your career.

Resources

Miles, Sandra. *Left Behind: The Status of Black Women in Higher Education Administration.* Florida State University Libraries: Electronic Theses, Treatises, and Dissertations, 2012. https://diginole.lib.fsu.edu/islandora/object/fsu:183012/dat astream/PDF/view

Moody, Josh. "Where Are All The Female College Presidents?" *Forbes*, 6 July 2018. www.forbes.com/sites/joshmoody/2018/07/05/where-are-all-the-female-college-presidents/

About the Author

Dr. Sandra Miles is the Vice President for Student Affairs and Chief Diversity and Inclusion Officer at Flagler College. She has spent the last 15 years serving as a leader and administrator in higher education. Specifically, she has extensive experience managing crises, strategic planning, developing leadership programs, working with persons with disabilities, serving as a Dean of Students, Chief Student Affairs Officer, Chief

Diversity Officer, Deputy Title IX Coordinator, and mediating disputes.

Dr. Miles completed her doctoral work at Florida State University in 2012, earning a Ph.D. in Higher Education Administration. She also completed her Bachelor's and Master's degrees at the University of Central Florida. In addition to her career and educational achievements, Dr. Sandra Miles is the Chair of the NASPA Center for Women Board, a national speaker for Campus Outreach Services, the Immediate Past National Director of the Black Female Development Circle, Inc, and is an active alumnae member of Delta Sigma Theta Sorority, Inc.

CHAPTER 31
THE INTERVIEW: EXERCISE CONTROL OVER THE OUTCOME

by Lucy Leske
Senior Partner, WittKieffer

"I try to perfect my strong points and make my weaknesses adequate."
- Billie Jean King

The Skill of Interviewing

Interviewing for leadership positions is a lot like a competitive tennis match. If you stand at the baseline waiting for the ball to come to you, you will lose, but if you approach the net and anticipate shots, you can be more strategic and control the outcome. In nearly 30 years as an executive search consultant for higher education, I have observed hundreds of candidate interviews. I have to say that when women understand that they have the ability to influence the outcome with better planning, strategy, and control, they stand a better chance of moving forward in the process. Because institutions of higher education say they want more diverse leadership teams, they insist that we help recruit diverse pools. However, sometimes they can't seem to get out of their own way, and they trip up on process or unintended bias, especially when it comes to women. I have observed deliberate bias and discrimination, but only rarely. I believe that the inability of more women to advance in leadership searches is due to far more subtle reasons rooted in stereotype. Effective interview technique can help break that trend.

An Action Plan

Model leadership behavior

None of this is a game, of course. I often describe the interview to candidates as more like an audition. The fact is that committee members or decision makers are actually judging performance and behavior just as much as, if not more than, content. This suggests that you play the part during the interview and model the leadership behavior you will bring to the role. If you imagine the interview as your first meeting with your first group of colleagues, be the leader they want you to be by facilitating their task. They need to hire a leader; help them reach their goal. Plan ahead by considering what the committee needs in order to achieve that goal and prepare in advance to deliver. In the meeting, engage committee members or interviewers the way you would on your first day of work.

Start by listening and seeking to understand. While the committee or interviewer is asking all the questions, they are also communicating information through their questions about what is important to them and what they care about.

Digest and reflect on the question, consider different approaches, and provide answers or information they can use. You are not defending your dissertation, dazzling them with your intellect, or selling yourself. You are demonstrating through action what kind of a leader they are hiring.

Show them how you work. Use the interview as an opportunity to uncover their values, what binds them together or drives them apart, how they celebrate success and to what extent they tolerate risk and failure. In return, share observations and stories that are relevant to what they need done, their culture, and their aspirations.

Use examples that are appropriate for the role you are interviewing for. I coached a candidate once who was consistently washing out of searches as the runner-up. When I asked her to describe some of the questions and her answers during interviews, we realized that she was relying heavily on detailed examples from prior, more junior roles. By returning to prior roles, she wasn't fitting the examples into a broader institutional context appropriate for the role under consideration. Together, we reframed her examples to reflect how her actions and results were critical for moving the institutional agenda forward. This helped her overall thinking and strategy for her next interviews, in which she was successful in landing her next role.

Beware of gender traps

Interviewers in higher education typically ask the same questions of each candidate during the first round, but in the second or third round, candidates find themselves in one-on-one conversations or free-for-all forums. Interesting research published by the *Harvard Business Review* about venture capital funding results for men and women entrepreneurs shows that the two genders are frequently asked different types of questions in open-ended interviews, which ultimately skewed results in favor of male entrepreneurs. The men were more often asked "promotion" questions about hopes, achievements, advancement, and ideals, while women were asked "prevention" questions concerned with safety, responsibility, security, and vigilance. Women are socialized to be dutiful and truthful, so following the questioner's lead confined their answers to safety, security, and prevention, instead of boldness, risk taking, and vision. The good news is that the research also showed that reframing prevention questions with promotion answers reversed the trend. Lesson learned: women need to be better prepared to recognize these traps in interviews, control their responses (remember, approach the net), and to either reframe the question or build in discussion of vision and promotion. One strategy I often recommend is to bring two or three things to every single interview that you want to make sure the committee knows about you by the time the interview is over, including developing and pursuing a vision, strategy, or bold direction. Don't let the interview end without demonstrating that you can think big.

Own the skill

Often, succeeding in the interview is about recognizing, describing, and claiming the transferable skill, even when you don't have direct hands-on experience. In my observation, men are more often assumed to have skill, while women must prove it. A classic example of this is in fundraising. Many higher education administrators are not directly involved in fundraising. Even though they are often asked to show up at events, talk with alumni or parents, or identify potential donors from among their former students or professional network, they commonly do not have direct experience "making the ask." But as any professional fundraiser will tell you, it is not rocket science. Rather, it is about forging and cultivating strong relationships, then helping the individual to act. The transferable skill is building effective relationships while engaging people in strategic partnerships to help move an institutional agenda.

So, claim the skill and put it into the context of the role. And what better place to model relationship building than in an interview? Make sure you have done your homework on the individuals in the room and make a point of connecting with one or more of them in some way during your time together. One of my favorite questions asked by a female candidate for a presidency, who was assumed by some committee members to be an inexperienced fundraiser, was, "How did you initially get involved with this university and why is it important to you?" In following up, she moved the conversation forward, indicating she could develop an action plan. The committee members completely changed their minds and stated categorically the candidate would be a success in this role.

Share credit while claiming responsibility

In reviewing the last several years of search committee comments on female candidates who did not move forward, I noted the frequent committee observation that women either take too much credit or not enough. Taking credit is atypical, unexpected behavior in women and is more often expected in men, while not taking credit reinforces stereotypical notions of how women should behave. Either way, you can't win. One solution is to give credit first, then take credit second. In doing so, you demonstrate that you know this is a team effort, while also taking responsibility for the outcome. A good example is in strategic planning. Institutional planning takes a team of people, but someone has to lead the effort. If you did it, say so.

At the same time, practice balancing "I" with "we." Don't be afraid to highlight your role. There is a great deal of research on this topic, with one recent study (Reuben, et al.) showing that "men tend to exaggerate their acumen, while women downplay theirs." If asked whether you have accomplished X, instead of saying, "No I haven't done X," try this for a change: "I understand how important X is to this institution. As a senior administrator I have been heavily exposed to X, what was involved, what lessons we learned as an institution, and what skills and competencies were required to deal with X. I have developed those skills and competencies in other ways doing Y, so I know I am prepared to take on this challenge."

Another stereotypical misperception arising in interviews is that women candidates aren't prepared to make tough decisions because they are "too nice." I love this one—as if we don't have to make tough decisions every day of the week. You can be kind and empathetic and still make hard calls. How you talk about it is critical. Take an inventory of every tough call you've ever had to make and build a compelling narrative arc that you can use during interviews. Start big (e.g., during the last economic downturn, our university had to furlough employees to meet budget shortfalls), go small (I was asked to look at my departmental budget and examine which elements were most closely aligned with mission and strategy, and I made the tough call to eliminate three staff; here is how we went about it), communicate the values basis for the decision, and then bring it back to big again (this experience taught me that mission alignment is the best framework, etc.). Beware of stereotyping here: making a tough decision is not the same thing as being tough.

Apply knowledge strategically

Do your homework and anticipate the themes likely to surface in an interview. I have seen women get dinged on this a great deal more than men. The previously mentioned study shows that interviewers are more likely to assume that men know how to do a task. Women have to prove it over and over—so don't get caught short with no proof. Billie Jean King's quote about focusing on your strengths offers an important lesson; know what you know and don't shy away from being a subject matter expert in the meeting. Make it your goal to ensure that committee members leave with a takeaway. At the same time, interviewers are socialized to expect women to be humble, nice, welcoming, uncritical, and accepting. Boasting or coming across as the smartest person in the room doesn't work well for either gender. So, know what you don't know, also, and don't apologize for it. Reveal your knowledge through well informed, thoughtful, strategic questions that get them thinking. That is how you demonstrate leadership.

Demonstrate your potential

A frequent biased observation is that women aren't ready for the job, while men are valued for showing potential. I have seen interviewers express more willingness to hire men who will learn on the job, while if women have to learn on the job, the interviewers use lack of preparedness as an excuse for eliminating them from the pool. Get rid of the differential by showing the committee or the interviewer your chops. Start to work during the interview. Get them talking with each other. Facilitate the dialogue. Ask them to tell you what their biggest obstacle is to success, listen, analyze, ask questions, digest and distill, offer observations or examples of similar situations. In other words, establish authority through action, not claims.

Practice

Some of the most valuable feedback I ever received was in a marketing training workshop. We were asked to perform in a mock Q&A session with a panel and were recorded on video. When I watched my performance, I was immediately struck by the weak points in my physical and verbal presentations. I had been so unaware, and it was so easy to fix. Try this yourself: record answers to typical questions on video and replay. You might be surprised at how much you uptalk (i.e., ending every sentence as if it is a question), or at how much you say "umm" or "you know," or stray from the point, look down, wave your arms, bite your lip. All of these habits portray a lack of confidence. And strike this language from your repertoire: "Have I answered your question?" or any phrase that starts with "I am not sure…" These all indicate to audiences that you don't know what you are doing. At the same time, conveying empathy, understanding, and authenticity can make all the difference. So, use the positive phrase, "I understand…" Example: "I understand that this may not answer your question completely and that you might have another perspective. I am keen to hear your response; please, push back."

Anyone who has ever played tennis or performed on stage knows that preparation, practice, and rehearsal are essential for strong performance. As long as interviews are prerequisites for moving into leadership positions, women will need to succeed in them. These guidelines and tips, gathered from years of observations, may make all the difference for you.

Resources

Kanze, Dana, Laura Huang, and Mark A. Conley. "Male and Female Entrepreneurs Get Asked Different Questions by VCs—and It Affects How Much Funding They Get." *Harvard Business Review.* June 27, 2017. https://hbr.org/2017/06/male-and-female-entrepreneurs-get-asked-different-questions-by-vcs-and-it-affects-how-much-funding-they-get

Latu, Ioana M., Marianne Schmid Mast, and Tracie L. Stewart. "Gender Biases in (Inter) Action: The Role of Interviewers' and Applicants' Implicit and Explicit Stereotypes in Predicting Women's Job Interview Outcomes." *Psychology of Women*. March 18, 2015. https://doi.org/10.1177/0361684315577383

Mamlet, Robin. "Gender in the Job Interview." *The Chronicle of Higher Education*. 24 Mar. 2017. chroniclevitae.com/news/1743-gender-in-the-job-interview.

O'Sullivan, Tara. "How Interviews Increase Bias Towards Women of All Ages." *Sourcing and Recruiting News*. 11 Apr. 2019. recruitingdaily.com/how-interviews-increase-bias-towards-women-of-all-ages/.

Pazzanese, Christina. "Women Less Inclined to Self-Promote than Men, Even for a Job." *Harvard Gazette*. 11 Feb. 2020, news.harvard.edu/gazette/story/2020/02/men-better-than-women-at-self-promotion-on-job-leading-to-inequities/.

Meyers Pickard, Jen. "The 'I' vs. 'We' Balance: Highlighting Your Collaborative Prowess When Interviewing." *The EvoLLLution*, 18 Oct. 2019. evolllution.com/managing-institution/operations_efficiency/the-i-vs-we-balance-highlighting-your-collaborative-prowess-when-interviewing/.

Reuben, Ernesto, Paola Sapienza, and Luigi Zingales. "How Stereotypes Impair Women's Careers in Science." *PNAS*. March 25, 2014 111 (12) 4403-4408. https://doi.org/10.1073/pnas.1314788111

About the Author

Lucy Leske is a Senior Partner with WittKieffer, a global executive search firm that specializes in senior-level, mid-level, and interim executive search, leadership solutions, and board services in healthcare, education, the life sciences, and the not-for-profit sector. During her nearly 30-year career as a search consultant, Lucy has led a broad range of searches, including presidential, vice presidential, decanal, and provostial searches. Her areas of expertise include presidential and CEO positions; academic leadership in arts and sciences, law, engineering, education, and business; finance and administration; inclusion and diversity; international leadership; and advancement and philanthropy. She has volunteered as a panelist for professional development workshops offered by the American Council on Education, the National Association of Diversity Officers in Higher Education, the Millennium Leadership Institute of the American Association of State Colleges and Universities, Association of Public Land Grant Universities, AACSB, Women's Leadership Academy, HERS Institute, and TIAA-CREF Institute, and has written extensively about leadership development for women and underrepresented individuals in numerous publications.

Lucy is a founding member of the WittKieffer Diversity, Equity and Inclusion Council and works with clients to enhance diversity and inclusive excellence in leadership recruitment. She has played a key role in expanding WittKieffer's international executive search practice. She served for ten years on the Board of Trustees at Mitchell College in New London, Connecticut, and on numerous boards and committees related to environmental and community sustainability in her hometown of Nantucket, Massachusetts. She earned her B.A. from Mount Holyoke College.

CHAPTER 32
HOW TO CULTIVATE AND LEVERAGE A STRONG NEGOTIATION REPUTATION

by Sandra Mohr, Ph.D.
Dean of Academic Resources and Administration
New England College of Optometry

SCENARIO A

You have just started a new job and it's your first senior-level leadership position at a university. When you were offered the position, the salary and benefits package had seemed reasonable to you, and you accepted the position with minimal negotiation. You hear from a colleague that your predecessor who had significantly less experience earned $20,000 more than you do in the same position. They share that during the hiring process, that person had negotiated multiple aspects of the offer by referencing their ability to fundraise and citing salary data from comparable institutions.

SCENARIO B

It's budget-approval season and you will be presenting to the Board of Trustees. You and your team have assembled a lot of data on effectiveness and outcomes to support your argument for requesting additional resources.

> Meanwhile, the vice president of another division focused more on collecting anecdotes and sharing stories about how funding would be used. When the Board approves the budget and it's released, you discover that the vice president was awarded additional funding and your request was denied.

Did either or both of these scenarios sound familiar? How did you respond at the time? Both of these scenarios demonstrate the significant role that negotiation has in our careers in higher education and why it is critical for us to strengthen our skills in this area. They also highlight how institutional culture and the people involved in a negotiation impact outcomes—and the importance of assessing whether a data-driven approach or a story-driven, emotional appeal will be more effective.

While there can be institutional factors at play that we do not have control over, we do have the power to negotiate both upon accepting a role, as well as in-position. Recognizing and capitalizing on opportunities to successfully negotiate can be essential moments that help promote your political capital and enhance your personal brand, enabling you to further your career success. Negotiation can also be a pathway to building trust and expanding connections both within your campus community and beyond. So, how do we shift our mindset about negotiation from regarding it as an uncomfortable but necessary evil, to considering it an opportunity to strengthen our reputation?

DEFINING NEGOTIATION IN A HIGHER EDUCATION CONTEXT

Before examining how to expand your negotiation skills and how that fits into your personal brand, let's establish a working definition of the term. Negotiation is a deliberative process that works to navigate through an issue or problem from two or more sides that have value in seeking an agreed-upon solution (Beers, Boshuizen, Kirschner, and Gijselaers, 2006).

Within higher education, both formal and informal negotiations happen in our roles every day. You may be leading a team on a major initiative and negotiating with your colleagues that have different job responsibilities but who need to work together to achieve bigger goals. It may be budget submission time and you are negotiating and advocating for the resources you need going forward. If you are in an advising role, you may be negotiating with a student or faculty member to help resolve a concern. Often negotiation is so woven into our lives, we don't even consciously realize we are doing it. At best, negotiating on autopilot is a missed opportunity, and at worst, it can damage working relationships and negatively impact your reputation. This is why being intentional and strategic in all aspects of a negotiation is so important.

Negotiation Reputation as Part of Your Personal Brand

Like it or not, every negotiation we are involved in contributes to how we are perceived. Even if we have worked very hard to build our brand, one negotiation can tarnish it. For example, let's say you have carefully cultivated an empathy-driven leadership style, but then, in a negotiation, you resort to tactics that others perceive as very harsh and ruthless. You may end up with the outcome you want, but it can come at a significant professional and personal cost. As we have all seen in higher education, gossip spreads quickly and often leads to broken trust and a loss of respect. Being mindful of how our negotiation reputation impacts our personal brand is key and needs to be considered during all phases of the negotiation.

Tapping into Our Strengths

As women leaders in higher education, relationship building is an essential part of our roles, and this is especially helpful in negotiations. When negotiating at work, the nature of your relationships impacts your negotiation ability—through building shared trust, the potential for cooperation on shared interest areas, and the ability to gather information about those you are negotiating with (Babcock and Laschever, 2008). Successful negotiation agreements often occur from actively listening and responding to the other side's perspectives and needs while managing the emotions, biases, and faulty intuition that can impact your decisions during negotiation.

Another strength we can harness during the negotiation process is our ability to listen and ask questions to better understand other people's perspectives and what values they bring when working towards an agreement. Listening is at the heart of the way we lead in higher education, and it is a superpower in negotiations. It helps ensure that you gain historical perspective from your counterpart's vantage point, understand their perceived issue(s), and see where they intersect with the issues you have identified before the negotiation. Identifying shared values can be a way of agreeing on a path of working together through shared or common interests instead of focusing on differences among key areas.

Finally, our ability to plan strategically for the future comes into play in the negotiating process. It is important to think about how your current negotiations impact other people and the potential impact of future negotiations within your role. Reaching agreement on complicated items has the potential to set the precedent for the future.

Negotiation Preparation

As a leader, one of the most important things you can do is create a plan to help you work your way through any discussion or negotiation. Taking the time to plan for your negotiation better equips you for the conversation, allowing you to set realistic targets and practice the ability to position your points of view confidently and persuasively. Preparing before a negotiation allows you to think more about the issues and context of the negotiation, as well as the personalities of those negotiating, and allows you to strategize how to best position your points to communicate your perspective persuasively (Babcock and Laschever, 2008). Additionally, planning ahead of a negotiation allows you to lessen your fears and anxiety and understand your value as well as potential risks involved with the tactics you utilize during the negotiation.

Negotiation has three main elements: information, time, and power (Cohen and Mackenzie, 1991). *Information* relates to what both sides know about you and your needs in the negotiation; *time* relates to the pressures, constraints, and deadlines you are facing around the issue; and *power* relates to the perceived authority you think the other side has over the capacity or ability to get things done (Cohen and Mackenzie, 1991). During the negotiation planning phase, you should assess all three of these elements so that you have clearly defined the central problem you are trying to solve or address, your timeline, and exactly where you can be flexible or where you need to stand your ground.

Once you know what you are working through, think about the person or the people you will be negotiating with. It is very easy to focus solely on your own goals in a negotiation, which creates opportunities to miss something important that can have an impact on the negotiation outcome. Knowing more about those people's backgrounds can be helpful, and this links back to the concept that negotiation reputation is a part of your personal brand.

PLANNING QUESTIONS BEFORE BEGINNING A NEGOTIATION

What are the accepted norms for negotiation in your workplace?

What do you want from the negotiation? What alternative outcomes are possible in the negotiation?

What items or problems do you foresee being negotiated?

What strengths do you come to the negotiation with?

What weaknesses do you come to the negotiation with?

What brings the other party to the negotiation? Do you have anything that they need?

What relationship do you have with those you are negotiating with?

What are the other sides' interests in the negotiation? What expectations might the other sides bring to the negotiation?

How important is timing in the negotiation? What are the potential costs or benefits of delaying a negotiated agreement?

What relevant circumstances and relationship factors have the potential to influence the negotiated outcome?

What have you learned from past negotiations that might be helpful with this negotiation?

What value does an agreement to the negotiation bring, and to whom?

Spending time researching the problem, your potential bargaining power, and other factors influencing your problem helps you prepare your negotiation strategy. The more that you practice your negotiation skills and planning, the more likely you are to adopt better patterns of thinking, which can also be applied to future negotiations.

Strategies during the Negotiation

During the negotiation itself, rely on what you have prepared but also read the room. Be ready to shift your tactics based on what's being said and the body language of the people involved. Pay attention to any questions that are being asked and use them to help you decide whether the situation calls for you to give more data-driven responses or whether a narrative-based style will be more effective. Look for chances to keep the overall tone of the negotiation positive and collaborative rather than adversarial. A good guideline to follow is the Social Change Model of Leadership's concept of Controversy with Civility and how differences in opinion "must be aired openly but with respect and courtesy" (Komives and Wagner, 2016).

Post-Negotiation Assessment

Remember, negotiation is a skill that takes practice and reflection to improve your negotiation ability. Taking the time to evaluate your skills after a negotiation allows for reflection around the dialogue to help determine if your planning correctly identified the issues at hand, the other side's positions, and strategies used to reach an agreement. Reflection is also an opportunity to think about other potential strategies that might have been effective if used, which can help build your negotiation toolkit for future negotiations. As you apply new negotiation strategies through multiple environments, they become normalized strategies for gaining consensus in unlimited ways.

EVALUATION QUESTIONS AFTER A NEGOTIATION

What worked well in the negotiation?

What would you change if you were to begin the negotiation again?

What successes and losses did you come out of the negotiation with?

What successes and losses did the other side come out of the negotiation with?

How might the other side perceive the outcome of the negotiation?

Depending on the other people who were part of the negotiation and on the nature of the conversation, you can also seek feedback. For example, if you and a colleague from another department had teamed up to negotiate, you could ask for her/his assessment of the negotiation.

Final Thoughts

Effective negotiation skills allow you to capitalize on chances to find a mutual benefit for all parties and establish yourself as a respected and valued leader at your institution and overall. It is within our power to foster cooperative relationships and to look for ways of creating mutual benefits when working through challenging situations. Instead of pointing fingers or assigning blame, handle situations with a collaborative approach of problem solving that allows all sides to commit to an agreement that works for everyone (Shapiro, 2017). When you approach negotiations with the right mindset, you will greatly enhance your reputation and personal brand, thrive in your current role, and position yourself for future opportunities aligned with your professional goals.

Also, as leaders within higher education, we are role models for the next generation of women entering our field. We are responsible for modeling successful negotiation behaviors and mentoring others along the way. If we embrace the full potential of negotiations, it will significantly benefit us as individuals, improve our institutions, and positively impact those we serve.

Resources

Babcock, Linda, and Sara Laschever. *Ask for It: How Women Can Use Negotiation to Get What They Really Want.* Bantam, 2008.

Beers, Pieter J., Henny P.A. Boshuizen, Paul A. Kirschner, and Wim. H. Gojselaers. "Common Ground, Complex Problems and Decision Making." *Group Decision and Negotiation.* 15(6), 529-556, 2006.

Cohen, Herb, and R. A. Mackenzie. *You Can Negotiate Anything: How to Get What You Want.* Newbridge Communications, 1991.

Komives, Susan R., and Wendy Wagner (Eds.). *Leadership for a Better World: Understanding the Social Change Model of Leadership Development.* John Wiley & Sons, 2016.

Shapiro, Daniel. *Negotiating the Nonnegotiable: How to Resolve Your Most Emotionally Charged Conflicts.* Penguin, 2017.

About the Author

Sandra has over 20 years of leadership experience within higher education, where she has found practical ways of advancing impactful learning in all of us. Sandra currently is the Dean of Academic Resources and Administration at New England College of Optometry. Prior experiences were at the Online Learning Consortium as the Director of the Institute for Learning; Wentworth Institute of Technology as the Director of Faculty Services; and the Director of Financial Aid and Grants Management at the Urban College of Boston. Her research has focused on faculty professional development and educational sustainability. Dr. Mohr earned her Doctorate Degree in Global Educational Leadership from Lamar University, a Master's Degree in Educational Leadership and Administration from West Virginia University, and a Master's in Counselling and a Bachelor's in Psychology from California University of Pennsylvania.

Sandra is a people and culture-first leader who is passionate about defining organizational purpose, galvanizing teams and developing next-gen leaders, especially women. She is also an active mentor, public speaker, and non-profit board member.

PART 10

DEFINING YOUR SUCCESS

CHAPTER 33
MAKING THE CASE: USING QUALITATIVE AND QUANTITATIVE DATA TO TALK ABOUT YOUR ACHIEVEMENTS

by Chaudron Gille, Ph.D.
Provost and Senior Vice President for Academic Affairs,
University of North Georgia

What are you really worth? As academic professionals, we present ourselves through our curriculum vitae, annual evaluations, promotion and tenure portfolios, cover letters, and other similar artifacts. In each of these formats we make the case for our value to the organization. We tell our story— the qualitative data—but are we effectively using quantitative data to speak of our achievements, as well? Research into the income disparities and the attainment of promotions by women often cite the fact that men negotiate and promote themselves more effectively than women do. Women are taught to be modest and tend to attribute success to the results of teamwork rather than to their individual accomplishments. Women are more likely to accept what is offered as a salary than to negotiate for what they think they are worth. Women also tend to underestimate their own value, hesitating to claim a skill unless they think they have mastered it. In order to succeed professionally, a woman must learn to be her own best advocate.

I learned to be a better advocate for myself in my journey from faculty member to provost through a series of realizations and subtle shifts in how I have presented myself and my work over the last 25 years. The traditional path to provost is to serve as a department chair, dean, and associate provost first. There is an assumption of shared knowledge about what that path represents in terms of leadership preparation and responsibilities. My own path was not traditional. I moved from faculty into roles that were half teaching/half program coordination, and subsequently, a variety of leadership roles both in academic affairs and in related areas before becoming vice provost and provost. Women often advance in their career through alternative leadership paths. Many times, I have spoken with colleagues who knew my title in the organization, but who would ask, "What is it that you do?" I often acted as though the title of the position was shorthand for all it encompassed, assuming that my audience understood it in the same way I did. Yet the shared knowledge of what the role entailed was missing from their understanding. Because my journey to provost did not include the typical role of department chair or dean, learning to effectively communicate both the scope of responsibilities I had in a position as well as the impact I had as a leader was key to my professional advancement. I didn't develop this skill at once, but through a series of lightbulb moments.

My first lightbulb moment was as faculty member, teaching, coordinating a program, and serving as an advisor for international students. Serving as an advisor for international students went far beyond the typical academic advising responsibilities. It was very time-consuming, and I found it frustrating that the standard annual evaluation format did not adequately capture what I was doing. The number of advisees alone did not communicate the workload that I had. I began tracking the number of student appointments and the time devoted to these each week so that I could include that in my annual evaluation. The quantitative data—number of advisees, number of appointments, hours per week, total hours in the semester—helped me define and demonstrate the level of service I was providing to the university. It also helped to make the case for additional services and resources to support those students.

Another lightbulb moment occurred for me when I realized that in writing my CV or talking to people about my job, the same title at different institutions can carry vastly different responsibilities. This is particularly important to realize if you have a less traditional position in the administrative structure that may involve wearing a lot of hats. I learned it was important to include all of the programs I administered as part of that particular job and to describe my role, giving more detail about what I did. I found this to be particularly important in trying to benchmark the salary for a position—not only in advocating for myself, but also for those I wanted to promote or hire. The title of a position is only the starting point in looking at equity for many administrative positions. The scope of responsibilities also must be considered.

Compare the following *before* and *after* CV entries:

BEFORE:

Director of the Center for Teaching and Learning

Responsible for the activities of the University Center, the Center for Teaching and Learning, and Study Abroad. Direct faculty development program, the Teaching Excellence Preparation program, the Mentor Program, the hybrid course project, and the Innovative Teaching grant program. Teach faculty workshops. Coordinate all study abroad programs on campus and administer related scholarships and work-study programs. Represent the college at the university system level.

AFTER:

Director of Center for the Teaching, Learning, and Leadership

Responsible for the activities of the Center for Teaching, Learning, and Leadership (CTLL) and the Institute for Global Initiatives. Activities of the CTLL include faculty and staff development programs, new faculty/staff orientation, the Teaching Excellence Preparation program, the Mentor Program, hybrid and online course development, coordination of the promotion and tenure process, and the Innovative Teaching Grant program. Teach faculty workshops, serve as a liaison to other institutions to develop international partnerships, coordinate all study abroad programs, draft policies and procedures for international education, supervise faculty study abroad leaders, and administer related scholarships and work-study programs. Represent the college at the University System level in the areas of international education, distance education, and faculty and staff professional development. Supervise a staff of two, a faculty associate to CTLL, six faculty study abroad leaders, and the work of three committees.

Major Accomplishments:

- Teaching Excellence Preparation program, a year-long academy for new faculty with limited teaching experience

- Established the Innovative Teaching Grant program

- Establishment of the first study abroad programs for academic credit in POS for bachelor's degrees rather than general Core Curriculum

- Establishment of eTuition rate to support online course development and professional development program for faculty to create first online courses offered

Note that in the second example, there is more detail about the actual activities and responsibilities. The additional details clarify the scope of the job, indicating coordinating responsibilities across the institution and with external partners, both international and domestic. The level of supervisory experience both direct and indirect is included. The indirect supervision highlights experience working with faculty, which is particularly important for those who wish to advance in Academic Affairs. Highlighting key accomplishments also signals innovation, problem solving, and results, letting the reader know that you were not simply maintaining existing programs.

As I participated in searches for administrative positions and reviewed the CVs of other people, particularly men, I saw that they included the budget figures and personnel figures for the units that they led. That added bit of information gave a better sense of the scale of their responsibilities than the title or the description of their responsibilities alone. It was such an obvious data point, but one that I had not thought to include previously. Generally, the larger the number, the more implied responsibility and experience. There is a significant difference in leading a team of four people versus leading a team of twenty, and in leading a single office versus leading a unit that is dispersed over multiple locations. I began to include on my vitae the number of people in each of the areas I supervised, the budget I had oversight of, the dollar amounts of the scholarships I administered, and the grants I received. Sometimes, including information about the institution at the beginning may be an effective strategy.

EXAMPLE:

<u>Administrative Appointments</u>

The University of X is a public university with academic programs ranging from associate to doctoral levels, serving approximately 20,000 students on five campuses and online programs.

Provost and Sr. VP Academic Affairs | January 2019-Present

Serve as chief academic officer, providing leadership and integrity in the areas of academic program development, curriculum, evidenced-based research, and organizational effectiveness. Serve as a member of the President's cabinet. Oversight of six academic colleges, all departments and academic programs. Responsible for putting into action all academic policies, including those affecting faculty appointment, development, promotion and tenure. Responsible for a budget of $99,170,000.

Major Accomplishments:

- Drafted strategy and allocated $500,000 in faculty equity adjustments as part of a multi-year commitment by the President, integrating recommendations from college deans, a committee-based faculty equity study, and the Faculty Senate

- Established the Provost's Faculty Fellows program, a professional development program for faculty interested in entering or learning about administration

- Launched an academic strategic planning process to complement the work of the institutional strategic planning committee

Vice Provost | July 2016 - December 2018

Ensure that Academic Affairs remains compliant with laws and regulations. Facilitate the development of new policies/procedures. Ensure a collaborative environment and effective communication in working with all five campuses. Assist the Provost in the review of faculty/staff issues, budget planning and allocation, strategic planning, respond to issues/matters on behalf of the Provost, and in the temporary absence of the Provost, exercise the functions of the Provost Office. Serve as liaison to the University System in the submission and approval process for new courses, new programs, and program modification. Serve as academic conduct officer related to student academic issues. Serve on the Provost Council, the Academic Affairs Committee, and chair those meetings. Serve on Executive Council, Investigations Committee, Strategic Enrollment Council, Strategic Enrollment Management Steering Committee, Dual Enrollment Committee, General Education Council, Persistence Steering Committee, QEP Advisory Committee, Banner Committee, Behavior Intervention Team, Student

Suspension Hearings (chair), University Internationalization committee, and the Diversity Council.

Direct Reports: The three Associate Deans for Academic Administration (Academic officers for the regional campuses); the Associate VP for Academic Affairs, Honors Program, Graduate Studies, and Libraries; the Assistant Vice President for Strategic Student Success Initiatives; the Executive Director of Academic Advising and the QEP; the Director of Distance Education and Technology Integration; and the Academic Affairs liaison.

Major Accomplishments:

- Co-authored Title III grant, SOAR: Success Oriented Academic Reform, to support student success initiatives for the freshman year. $2.1 million over three years.

- Collaborated with an interdisciplinary group of faculty representing three colleges to establish Center for Healthy Aging. In its first year, the Center has facilitated a grant application collaboratively with a community partner, participated in panels for a regional economic conference, and is actively pursuing community partnerships to bring programs to the university.

- Guided the development of a Guttman-style cohort model of integrated general education curriculum delivery with required co-curricular components for the freshman year.

- Served on the core leadership team for a successful SACSCOC reaccreditation visit, including responsibility for review of all faculty credentials and faculty roster.

- Facilitated expansion of Master Faculty Advisor model for orientation to include departments and campuses not currently in the QEP.

- Coordinated the university's launch of the predictive analytics platform and the incorporation of those resources into Academic Advising and the work of the Persistence Steering Committee by building a cross-functional group of ten "super users" from student affairs, institutional effectiveness, enrollment management, and academic affairs, and the infrastructure and communication structure to support integration of all the university's student success initiatives.

- Developed the infrastructure to support the university's rapidly growing dual enrollment program serving 1200+ students to ensure quality and rigor of the academic experience, as well as customer service to students, parents, and participating high schools.

A seminal moment occurred for me when I listened to a colleague at another university discuss their very successful student retention program. I was struck by the way in which he translated the data about the number of students retained into the equivalent tuition dollars the university gained as a result. He then used that information to advocate for greater investment in those successful programs. This powerful lesson helped me shift my thinking about how programs are assessed, to ask about their impact.

While I learned the power of being able to talk about impact first through advocating for programs or projects I was working with, the lessons are transferable to advocating for your own professional advancement. The ability to align your projects and your ideas with the priorities of the university, and to demonstrate that they have had an impact, is very persuasive. For example, tracking the number of faculty who attended a writing workshop and their satisfaction with the workshop is one measure of success, but being able to speak about the number of faculty who actually submitted grants or articles for publication that were begun or polished through that workshop speaks more directly to the impact of the program.

Some key university priorities to keep in mind are student retention and graduation, student achievement, faculty achievement, and efficiency or good stewardship of resources. Think in terms of what you can measure, and how that measurement can be used to demonstrate impact on key priorities. Track the change over time. For example, a shift in the type of courses you as department head have scheduled in the summer term might have resulted in an enrollment increase compared to previous years. There are two ways to talk about this decision and its impact. The story, or the qualitative part, is that more upper-level courses were scheduled to relieve pinch points for majors and keep students on track to graduation. The quantitative side is the increase in the number of credit hours produced by the department during the summer term, resulting in higher tuition dollars. This accomplishment can be further developed by tracking the resulting improvement in the number of semesters your majors have taken to graduate, shortening time to degree and increasing the overall number of graduates. Providing that data explicitly connects your actions—the result of your leadership—with the essential goals of the institution.

A story can be compelling. People relate to the human detail in a story, but combined with quantitative data on the number of people who benefitted from a program, the impact on the budget of dollars saved, the additional revenue generated, the students who graduated, it becomes more powerful. The story, or qualitative side, speaks to your motivation, to the why and how of your accomplishments. The quantitative speaks to what you accomplished, the results. As you think about how to communicate your accomplishments, think about the scope of what you have done and about the impact you have had in each project, role, or program.

QUESTIONS TO ASK YOURSELF

Would a layperson or someone not in my field understand what I accomplished?

Does my title reflect fully all aspects of my job?

What resources did I use?

Who did I work with?

Which areas of the university did I collaborate with?

How many people were involved?

Who benefitted from this program or project? How did they benefit?

What was the budget?

What actions did I take to make it happen? How did I decide what action to take?

THEN THINK ABOUT THE IMPACT:

What was the product or outcome?

How did I measure my success or the success of my team in this endeavor?

How many people were affected?

What was the impact on students? Faculty? Staff? Alumni? The public?

What did they do as a result?

Did this have an impact on retention? On recruitment? On graduation?

Did it bring in additional revenue or tuition dollars?

> Did it result in any efficiencies or improvement in customer experience?
>
> Did it bring any positive publicity to the university?
>
> Did it strengthen a community relationship?
>
> What need did it meet?

These questions can be used to think about a particular program, about a particular position you hold, and ultimately about your achievements throughout your career. No one else is as well equipped to tell people what you have done as you are. Additional detail, both quantitative and qualitative, provides a clearer picture of your accomplishments and the value you bring to the organization.

About the Author

Dr. Chaudron Gille currently serves as Provost and Senior Vice President for Academic Affairs at the University of North Georgia, a five-campus university of approximately 20,000 students. Gille began her career teaching French and English as a Second Language. She has experience in the areas of curriculum development, strategic planning, accreditation, international education, distance education, academic advising, student success initiatives, and faculty professional development. She has a Ph.D. in French Literature from Emory University and a M.A. in Applied Linguistics and

Teaching English as a Second Language from Georgia State University.

Gille currently serves on the advisory board of Atlanta Botanical Gardens-Gainesville, as well as the Strategic Facilities Planning group and the Vestry for Grace Episcopal Church.

CHAPTER 34
DEFINING SUCCESS:
A PROCESS FOR DETERMINING
YOUR PATH FORWARD

by Dr. Therese Lask
Talent Development Specialist
Colorado State University

What is success? According to the Merriam-Webster dictionary, success is defined as: "a degree or measure of succeeding; favorable or desired outcome; attainment of wealth, favor, or eminence." For those of us in higher education, do any of those definitions ring true? Is moving up the hierarchy in an institution the only benchmark for success? Or are there other variables to consider? At the end of careers, is there comfort in letting go, knowing we contributed our best? Or a sadness believing more could have been done?

The purpose of this chapter is to provide a framework for the question of success. Based on various books, articles, and videos on career satisfaction, certain variables are important to professional fulfillment. But success is not only defined by career fulfillment. All aspects of our lives, including our relationships, communities, and health are key in our journeys. Although success is often defined for us by society, let us approach this from a different vantage point. For our purposes, as individuals, looking through the unique lenses of our lives, let us create our own meaning of success through this definition:

Success is to honor your purpose, live your defined values, and utilize and continually develop your strengths.

The following are definitions for each of the variables:

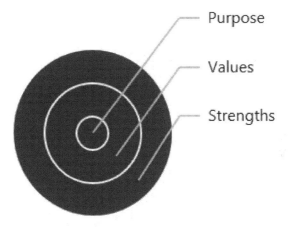

HONORING PURPOSE

Designed to inspire, motivate, and provide clarity, purpose statements become your compass, providing the direction for your future.

DEFINED VALUES

Values are the foundation for how you live your life—timeless beliefs that guide the hundreds of decisions made in a day. Consider these your personal bottom line, how you define expectations for behavior for yourself and others.

YOUR STRENGTHS

What you do best is your opportunity for excellence. Think about how you best contribute to your home, work, and community. Using your strengths provides a boost in energy, as time flies by due to your engrossment in activity. Others notice your excellence.

Why will these three variables of *purpose, values,* and *strengths* lead you to your definition of success? In the book *What Will I Do With My Life?,* author Po Bronson profiles individuals who search to find answers to the question of life's purpose. Many of their journeys begin with the realization that something is missing, off, in the way they are living their lives. Some leave lucrative jobs, searching for a more meaningful existence. All find that the honoring of purpose, living of values, and the utilizing of strengths helped answer the difficult question of what to do with this life they were given.

For many of us, we are drawn to our roles due to the overall mission of higher education. The opportunity to explore knowledge, create new discoveries, transform individuals, and be a part of a community draws us into our work. However, in certain situations, the role becomes blurred. Maybe you go home every night, wondering why you got into this field in the first place. Perhaps you experience a strong reaction to the implicit beliefs in the system. You may have lost all your energy for your role, dragging yourself to the office each day only to feel like you are not contributing your best.

What if your role is no longer blurred? You realize exactly why you are in higher education and only pursue opportunities that fulfill your purpose. Your work is for a system that demonstrates a consistency of values—beliefs you can honor. There is an energy you have when doing aspects of your job, where you can grow continually and develop in the responsibilities you do best. What if?

The first step in this process is to examine a timeline of your life, designed to explore the important themes that emerged based on your roles and experiences. This timeline will provide the information necessary to craft your definition of success.

Your Timeline

The question of success and the three variables of purpose, values, and strengths seems easy to define. However, many of us struggle, convinced the only success is upward movement through titles and standing within our institutions. But true success can only be defined by you, through the process of exploring what matters to you in the course of your life. It seems so simple—like our purpose, values and strengths are obvious to each of us. It is not always simple. Defining all three variables requires reflection on your past, including the roles you chose, and lessons from your experiences. Through this reflection, you will see patterns emerge through the various turning points of your life.

What were the roles that defined you, the experiences that shaped who you are? What lessons did you learn that are a part of you today? What themes are evident along the way? Creating a timeline of your key roles/experiences provides the framework necessary for exploring the important patterns of your life.

There are no defined rules for the development of this timeline, only the goal of creating a timeline that is meaningful for you. You may choose to create this timeline to explore your professional path, or you may choose to approach this exercise from a broader perspective of your life.

For each role/experience listed, answer the following:

- Why did you list this role/experience on your timeline?

- What positive takeaways do you have as a result of this role/experience?

- What difficult takeaways do you have as a result of this role/experience?

- Would you do this again? Why? Why not?

- What did you take forward as a result of this role/experience?

After answering the above questions for each role/experience on the timeline, consider the following questions:

- Is there a common thread to the roles/experiences you listed on your timeline?

- Is there a common thread to the positive roles/experiences you listed?

- Is there a common thread to the difficult roles/experiences you listed?

- What roles/experiences would you do all over again? Why?

- What are the overall themes of what you have learned?

A draft of a timeline that you can use for this exercise is included at the end of this chapter.

Honoring Purpose

Imagine yourself on a scenic drive, in the mountains, along the ocean, or wherever a place of beauty is for you. You are relaxed, enjoying the peacefulness of the beauty that surrounds you. Suddenly, the weather turns; the rain and wind pound against your car windows, making it impossible to see. You grip the steering wheel, decrease your speed, and feel a panic rushing through you, as you cannot see the road ahead. After lasting for what seems forever, the storm finally lifts; the sun peeks out from behind the clouds. You loosen your grip on the steering wheel and feel a sense of relief. The journey is much easier when you can see where you are going.

With the exceptions of a few storms, do you know where you are going? Through the critical choices of your life, what guides you to make the best decision? A purpose statement can serve as a guide, providing direction for what is the most important to you.

In order to draft your purpose statement, return to your timeline. What are the themes that emerged from your roles and experiences? Consider the following questions as you develop your purpose statement:

- What essential beliefs guide you in the choices you make?

- What gives you energy in your life?

- How can you best contribute?

- How do you want to contribute?

There is no right or wrong for purpose statements, only that the statement is meaningful for you. The past will provide the clarity necessary to create the purpose statement to guide your future.

Living Defined Values

In work environments, relationships, and other experiences in our lives, our values are the beliefs that shape our decisions. Often referred to as our personal bottom line, values influence the hundreds of decisions we make in a day. How we treat people, how we manage our money, our expectations on the job, and our beliefs on what is right and wrong are all determined by our values.

There are several ways to conduct a value sort, a process where you identify your top three to five values. A list of values has been included in the exercises at the end of this chapter. By no means is this a complete list—feel free to add values omitted from the list. Using the list, complete the steps listed below:

- Sort the list of values into three categories: always value, sometimes value, never value.

- After sorting into the three categories, focus on the list of values in the "always value" category.

- Review the values in the "always valued category to determine if any should be moved into the "sometimes value" or "never value" category.

- With the remaining values in the "always value" category, determine if there are themes that could be grouped together (for example: family, relationships, community). Out of the values grouped together, select the word that best represents your value.

- After completing the review, use the questions below to identify the three to five values that are your core beliefs.

Refer to your timeline exercise to answer the questions below:

- For the major decisions in your life, what values guided you?

- In the various roles in your life, what values are evident?

- During the most difficult times, what values guided your decision?

- Recall a time when your values were tested. What line would you not cross from a value perspective?

Living your defined values can be difficult. We all experience times when our beliefs are challenged, discarded, demeaned. What do we experience when we do compromise on our values? Many times, the price we pay for violating our core foundation is guilt, frustration, and often making a terrible decision. Living our defined values will provide the foundation we need to make all the key decisions in our lives.

Utilize and Continually Develop Your Strengths

Do you believe we continue to grow throughout our lives? So many of us gravitate to higher education for that very reason: to build on knowledge or theory; to pursue research that solves our challenges; to aid in the growth and development of others. Where is our best opportunity for growth and development? A focus on your strengths provides not only the opportunity to grow, but the prospect of contributing to your greatest potential.

Think about the times in your life when you were so engaged that time stood still. Think about experiences when you naturally knew the next steps and exactly where you were heading. Think about the compliments you disregard, even though others continually recognize your strengths. These times are important signals to your strengths.

Return to your timeline exercise to answer the following questions to explore your strengths:

- In each role, what gives you energy?

- What responsibility provided the optimal experience, meaning you experienced a heightened level of engagement?

- What are you continually drawn to?

- What are you doing when you receive the most compliments?

- If you had a free day to invest in one responsibility/ activity, what would you choose?

Seek opportunities to enhance your strengths by developing new skills and pursuing additional knowledge. Build a consistent focus on your strengths to continue to move towards excellence. You will discover how utilizing and continually developing your strengths provides an opportunity to fully engage in life, increasing your sense of happiness and wellbeing.

Live Your Successful Life

For all of us, life has endings. Some endings we have no control to change. But for the endings we do control, how do we want those to conclude? We want to feel that the paths we chose served a purpose, to enhance not only our lives, but the lives of others. We want to believe we acted honorably, living a life that reflected our values. We seek to reflect on the closed chapters of our lives with a sense of pride, knowing we did our best by utilizing our strengths. Knowing all this, will you experience success? You will.

Find the exercises for this chapter on pages 448-454.

About the Author

Dr. Therese Lask is a Talent Development Specialist. Therese has worked in higher education for more than 25 years and as a consultant for the Gallup Organization for four years. As a consultant, Therese has helped organizations infuse a strengths-based philosophy to assist with building teams and helping individuals contribute their best at work. She has a Bachelor's and Master's degree from Colorado State University and a Doctorate in Higher Education Leadership from the University of Northern Colorado. Therese has published numerous articles, workbooks, and a book, *Your Life as a River*, on the topic of strengths development.

Her areas of expertise include strengths development, strategic planning, wellbeing, hope, multi-generational workforce, change, professional resilience, and career exploration.

Timeline

Directions

Reflect on your most important roles/experiences in life. What were the roles that defined you? What experiences shaped who you are? In each box provided below, list one role and answer the following questions. Your goal is to find key themes to help you define success.

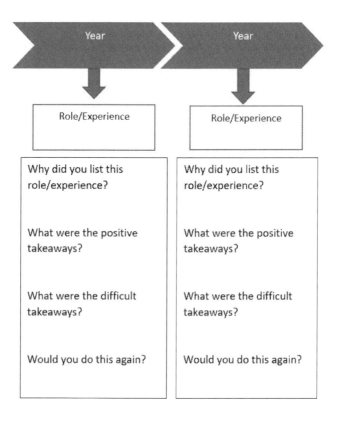

Year	Year
Role/Experience	Role/Experience
Why did you list this role/experience?	Why did you list this role/experience?
What were the positive takeaways?	What were the positive takeaways?
What were the difficult takeaways?	What were the difficult takeaways?
Would you do this again?	Would you do this again?

As you complete this timeline worksheet, consider: Is there a common thread to the roles/experiences you listed on your timeline? Is there a common thread to the positive roles/experiences you have had? Is there a common thread to the difficult roles/experiences you have had? What roles/experiences would you do all over again? Why?

What are the overall themes you see?

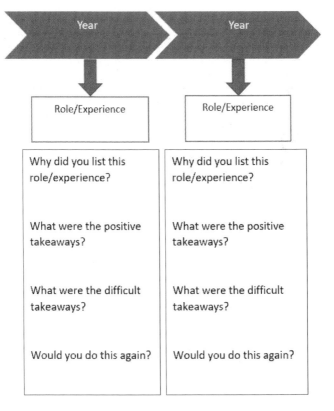

Crafting a Purpose Statement

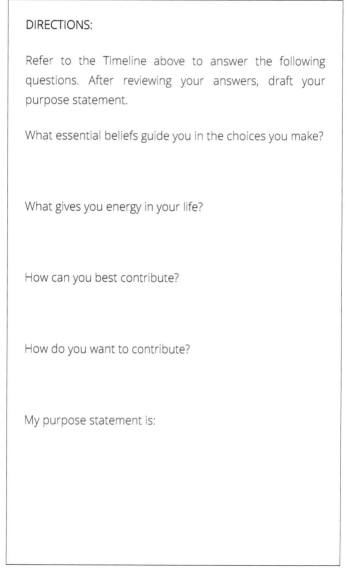

DIRECTIONS:

Refer to the Timeline above to answer the following questions. After reviewing your answers, draft your purpose statement.

What essential beliefs guide you in the choices you make?

What gives you energy in your life?

How can you best contribute?

How do you want to contribute?

My purpose statement is:

Living Defined Values

Directions

The list provided below provides a sample list of values. The overall goal is to narrow the list to the three to five values that guide your life. Sort the list into three categories: *always value, sometimes value, never value.*

After sorting into three categories, focus on the list of values in the "always value" category. Review the values in the "always value" category to determine if any should be moved into the "sometimes value" or "never value" category.

With the remaining values in the "always value" category, determine if there are themes that could be grouped together (for example: family, community, relationships). Out of the values grouped together, select the word that best represents your value.

After completing the review, use the questions below to identify the three to five values that are your core beliefs.

Value	Category
Achievement	
Aesthetics	
Altruism	
Ancestry	
Autonomy	
Community	
Competency	
Control	

Creativity	
Dignity	
Emotional Wellbeing	
Family	
Harmony	
Health	
Honor	
Honesty	
Humility	
Inclusion	
Justice	
Knowledge	
Love	
Loyalty	
Passion	
Pleasure	
Physical Appearance	
Recognition	
Relationships	
Spirituality	
Wealth	

Questions to consider:

- For the major decisions in your life, what values guided you?

- In the various roles in your life, what values are evident?

- During the most difficult times, what values guided your decision?

- Recall a time your values were tested, what line would you not cross from a value perspective?

Utilize and Continually Develop Your Strengths

Directions

Return to your timeline to explore the following questions concerning your strengths:

- In each role/experience, what gave you energy?

- What responsibilities provided the optimal experience, meaning you experienced a heightened level of engagement?

- What are you continually drawn to?

- What are you doing when you receive the most compliments?

- If you had a free day to invest in one responsibility/activity, what would you choose?

Defining Your Success

My purpose is:

My values are:

My strengths are:

DEFINING SUCCESS

WORKSHEET: 15 QUESTIONS FOR REFLECTION

1. Where do you see your current leadership experience in relation to a more national or global scale? Does the success of other women impact your daily experience? Has the lack of women leaders and role models hindered you or motivated you?

2. When you consider intersectionality in your identity, what comes to mind (race, gender, sexual orientation, generation, childhood experiences, etc.)? List each of these and how they have impacted your view of the world. How can you harness each of these to be an advantage in your leadership journey?

3. Do you have "facets" of yourself that you consciously or subconsciously hide? Why might this be so? What are steps you wish to take towards presenting a more authentic version of yourself?

4. Consider a journaling activity: "Would I ever hold a colleague to the same harsh standards to which I hold myself? Do I fear being seen as imperfect? Why might this be so?"

5. As you rise in leadership, what are potential "blind spots" you may develop? How might you mitigate those while remaining focused on your career and personal goals?

6. If you are considering taking a risk in your professional or personal life, consider creating a matrix and answering

these four questions: What's the best thing that could happen if you take this risk (i.e., how might this impact your future goals?)? What's the worst thing that could happen (and if that happens, what skills and strategies could you use to get back to a place of equilibrium?)? What's the best-case scenario if you don't take this risk? What's the worst-case scenario?

We have provided a table below to assist you in creating this matrix:

	Worst-Case Scenario	Best-Case Scenario
If I take on this new challenge:		
If I don't take on this new challenge:		

7. What's a first step you could take to create, join, or improve a support system for women of color at your institution with the mission to advance their careers?

8. Do you witness colleagues who are women of color being asked to take on projects and lead conversations on diversity to the point of overwhelming them emotionally and in terms of workload? What would be a safe space to engage in a dialogue to hear their perspectives and to see how you can be most supportive?

9. Introverts often work in such a way that can contribute to their "invisibility" in the workplace. If you are or know an introvert, what are ideas for getting contributions and leadership noticed?

10. How might you be saying "yes" to "unpromotable tasks" for the sake of being seen as a team player? Consider ways you could communicate to your supervisor your professional goals, and how saying "yes" to some of these tasks may ultimately hinder you in your ability to do more strategic work.

11. Several of the chapters highlighted the need for women to have and to be advocates for one another. If you are in a leadership position, reflect on your current support of women who report to you. If you are not currently in a leadership position, reflect on whether you have someone who will advocate for you. If your current situation is not ideal, what steps could you take to start a conversation with someone on campus?

12. Reflect on your current influence at work. Are there decisions being made or projects being completed that would benefit from your insights? What are diplomatic ways you might go about joining those conversations? Who could connect you to those involved?

13. What is an action you could take to progress a conversation on your campus or in your department about current hiring practices and their commitment to diversity? If you already feel your institution has made good progress in this area, how could others learn from your example?

14. When you think about equity in your most immediate personal and professional world, where do you think your focus should be in the short-term? In the long-term?

15. Consider a writing or drawing activity where you conceptualize your success two years from now. What does your life look like? What challenges have you overcome? Use this activity as a springboard for your next steps in personal and professional negotiations.

ABOUT THE EDITORS

ELIZABETH ROSS HUBBELL, M.A., serves as a Senior Program Manager at Academic Impressions, where she conducts market research on current trends and issues impacting higher education, collaborates with subject matter experts, and designs professional learning experiences. Her primary areas of focus are developing women leaders in higher education and creating professional learning and networking opportunities for Chiefs of Staff. Prior to joining Academic Impressions, Elizabeth served as a K12 consultant, focusing on instructional technologies and co-authoring a number of books on instruction. Elizabeth is a former Montessori teacher.

DANIEL FUSCH, Ph.D., contracts with Academic Impressions as a developmental editor, working to publish books on current and challenging issues in higher education, such as the recent *Fix Your Climate: A Practical Guide to Reducing Microaggressions, Microbullying, and Bullying in the Academic Workplace* by Myron R. Anderson and Kathryn S. Young, and *The Future of Fundraising: Adapting to Changing Philanthropic Realities* by James M. Langley. Previously, he served for thirteen years with Academic Impressions variously as a program manager developing conferences and symposia for higher ed and as a publications director producing research reports and curating a library of 800 articles and papers focused on practical strategies for administrators and academic leaders. He directed several iterations of Academic Impressions' biannual *State of Professional Development in Higher*

Education survey, a study of views and practices for empowering higher-ed employees' professional development, drawing on responses from 2,500 higher-ed faculty and staff. Prior to his work with Academic Impressions, Daniel served as an adjunct instructor at the University of Denver. Daniel holds a Ph.D. in English from the University of Denver.

Made in the USA
Columbia, SC
27 June 2021

40806977R00259